This book belongs to

Rachel Hayward
Feb. 1993

The
Byrom Collection

John Byrom, M.A., F.R.S.
'Ha!' quoth I to his Face, 'my old friend are you there' –
And me Thought the face smil'd. *Collected Poems*, Vol. 1, 1814 edition.

The
Byrom Collection

JOY HANCOX

JONATHAN CAPE
LONDON

Most of the geometric drawings included in the book have
been reduced to fit the size of the page.

First published 1992
© Joy Hancox 1992
Jonathan Cape, 20 Vauxhall Bridge Road, London SW1V 2SA

Joy Hancox has asserted her right under the Copyright,
Designs and Patents Act 1988 to be identified as the
author of this work

A CIP catalogue record for this book
is available from the British Library

ISBN 0-224-03046-9

Phototypeset by Falcon Graphic Art Ltd
Wallington, Surrey
Printed by Butler & Tanner Ltd,
Frome and London

Contents

'Whatever deserves to exist deserves
also to be known, for knowledge is
the image of existence.'

Francis Bacon

CHAPTER ONE

Discovering the Collection

THE STORY OF the Byrom Collection begins with the purchase of a house in Salford in August 1965. Drawn by its old world charm and elevated position behind an old stone wall, surrounded by trees and yet so close to the city, I found it irresistible. The deeds began in 1923, the time when much of the property round about had been built. Intermittently during the first four years I came across people who knew it and was told various tales from which one thing soon became clear: before 1923 the house had been a farm. Some of my oldest neighbours remembered calling daily for milk. There were even rumours of a tunnel. At first I was simply amused by these stories and regaled my friends with them. Then, in January 1969, when central heating was being installed, plumbers made two unexpected discoveries. The chimney flues at the back were found to be vast cavities and had to be specially modified – they were certainly not the flues of a house built in 1923, and under floorboards at the back of the house, one workman discovered a chamber with a flight of stone steps disappearing into a brick wall. Suddenly the pedigree of the house was incomplete.

The farm had been altered to a family house. Descendants of the builders responsible were able to tell me a little more about the tunnel. It was 'a passage going from the house under the road towards Manchester' and, in the interest of expediency, had been blocked up, while the underground chambers had been filled in with soil and rubble.

I suppose it was out of curiosity that I began a systematic investigation into the history of the area, with the help of maps, street directories, local archives, in the wider context of Manchester's and Salford's past. Through the tenant rolls of the old manor court I was able to trace the history of the farm back to the early eighteenth century. Later, the discovery of a priest hole beside one of the flues linked the house with the Reformation. At that time there was nothing else around but fields and a lane leading to the farm which stood on a ridge. This was the highest point on the Roman road north from Manchester which passed directly through the farm. The house occupied a commanding, not to say strategic, position, and by the early nineteenth century the adjacent fields were called 'Siddal's Fields'.

I noticed from the tenant rolls that the new tenant in 1729 was a 'Mr Thomas Siddal' but that when he left in 1745 he was listed simply as 'Siddal'. This was the only entry on the page which omitted the Christian name of the tenant. The omission reminded me of reports in criminal cases where a convicted felon is no longer deemed worthy of the ordinary courtesies. The year 1745 marked the second Jacobite uprising, when the town of Manchester played a part in the disastrous attempt to restore the Stuarts to the throne. It looked as if Siddal's departure from the farm and the uprising might be connected.

This proved to be so. Thomas Siddal was one of nine 'Manchester martyrs' executed for their role in the '45 rebellion. Moreover, Siddal's father (Thomas senior) had been a Jacobite in the 1715 rebellion on behalf of the Old Pretender, James Stuart. His head had been stuck up on a pike in Manchester as a warning to other would-be traitors. His widow and children could see it from their home. At the time young Tom was a boy of seven. Yet when Bonnie Prince Charlie raised his standard in 1745 Thomas junior undeterred rallied to the cause. Serving as an Ensign, he was arrested in Carlisle and sent for trial to London. But before the trial something strange happened: someone in Manchester obviously hoped that Siddal might be persuaded to turn King's evidence and save himself. An anonymous, undated letter was sent to the Secretary of State, the Duke of Newcastle, which stated: 'If Tom Siddal was to be examined (tho I think he would prove very stiff) it would not be amiss, for it's certain that fellow knows enough to save 20 such heads as his.'[1]

The ruse failed and Siddal stood trial on 18 July 1746. He boldly declared that the prosecution dared not put him in the witness box, but remained silent about the reason for this assertion. After a trial lasting only an hour he was found guilty and moved to the New Gaol, Southwark, to await his end. The executions of Siddal and his fellow Jacobites were carefully stage-managed. Preceded by 1,500 soldiers, the nine men were taken in three sledges to Kennington Common, where they were hanged, drawn and quartered before the London mob. The information deemed worth the lives of twenty men died with Siddal. His head, too, was sent back to Manchester to intimidate the townsmen.

Before the uprising, Siddal, in addition to tenanting the farm, had been a peruke-maker and barber. All the contemporary evidence points to his sober, devout nature, the probity of his life as husband and father, and his unswerving loyalty to the cause his own father had espoused. His father's death had demonstrated the price of failure. Why, then, did he not seize the opportunity to save himself for the family he loved? What was the secret he refused to divulge? No contemporary accounts offered an answer.

Each new fact I discovered led to fresh questions; the history of the house resembled a constantly changing kaleidoscope. One of the best accounts of Manchester during the '45 is the diary kept by Elizabeth (or Beppy) Byrom, who writes with excitement about her visit to see the young Prince and of his progress through the streets. Her vivid description can be found in the four-volume edition of the journal written by her father, John Byrom. His *Private Journal and Literary Remains* were published, after careful editing, by the local antiquarian society and paid for by his last surviving descendant. After reading Beppy's diary, I scoured this journal for any reference to Thomas Siddal. I felt sure Byrom must have known him.

In 1748, the Reverend J. Owen published *A Letter to the Master-Tool of the Faction at Manchester* attacking the principles of the Jacobites and Non-jurors. Byrom was known to be a Non-juror and had forfeited an ecclesiastical and academic career as a result. Owen was convinced he was the master-tool of the Jacobites. From the journals it is clear Byrom knew Siddal, whose business in Manchester was not far from the Byrom family home, yet they had not suffered the same fate.

My search for the facts about Siddal led me to look more closely into the life of John Byrom, whose public image as presented in the journals lacked conviction. His Victorian great-granddaughter had made him out to be far too good to be true. In an effort to find the original manuscripts from which the edited journals had been compiled, I traced four different Byrom legacies, always hoping to discover more about Siddal. Openly a Jacobite, he had died cruelly in consequence. Byrom, a secret Jacobite, had escaped. Had he gained his freedom with Siddal's silence? I began to feel this was so, particularly when I discovered that Byrom once owned the cloth used to wrap Siddal's head in when it was sent back to Manchester, where it remained with the Byrom family for years afterwards. Seeing it myself confirmed my suspicion that Byrom's role in the '45 had been protected by Siddal. Byrom must have kept the cloth, almost as a religious relic, in honour of his friend. As I learned more about Byrom's hidden life, I began to get a clearer picture of what had caused Siddal to remain 'tantalisingly silent'.

The Byrom legacies revealed a wealth of hitherto untouched material, included in which was the collection of geometric drawings Byrom once had in his possession. Their extent and diversity indicated their import-

9

ance. Centred on mathematics, they are unique source material, starting in the reign of Elizabeth I and ending in that of George II, some 174 years. They belong to a time when the delight in the power of number, particularly geometry, was first emerging in England. They span the period when recourse to magic gradually yielded to belief in science.

The tradition they draw on can be traced back to the Babylonians and some of the ideas still have a relevance today. A simple instance of the early delight in number is the presence in the collection of number squares, with their intriguing property of common totals no matter which way they are added – horizontally, vertically, or diagonally. (The artist Dürer was equally fascinated by them and included one in the background of a painting.[2]) With the advent of the calculator there is little wonder left, since the manipulation of number has been transferred from an agile brain to dextrous fingers. The symmetry of number and the many applications of geometry displayed in the collection may come to many as a revelation.

One of these applications is the representation in geometrical form of philosophic ideas. One can see in the drawings attempts to comprehend and explain the unity of creation and man's place in it. Such ideas may seem strange to us now, since science has swept away many of the assumptions on which they were based. Ultimately, it was left to such poets as Wordsworth to try to reformulate the idea of man's oneness with the world around him, as in his lines on Tintern Abbey:

> And I have felt
> A presence that disturbs me with the joy
> Of elevated thoughts: a sense sublime
> Of something far more deeply interfused,
> Whose dwelling is the light of setting suns,
> And the round ocean and the living air,
> And the blue sky, and in the mind of man;
> A motion and a spirit, that impels
> All thinking things, all objects of all thought,
> And rolls through all things . . .

Ideas can be as much a matter of fashion as clothes or furniture, and a new view is beginning to be expressed by some scientists, based on developments in quantum physics, suggesting that Nature after all *is* ordered. If order is common to all things, the appearance of the Byrom Collection is timely, for it displays both diversity and unity.

CHAPTER TWO
The Challenge Outlined

THE COLLECTION ARRIVED on Tuesday 19 June 1984 in two bulky envelopes. Literally hundreds of pieces of card and paper covered with geometrical drawings of mathematical precision, many intricately detailed, all exquisitely constructed, tumbled out of the packets. Who had originally assembled these drawings and for what reason was unknown, though John Byrom (1691–1763) had certainly been their keeper.

The present owners of the collection did what they could to enlighten me. The drawings had been rescued from a cupboard some years earlier almost by accident. Then they had been put aside with the casual assumption that one day they would mean something to someone. So they were left to lie forgotten once more. It was my research for a biography of Byrom which had prompted the owners to remember their existence after I had visited them, and the family readily agreed that the collection should come to me for further study. The drawings had remained carefully preserved but in no particular order for over a hundred, possibly two hundred years. There were 516 separate pieces of paper, many with drawings on both sides, but not one accompanying sheet of notes to explain their significance.

Over the years I had come to know Byrom well. He was a complex personality with a brilliant mind and a predilection for subterfuge. Everything about him indicated that the collection would be purposeful and coherent. So to what part of his life could one allot this extraordinary series of diagrams?

Byrom had invented the first phonetic system of shorthand. Today this is a language of obsolete signs and symbols, although it is the one from which Pitman's shorthand was developed. The late Sir James Pitman put all his shorthand archives at my disposal, but it soon became clear that I had to teach myself the system in order to decipher the shorthand book of Byrom's which was to provide me with a new insight into his life. I had earlier suspected that Byrom was a freemason, and I wondered now if the collection were connected with Freemasonry, and whether that might hinder my investigations.

I began by covering every available surface in a large room at home with drawings set out and sorted into groups, like with like. Squares, triangles, circles, polygons, three-dimensional cubes and cones piled up to show the diversity of the collection. I invited to supper a carefully chosen group of colleagues which included an engineer, an artist, a bookbinder, an historian, a freemason and a scientist in the hope that they might recognise some feature which would provide a clue to the nature and purpose of the collection. They were all fascinated, but few facts emerged. The engineer reproduced a copy of one of the simplest drawings, which took him two and a half hours to complete. The artist thought that some of the diagrams might have mystical associations. The freemason, who spent much longer studying the drawings than anyone else, was quite decided that they had nothing to do with Freemasonry. My other guests could offer nothing tangible, though everyone agreed that the workmanship was highly specialised and the content far from commonplace. The order and beauty of the drawings demanded to be understood.

Some of the drawings had writing on them, others had not. Some were dated, and the latest was 1732. A number appeared to have instructions on them, but these were brief and cryptic. Some even bore initials and, here and there, a name. One or two mentioned the Royal Society, of which Byrom became a Fellow. Others contained biblical references with the measurements of the Ark of the Covenant. One very small piece contained English words strangely put together but including the word 'Cabalists'. This was to help me find a way out of the labyrinth.

Byrom and his Circle

I returned to John Byrom's Journals. Starting in 1707 and ending in 1763, the year of his death, they are still, despite the editing, the prime source for the facts of his life. Early in the first volume I came across the following entry for 25 February 1725:

> I writ a bit for Phoebe to read from Holmes Chapel, and a bit for the Cabala Club . . .[1]

Byrom was riding from Manchester to London at the time. The second clue appeared two weeks later. The date is 9 March:

> Thence to the Club in Paul's Church Yard, where we had two barrels of oysters, one before and another after supper. Mr Leycester, Glover, White, Bob Ord, Graham, Folkes, Sloane, Derham, Heathcote, a talking gentleman I had never seen before; paid 2s.6d. apiece ... I told them I was going to establish a Cabala Club that were guessers.[2]

The club at Paul's Church Yard was in fact the Sun Club, a group mentioned continually by Byrom and one which I had already studied. Meetings took place directly under the room where the Lodge of Antiquity met, one of four founder-lodges of the Grand Lodge of Freemasonry in England. Some members of the Sun Club also belonged to this lodge, and in addition were members of the Royal Society.

Sun Club associates of Byrom to whom he spoke of his intention to form a 'Cabala Club' were no strangers to me. One or two gained for themselves lasting reputations. George Graham (1673–1751), one of our greatest clockmakers, brought several improvements to Greenwich Observatory. Martin Folkes (1690–1754), a leading mathematician of the age, was elected President of the Royal Society and a member of the Royal Academy of Sciences in Paris. During the course of his life he gathered a library so vast that it took forty days to sell when he died. Sir Hans Sloane (1660–1753) was first physician to George II, and became President of the Royal Society in 1727. He had admitted Byrom as a Fellow in March 1724. Sloane bequeathed his scientific collections and books to the nation and thus laid the foundation of the British Museum.

These men were leading figures in the intellectual and scientific establishment of their day. Perhaps the collection of drawings was bound up in what they stood for as a group, though there is an unexpected silence about further meetings of the Cabala Club. Was this another exasperating consequence of the editor's heavy hand? Or had the Cabala Club gone underground? The collection of drawings possessed a shape and personality of its own, and Byrom had been custodian, but had he chosen the form it took? Had he indeed created the collection? What did he mean by his 'Cabala Club'? Throughout his time in London Byrom was involved in clubs, societies and lodges of one kind or another, but could I suppose some special and direct link between his Cabala Club and the drawings merely on the grounds that one of them mentioned 'cabalists'?

I decided to pursue the mystery of this club further. But first I needed to know more about the Cabala. The word itself appears in different forms – Cabala, Cabbala, Kabbalah and even Qabalah – and has its origins at the time of Christ as a mystical system within a Jewish sect known as the

Essenes. Over the centuries the Cabala developed into a highly complex body of teachings which are an attempt on the part of the practitioners to attain union with God. Eventually Christian mystics borrowed some of its doctrines and techniques to evolve a Christian form of cabalism. So what had started as a secret store of knowledge with theological, metaphysical and even mystical associations for ancient Jewish rabbis, who claimed to read hidden meanings in the Old Testament, had attracted Byrom sufficiently to form his own cabala club in eighteenth-century London.

The claims made for the Cabala as a way of enlightenment are vast; the spiritual and intellectual demands formidable. The language of many commentators on it almost inevitably becomes grandiose:

> The Qabalah has its ideal geometry, its philosophical algebra and its analogical trigonometry. Thus it forces, so to speak, Nature to render up her secrets.[3]

Even allowing for the writer's love of metaphor, was there such a thing as an 'ideal geometry' and were any of the drawings examples of it? This seemed a distinct possibility since apart from the word 'cabalists' there was a striking resemblance between one group of drawings and the cabalistic figure of 'The Tree of Life' – a diagram which represents the road to perfection and the various stages of development along the way. That is something of an over-simplification, for the symbolism of the Tree of Life is rich and manifold, and these drawings were much more geometrically detailed. It seemed imperative to consult a twentieth-century cabalistic adept.

The Investigation Begins

Since it was claimed that some cabalistic systems required ten years of study and isolation to understand them fully, I needed someone who could separate fact from rhetoric. The staff at the British Library could only point me to more books, not a suitable exponent. In the end I was recommended to visit the Theosophical Society in Gloucester Place, where it was suggested that I should speak to one of its members, who not only lectured on the Cabala but had published a beginner's guide. Over the telephone he described himself as 'The Principal of the International Cabalistic Movement'. What that meant I did not know. The title had a grand ring to it like some of the language in the commentaries I had been reading. But what was this movement and how did one become its principal? In August 1984 I visited him.

I had placed my preliminary groupings in numbered envelopes and as I withdrew the contents from each one in turn I felt like a conjuror producing a succession of white rabbits from a top hat. Soon my host and his wife were uttering little cries of wonder, now the usual accompaniment wherever I hawked my geometrical wares. There was obviously far too much material for him to deal with there and then. I agreed to leave the drawings overnight and he promised he would see what he could make of them.

On my return I discovered that he had spent half the night examining the drawings and writing summaries. I realised I had asked too much of him. He thought that a large proportion of the collection was based on hermetic and esoteric principles while other drawings were more strictly mathematical and scientific. He believed some had been used for teaching purposes and would have been housed and displayed in a special room. This may well have happened in Byrom's Cabala Club. As I read the summaries through, key phrases leapt from the hand-written pages to arouse my curiosity: 'mathematical side of the occult', 'striving for perfection', 'alchemy', 'astrological charts', 'excellent magician' and 'magnetic forces and rays'. Mathematics and the occult, science and magic, these opposing concepts were to occur again and again in the course of my investigations, but as yet there was no mention of buildings or architecture.

I had noticed that some of the drawings were connected with navigation and that one was the plan of the interior of a building. A few cards were dated 1724. Were these directly concerned with Byrom's club? I was also beginning to refine the categories of the drawings in sets and series – like playing cards – by shape, colour, number and other subtle variations in design. During this necessary process I collected together the names written on individual cards. Some of these were embedded in explanations or instructions which were themselves mysterious. The roll call grew: John Colet, George Ripley, Robert Fludd, Jacob Boehme, Michael Maier, Heinrich Khunrath, Lord James Paisley.

These men were scholars, doctors, mystics and scientists across the centuries. Colet and Ripley flourished in the fifteenth century, Fludd, Maier, Khunrath and Boehme straddle the sixteenth and seventeenth centuries. Lord Paisley, later Earl of Abercorn, was a member of the Royal Society in the eighteenth century. Some drawings mentioned his membership. Another person named was Matthew Gwinne, who became the first professor of physic at Gresham College on its foundation in 1597. On those drawings connected with navigation were, among others, the names of John Henshaw and Henry Sutton, prominent mathematical instrument makers in London during the seventeenth century. Several other drawings bore initials which, though meaningless at the time, were to provide an identity for much of the collection. Many more were unnamed.

It was obvious that these rich and various drawings had held a more than usual importance for Byrom. He had carefully preserved them during his lifetime. What should have happened to them thereafter? Were they of any relevance today? Or was their importance merely archival? Could any of them still be of practical use? Because there had been a suggestion of an association with magic, I thought it best to proceed with caution. One thing was certain; Byrom had not the skill to execute the drawings himself.

Since a form of Christian cabalism had emerged in the early Renaissance, perhaps the archives of the Church of England contained information about the tradition in this country. Byrom had studied for a career in the Church, though in the end his loyalty to the Stuarts prevented him from taking Orders. However, in the course of his studies he would have read the early fathers and the doctrines of many mystics. In response to enquiries at Lambeth Palace Library, the ancient library of the Archbishops of Canterbury, I received a list of obscure Latin texts on the subject but no mention of any manuscripts on cabalism. Perhaps these, if they existed, were housed in some other centre of Christian scholarship.

In October 1984, armed with a selection of the cabalistic drawings, I returned to the headquarters of the Theosophical Society. The librarian thought that the manner in which the Trees of Life had been extended and developed showed that the men concerned with those drawings had been deeply immersed in the Cabala and were not mere novices or dilettantes. It seemed evident to her, too, that the group using the drawings had come to a halt, otherwise they would have been passed on by Byrom to his successor.

The eighteenth century has been described as an age of enlightenment and the age of reason. Like all such labels these are only half-truths. Certainly in the early part of the century highly rational people still pursued modes of thought which we would not consider rational now. The boundaries of science and pseudo-science were less defined than they are today, and science could merge into metaphysics in a way that we would find unacceptable. Newton could propound on the one hand his theory of gravitation and display an interest on the other in alchemy and attempt to decipher the language of prophecy in the Book of Daniel and the Apocalypse of St John. He also believed in a secret tradition of learning which he thought could be traced back to the ancient Greeks.

After the accession of the Hannoverians, political instability continued until the Jacobites were finally routed in the '45 rebellion; it led to a confusion of loyalties in the first part of the century which encouraged the growth of secret societies. For some ambitious men time-serving and deception were the only means forward. Byrom's own choice of career instead of the Church was symptomatic. He perfected a form of phonetic shorthand and taught it privately. Despite its success, it was never published in his lifetime. He was thus able to provide his clients with a speedy but secret language in which they could lock away their confidences. At the same time it gave him an entrée to the great and the good and was responsible for his election to the Royal Society.

Appropriately the first drawing we look at is connected with his shorthand. In the collection it appears separately on a small piece of paper, but its true significance emerges when one sees it on the title page of Byrom's shorthand manual. Figure 1 shows a small square, quartered and inscribed with curves, straight lines and semi-circles and set within a circular border embroidered with flowers. At first glance the design is simply a neat construction of overlapping geometric shapes: circles, triangles, ellipses, but however pleasing to look at, they are also symbolic: Byrom's aim had been to devise a shorthand system whereby all the simple sounds of language were denoted by the shortest and simplest strokes. These, in turn, should join easily together and be 'always regularly and beautifully confined' within two parallel lines.[4] The signs which Byrom evolved are the same as the curves and diagonals which fill this square. It is both the master drawing for the title page of the manual and a summary of the system.

Sir Isaac Newton was President of the Royal Society when Byrom was elected. A few of the drawings had 'Royal Society' written on them. Byrom had studied at Trinity College, Cambridge, whose Master, Richard Bentley, had been responsible for the second reprint of Newton's *Principia*. He also enjoyed close links with Bentley and his family before joining the Royal Society. It was time to check for possible connections between Byrom and Newton. In February 1985 I paid a visit in Cambridge to Dr Simon Schaffer, who was a member of the Department of the History and Philosophy of Science and had been recommended as an expert on eighteenth-century science with a special interest in the pseudo-sciences and Newton's work. After examining a selection of the drawings, he concluded that they were part of an ancient tradition of learning and doctrines. He did not consider them to be particularly Newtonian, but felt that the philosophy behind them leaned more towards the work of Leibniz (1646–1716) and Robert Fludd (1574–1637). He felt that the particular samples he saw were working towards a specific end but was unable to divine what that end might be. Dr Schaffer confessed he had seen nothing like the drawings before, although certain features recalled the ideas of Andreas Freher[5]. A later study of Freher's own drawings confirmed this, though Freher's were created to explain while those in the Byrom Collection were intended to achieve an end.

The mention of Leibniz seemed significant. My research into Byrom had revealed a secret liaison between him and Queen Caroline, consort of George II. Leibniz had been her tutor before she came to England. Dr Schaffer could understand Byrom having the drawings if he were in

The Univerſal Engliſh

SHORT-HAND;

O R,

The Way of Writing Engliſh,

IN THE MOST

Eaſy, conciſe, regular, and beautiful Manner,

Applicable to any other Language,

But particularly adjuſted to our own.

Invented by JOHN BYROM, M. A. F. R. S.

And ſome time Fellow of Trinity College, Cambridge,

Now publiſhed from his Manuſcripts.

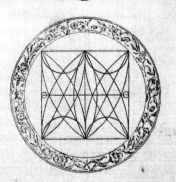

Fruſtra Per Plura.

M A N C H E S T E R:

Printed by JOSEPH HARROP, oppoſite the Exchange.

Figure 1: The Shorthand Manual, published in 1767.

any way connected with Caroline, for she was a bluestocking and her interest in mysticism has been well documented. He suggested a visit to the Warburg Institute as its archives contained material which might be helpful.

Despite Dr Schaffer's scholarship and willingness to help, I was not much further on the way to a fuller understanding. Certainly I was dealing with a very curious phenomenon. The reaction of everyone who saw the drawings was always the same: spontaneous delight and awe. Clearly they were important, but the precise nature of that importance was yet to be revealed.

I visited the Warburg Institute in April 1985 to show the drawings to the librarian, Dr Ryan. I arranged them in all their bewildering diversity on the table in the Director's office where Dr Ryan studied them in silence. He was obviously impressed by the material, but his chief concern was to warn me about becoming too involved in trying to fathom their mysteries. He explained that the Institute had source material for a number of fringe activities and consequently attracted more than a few eccentrics whose interests were in no way compatible with my own. This was the first hint of the dark side of the occult tradition in connection with the drawings. I was invited to return the next day to meet a colleague, who was equally impressed by the collection. Both men were most anxious to help but the only practical suggestion Ryan made was that I should talk to Sir Lionel Brett, a retired judge and a member of the Quatuor Coronati Research Lodge of Freemasons.[6] Dr Ryan had evidently seen masonic signs in the drawings.

As a woman I hesitated, but help came in the form of the Reverend Neville Barker Cryer, a senior freemason and, more to the point, Secretary to the Quatuor Coronati Lodge. For him I arranged the exhibits in a different order. I had learned enough about masonic symbolism to select those drawings with possible masonic associations and these were placed strategically for Mr Cryer's inspection. I had no wish to embarrass him by asking questions he might not want to answer. At the same time I wanted to establish the measure of his interest. If I had succeeded in creating some masonic order within the collection he would recognise it. So in June 1985, this ebullient and energetic cleric arrived to give one of the most spontaneous and demonstrative reactions to the collection I have seen. His delight was akin to that of a child let loose in Aladdin's cave. My selection and arrangement of the material paid a handsome dividend. He came to the conclusion that some of the drawings were part of a lost tradition belonging to the beginnings of Freemasonry in this country, and were of inestimable value in helping to establish ideas current in the earliest days of speculative Masonry. Through him I was able to draw responses from other senior masons, including Sir James Stubbs, a past Secretary of Grand Lodge, who recognised at once the cabalistic element in the drawings. Another mason, T.O. Haunch, wrote at some length that he could see an association of like minds, adding:

> Speculatives generally in the original and true sense of the word, e.g. members of the Royal Society, were attracted to the Craft. I wonder if, like Stukeley, they suspected it 'to be the remains of the mysteries of the ancients' and if so, cannot help but feel that, from what we know of the rudimentary freemasonry of the time, they must have been disappointed. Unless, that is, there really was some sort of inner esoteric circle, but of this my mundane and sceptical outlook makes me doubt.

I noted his reservations but was forced to consider that Byrom's Cabala Club might very well have been 'some sort of inner esoteric circle'. Byrom knew Stukeley well, for they attended the meetings of the Royal Society together. Stukeley even visited Manchester as a result of the recent discovery of a Roman stone inscribed to the Goddess Fortuna being brought to his attention by Byrom. Moreover, among the members of the Sun Club were prominent freemasons.

I turned my attention to the Royal Society, many of whose fellows – Newton, Stukeley and Byrom included – were interested in the mysteries of the ancients as well as the progress of science. In the collection there are drawings of 'The Ld Piesley's Load Stone'. A loadstone, being a form of magnet, can have a number of functions. Byrom knew Lord Paisley. At one time he had discussed with him the nature of Chinese characters. Later in the same year, 1725, the Royal Society was honoured by a visit from the Prince of Wales and the Duke of Lorraine during which various experiments were demonstrated, including some on the strength of Paisley's loadstone. It was evidently an advance of some importance, sufficient to interest Byrom.

Magnetism and cabalism, scientific experiment and esoteric investigation, the combination was characteristic of the age. With Jewish friends I studied the collection afresh. On one of the drawings were written the words 'Exodus 37 ch. Verse 6. Ark 5 to 3: or 10 to 6', the Biblical reference:

> And he made a mercy seat of pure gold; two cubits and a half was its length, and a cubit and a half its breadth.

We confirmed that the proportions of the Ark drawing were mathematically exact and corresponded to the reference. The Ark of the Covenant was a chest which was believed to have contained the stone tablets of Moses, a pot of manna and the rod of Aaron. It had been housed in the Temple of Solomon. Sir Isaac Newton's last work, published after his death in 1728, was *The Chronology of Ancient Kingdoms Amended*. In it he devoted considerable space to a description of the Temple. I knew that the Ark and the Temple had become important elements in masonic ritual and the more I learned about the collection the wider its provenance became. The last date recorded on the drawings was 1732. How could I bridge two and a half centuries to bring them nearer to our own day?

The Schweighardt Scrapbook

One summer evening in 1986 I was the guest of the Marquis of Northampton, who had heard about the collection from Mr Cryer. At that time Lord Northampton was Patron of the Hermetic Trust, one of whose functions was to publish facsimiles of Hermetic texts for modern scholars. The editor of the series, Adam McLean, was present at our meeting. As usual I had only a sample of drawings with me, but no sooner had I produced them than Adam McLean said something I had now given up hope of ever hearing. He recognised one or two. He had seen some comparable drawings in the British Library while engaged in translating a Rosicrucian manual by a German writer, Theophilus Schweighardt, published in 1618. In the back of the book containing this work were additional illustrations which he thought had been inserted at a later date. He had no doubt at all that the drawings in the Byrom collection were very similar. He explained that certain allegorical drawings of the sixteenth and seventeenth centuries often contained a geometrical substructure which conveyed a hidden meaning to initiates. Some of the drawings reminded him of those hidden geometrical patterns.

I returned to the British Library to track down the Schweighardt text and discovered several geometrical drawings, fifteen in number, in what can best be described as a scrapbook in which the German text has been inserted. It is this printed booklet which gives the 'book' its name in the library catalogue. The scrapbook is full of miscellaneous additions, including the geometrical drawings. On the inside cover is inscribed:

An account of the Rosicruc: Fraternity by Theophilus Schweighardt with the addition of several prints and miniature paintings by Mr. Rose.[7]

At this stage the other contents of the scrapbook were of secondary interest. More important was who had owned it, and how it had come to be in the British Library. It is generally accepted that Theophilus Schweighardt is a pseudonym, so I looked for other clues. The British

Museum was formed originally between 1753 and 1754. Later the old Royal Library was presented to the nation by George II. Both bequests were possible sources for the book. George had been married to Caroline of Ansbach, and she had possessed a magnificent library; the book might well have been hers. Her connection with Byrom could explain the presence of the drawings at the back. On the other hand, Sir Hans Sloane could equally have been the source. As members of the same clubs they evidently shared the same interests.

I needed to know something of the library's acquisitions and, as luck would have it, Professor Thomas Birrell was working on the library's catalogues, and in the building that very day. By an even greater stroke of good fortune he was studying the first volume of Hans Sloane's original collection of 1753, found the entry for T. Schweighardt, and was able to confirm that Sloane had owned the book and with it the fifteen drawings connected with Byrom's. For some reason they had become separated; now, two hundred and fifty years later they were brought together again.

It was now time to turn to the rest of the scrapbook. The Schweighardt treatise was published four years after the first of the Rosicrucian manifestos appeared in print in Germany. Frances Yates describes it as:

> Typical of such publications ... infused with Magia, Cabala and Alchymia, with its hint of earnest pursuit of learning and scientific activities, its prophetic side, its strong pietistic vein.[8]

Only today, perhaps, can the search for knowledge be seen as purely an intellectual activity. This has not always been so. Throughout the Western tradition, from Plato to the mediaeval scholar and, later still, in the Renaissance, intellectual progress has been automatically associated with moral self-discipline and piety. Milton, for example, believed that to be a great poet he had first to be a good man. Few, if any, artists would seriously hold that view today. Yet often the pursuit of truth for the seeker has been inextricably linked with spiritual growth. The good life is the prerequisite to wisdom. The upsurge of interest in Rosicrucian thought in seventeenth-century Europe is another example of this phenomenon. Stemming from idealism in the manifestos about a mythical person, Christian Rosenkreutz, and his brotherhood, this is best seen as an attempt to harmonise the finest elements of the occult tradition with Christian and humanist aspirations. A problem for us today in understanding the content of the belief is very often the context. We need to step back in time. References to alchemy and magic as if they are still serious possibilities are disconcerting, until the reader realises that, for the Rosicrucian, alchemy means the transformation of the human soul, not the transmutation of base metal.

The book is certainly a very odd compilation of esoteric verses, diagrams, small, extravagantly even crudely executed paintings, symbolic engravings and a handful of geometric drawings. One had the name 'Gerard Valck 1677' on it. Valck was a Rosicrucian. In addition there were the names of Elias Ashmole, the seventeenth-century freemason and alchemist; Khunrath, a seventeenth-century doctor and alchemist whose name appears on Byrom's drawings; Nicholas Flamel and Geber, both alchemists from an earlier era. The presence of these names was evidence of the underground stream of learning, the esoteric tradition, flowing in this instance from the fourteenth to the eighteenth century. The languages employed were just as varied: English, French, Latin and German. Much was cryptic and strange, and central to it all was the Rosicrucian pamphlet with its curious frontispiece. Frances Yates has drawn attention to this engraving:

> This print shows a peculiar building above which is an inscription containing the words 'Collegium Fraternitas' and 'Fama', and is dated 1618. On the building, on either side of its door, there is a rose and a cross. We are therefore presumably now beholding a representation of the 'Invisible College of the R.C. Brothers'.[9]

The compilation was clearly a source book of hermetic material, but who had been the collator? Mr Rose, mentioned in the front? Who was he? Disparate as the items might seem to the untutored eye, they were all unified by a philosophical ideal.

Two of the engravings stood out from the rest. Both were strikingly ornate, richly decorated, but one in particular caught my attention (figure 2). Behind, or embedded in, the immediate subject of the picture lay a geometric shape. I recognised with excitement the shape of one of my drawings. I had brought with me only a small cross-section, but fortunately, this one was among them. It consisted of a large square diamond flanked on two sides by two smaller diamonds (figure 3). The card had stuck in my mind because it had been cut out, not just drawn, to this unusual design. On one side were the initials 'MLB'. I placed it on top of the engraving in the scrapbook and it fitted perfectly. The inner geometry of the drawing and the card were an exact match. I was scarcely able to contain my delight in the restraining silence of the library.

The two engravings were major finds. Since they were both unnamed I shall for convenience refer to them as the 'Zeus' and 'St Michael' engravings. I shall deal with the St Michael picture in chapter seven where it properly belongs, but the Zeus print must be looked at here because of its place in helping to unravel the story of the collection and for leading me to some of the chief characters in that story.

The picture is filled with figures from Greek/Roman mythology. The main figure in the centre of the large diamond is Zeus. He can be identified by the thunderbolt in his left hand and the eagle above his head. He stands symbolically with his feet on the back of a turtle, a creature linked with the earth and with the God Hermes. The eagle perches aloft above a coat of arms which I spent many months in trying to track down, knowing it to be an important clue. The eagle indicates the extent of Zeus's domain from Heaven to earth. In each of the four diamonds which surround the main one are symbolical figures from Greek myth which represent the four elements which make up our world – Fire, Water, Earth and Air. Top left is Hephaestus, the smith God, an artist in metals with an anvil and instruments of Fire. Top right stands Poseidon on a vast sea shell, surrounded by sea beasts with trident and conch in his hands. He is Water. Below him we find Dionysus or Bacchus, the God who was worshipped as the source of the vital powers of nature, of tillage, and hence of early civilisation. The plough and the horse associate him with Earth. At the bottom left there is a younger, chubbier figure. He has with him symbols of Air, the birds, the peacock, musical instruments, the lute and a viol. (Music travels through the air.) Noticeable too is the ram with

Figure 2: The 'Zeus' engraving.

a bunch of grapes in his mouth. This figure is Ganymede, the beautiful youth who was carried off by the Gods to Olympus to be cup-bearer to Zeus. Some legends make Zeus fall in love with Ganymede whose story gave religious sanction to such a relationship. Ganymede was probably chosen as the Vitruvian figure to link Leonardo da Vinci by allusion to the man who, I discovered later, had commissioned the engraving.

In between the four elements are six other Gods inside oval frames. Starting again from top left we see Cronos in the act of eating his own child watched by Cerberus, the three-headed dog which guarded the way to death. The presence of Cronos reminds us of an earlier generation of Gods whom Zeus replaced. To his right stands Mars with his hound and arms. On the right below him stands Apollo, associated with the sun, hence the aureole around his head. He stands over the she-dragon Python on Mount Parnassus whom he killed. He is God of music and of prophecy. His oracle at Delphi proclaimed his maxim 'Know Thyself'. At the bottom right are Aphrodite and Eros symbolising human passion. To their left is Hermes, perhaps the most significant symbol of all. Here he is the messenger of the Gods, with his usual attributes of winged helmet and sandals and herald's staff. He is said to have helped the Fates compose the

Figure 3: The first clue, with the initials 'M.L.B.' printed on the back.

alphabet, and to have invented the musical scale, astrology and weights and measures. He is the prime symbol of, and gave his name to, the hermetic tradition. Finally we see Artemis, Goddess of the chase, sister to Apollo. Goddess of the moon, which we can see above her head, she was also the Goddess of virginity, and is shown so here. At her feet is Actaeon, the youth who, seeing her bathing, was punished by being turned into a stag. He was later eaten by his own hounds. Her presence balances that of Aphrodite and Eros, in keeping with another ancient Greek saying associated with Apollo: 'Nothing in Excess'. She also reinforces the platonic significance of the Ganymede figure below.

Outside, around the border of the picture, are the twelve signs of the zodiac in the traditional astrological sequence, from Aquarius through to Capricorn. Each is accompanied by a clock-face telling a different hour of the day. Finally, from each corner of the engraving blow the four winds from the four corners of the world. For this picture is an image of the world, the deities or forces which reign, the elements of which it is made, and the mathematical laws which hold it together. These laws are represented by lines which cross the circles and squares. They too may have an astrological significance.

If we return to the central diamond and Zeus, we find other hermetic symbols around him. The ape is an ancient figure, a symbol of Thoth, the Egyptian version of Hermes, the inventor of writing and hence the God of the Arts and Science. The ape came to be called the Ape of Nature and represents man's attempts through his skill and art to emulate the gods. The dog evokes ideas of fidelity and alchemy. The stag or hart is another emblematic creature whose antlers suggest the pattern of the cabalistic Tree of Life.

Later I learned of other impressive connections with the engraving. In the Sanctuary of Westminster Abbey is a cosmati pavement dating from the thirteenth century, whose geometrical concept is the same. Originally there was a Latin inscription set in the stones; translated it reads as follows:

Four years before this Year of Our Lord 1272,
King Henry III, the Court of Rome, Odoricus and the Abbot
set in place these porphyry stones.

If the reader wittingly reflects upon all that is laid down,
he will discover here the measure of the primum mobile:
the hedge stands for three years,
add in turn dogs, and horses and men,
stags and ravens, eagles, huge sea monsters, the world:
each that follows triples the years of the one before.

26

> Here is the perfectly rounded sphere which reveals
> the eternal pattern of the universe.[10]

The creatures listed here feature in the engraving, which also displays the 'eternal pattern of the universe'. Remnants of the geometrical motifs on the tomb of Edward the Confessor behind the pavement also reveal the same design. Evidently the engraver knew the tradition which inspired the pavement – which he may have studied. Moreover the geometry of the Great Pavement reflects the central geometry of the Abbey.

As can be seen, the engraving is remarkably rich in meaning and, in common with so much emblematic art, there are several layers of allusion. First, there is the most direct level of classical mythology. Then, there is the geometric substructure on which the classical figures have been arranged. This pattern is reproduced in different variations in the collection in more than one drawing. Third, there are other allusions to be revealed only to the believer. To illustrate these three layers, additional drawings have been prepared based on the inner geometry. Figures 4 and 5 are details of the geometry in the central diamond: figure 4 simply demonstrates the complex mathematical interconnections of this vision of the universe. Certain conjunctions, evidently more significant than others, are picked out by letters. Figure 6 shows how Zeus within the same pattern can produce in outline a frame for a Tree of Life, hinting again, like the antlers of the hart, at a cabalistic element in the picture, a Christian cabalistic element too. The right hand of Zeus is outside the framework of the tree, recalling Christ's injunction in the Sermon on the Mount:

> If thy right hand offend thee, cut it off, and cast it from thee.[11]

This is a reminder of the rigorous self-discipline required from the seeker after truth.

Finally, there is a fourth level at which we may look at the engraving, and that is with the use of a mirror to produce a mirror image. If a small mirror is placed at right angles down the imaginary centre line, running through the figure of Zeus and half-suggested by the upright sword in front of him, then either half of the picture can be reflected to create two new pictures for those who have the understanding again of this particular tradition. A mirror, present in the St Michael engraving, is a symbol for the multiplicity of meaning. It is said to be symbolic of the power of revelation, of fact or of the imagination. The myth of Narcissus is an example of the age-old fascination with mirror symbolism. The intangibility of a reflection carries with it associations of the supernatural. In figure 6 the mirror has been held to reflect the left half of the central diamond. The left hand of Zeus holding the thunderbolt disappears to be replaced by

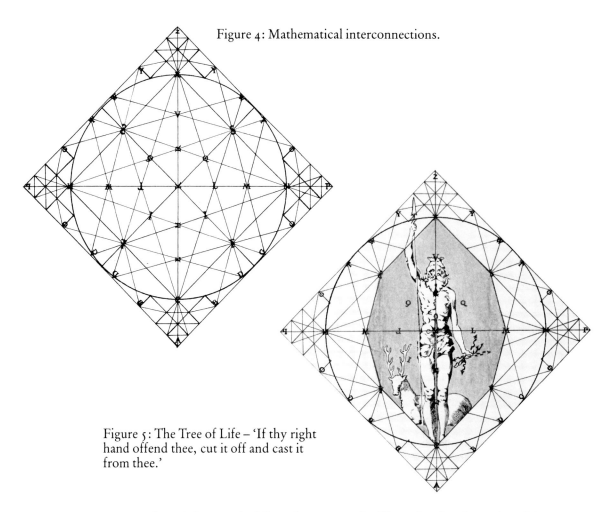

Figure 4: Mathematical interconnections.

Figure 5: The Tree of Life – 'If thy right hand offend thee, cut it off and cast it from thee.'

a second upright arm holding the spear of office, the dog is replaced by another ape of nature, re-emphasising the place of the arts and sciences in man's struggle to ascend. The head of the hart is also duplicated. If the mirror is reversed and you look into it from the right-hand, a similar process is repeated. Here, most significantly, the hart's head disappears and its body becomes a large stone, the Philospher's Stone. This is one of the most enduring, most potent symbols of the hermetic tradition. The neatness with which each side of the Zeus diamond can be so doubled is undoubtedly deliberate and has some arcane message for those for whom the picture was originally intended.

Not all these perceptions emerged at once. Over the months the emblems provided many hours of fascinating discussion with scholars and other writers. Each in his turn shed a little light to reveal more fully the texture of the engraving. However, while I was studying the content, I also bore in mind the other important fact: the relationship of drawings in the Byrom Collection to the engraving. There were various explanations for this, the most striking being that the same person had been responsible for both. Was I at last near to finding who had actually executed the drawings? A close examination of the engravings yielded up a name. Down towards the bottom right-hand corner of the Zeus picture, hidden away in a curl of a decorative scroll, were the words 'Blon fecit'. The same words appeared on the St Michael engraving as well, decorating the shield which lay at the feet of Mars in his chariot. The discovery of this name was a tremendous step forward, a leap from conjecture to solid fact, for it helped to elucidate the mystery of the drawings. I still did not know the identity of the coat of arms. It was so prominent that it too, I was sure, was important.

The drawings had come to me by way of Byrom; the engravings and some drawings were in a book once owned by Hans Sloane. Had both the collection and the scrapbook once belonged to the same person? If so, that might have been either Byrom or Sloane. But it was Byrom who had decided to form a Cabala Club, and the collection was so vast and covered such a wide spectrum of material that it looked much more likely that the scrapbook at one time must have been part of the collection.

Figure 6: The 'Mirror Image'.

The Two Le Blons

An examination of a Register of Engravers revealed a Huguenot family of engravers by the name of Le Blon. Jacques Christophe Le Blon was born in Frankfurt on Main in 1667, and after the death of his wife and child in 1715, when he was living in Amsterdam, he was persuaded by Lord Halifax to come to London. He did so around the year 1718, and two years later the art collector Colonel Guise, who had met Le Blon previously in Amsterdam, became his patron and the director of a company of noblemen who set him up in a printing office. Le Blon had invented a method of inexpensively reproducing oil paintings in colour. The Dictionary of National Biography lists some of his reproductions, which include a portrait of Queen Caroline. Though undeniably a man of great talent, Le Blon was a poor businessman. Bankrupt, he was forced to flee this country in 1732. That date I registered with interest, for it was the last date to be found on the drawings.

Some examples of Le Blon's work can be seen in the Print Room at the British Museum, at the Victoria and Albert Museum, and in the Gentlemen's Club at Spalding. His reproduction of Van Dyck's portrait of the children of Charles I shows the fine quality of his work. The only authoritative text on Le Blon is a biography by Otto Lilien, published in 1985. It concentrates on his work as an artist and makes clear his contribution to graphic art:

> Le Blon invented, followed and described the principles on which today all industrial colour printing is based and without which we cannot really imagine books, advertisements, magazines and newspapers.[12]

Unfortunately the book contains no reference to hermetic material or the engravings found in the Schweighardt scrapbook. There exists, however, a genealogy which shows Le Blon to be directly descended from the families of Matthaeus Merian and Theodore de Bry, who were known as eminent goldsmiths, engravers, printers and publishers on the continent.

Attempts to find the coat of arms on the engraving in British heraldry proved fruitless. It was evidently a European escutcheon, but that trail was intricate and, despite an extensive search, it remained an enigma. Nevertheless, there was among the drawings a group bearing the initials M.L.B. The Le Blon genealogy revealed a great-uncle of Jacques Christophe with the same initials. Michel Le Blon lived from 1587 to 1658. He, too, was born in Frankfurt. He, too, was an engraver as well as a goldsmith, highly respected in his day, specialising in coats of arms and book illustrations.

Michel Le Blon became sufficiently important or prosperous to have his portrait painted by Van Dyck. An engraving of this portrait carries an inscription which describes him as an agent to the Queen of Sweden and the King of Great Britain, who at the time was Charles I. Van der Kellen's catalogue of his known surviving works lists an impressive number, and entries 178 and 179 confirmed the identity of M.L.B. They were descriptions of the two engravings in the scrapbook which I had matched with some of the Byrom drawings. The descriptions and dimensions were exact. This meant that there were drawings in the Byrom Collection which were closely related to engravings by Michel Le Blon who preceded Byrom by more than a hundred years. In addition to this, at the end of the catalogue entry 178 came more intriguing information: 'The same composition engraved full size by Egbert van Panderen can be found in the work of Thibault, The Academy of the Sword.'[13]

So the 'Zeus' engraving existed in more than one form! The larger version had to be tracked down for any further clues it might hold about the collection. *L'Académie de L'Espée* by Gerard Thibault first appeared in Leyden in 1628. It is a most elaborate treatise on swordsmanship based on a highly complicated set of mathematical rules. The theory was certainly known to Shakespeare, who in *Romeo and Juliet* describes it aptly as fencing 'by the book of arithmetic'. By a neat coincidence it is Tybalt who is mocked for using a similar technique.[14]

The magnificent folio edition provided the key to the coat of arms in the Zeus engraving. It was in fact Thibault's own device. In the middle of the book, separating it into two halves and covering two pages each, were the larger versions of the engravings by Michel Le Blon. He had been commissioned by Thibault to do the engravings in 1615. Le Blon's versions differ in certain details. They were originally intended to publicise Thibault's method and the book he was planning. This took another thirteen years to complete, for it was conceived on a scale befitting such patrons as the Holy Roman Emperor and the King of France. Thibault died before it was published. Le Blon's engravings were to be used in a smaller edition which never materialised. They survived separately and appear to have come to England with Jacques Christophe Le Blon a hundred years later, together with other drawings bearing Michel's initials.

Certain facts had now emerged. There was evidence of a connection between Michel Le Blon, specific allegorical works of some stature and a number of Byrom's drawings. Le Blon's great-nephew, Jacques Christophe, was contemporary with Byrom and resident in London when Byrom was thinking of forming a Cabala Club. What was the link between Jacques Christophe and Byrom himself? In 1728 Le Blon was given permission to copy the Cartoons of Raphael at Hampton Court. A room was put aside for his use. He came from a group of German families well known for their long tradition of esoteric engravings and publishing. Queen Caroline, herself a German, would have known of them. She may well have been the intermediary between Jacques Christophe and Byrom.

Figure 7: Queen Caroline (1683-1737).

CHAPTER THREE

A Question of Origins

THE SUBJECT MATTER of the drawings was taken from a number of different areas. Many could be safely described as scientific or technical, mathematical and navigational. The boundaries of the rest were not so clearly definable. To the speculative student of Byrom's day, and indeed earlier, the subjects led imperceptibly, almost inevitably, one into another. Apart from those concerned with the Cabala, others illustrated ideas which were taken up into Freemasonry at the beginning of Grand Lodge in England. A fourth group is clearly connected with the Royal Society and its pursuits, both esoteric and orthodox. Some of the work was undertaken for a scientific purpose, while much seemed to be an attempt to achieve spiritual as well as intellectual enlightenment. Why else would Colet's work be mentioned? Different examples of handwriting, different names from different centuries suggested that the collection was source material for a group following specific aims.

A forerunner of the Royal Society was Gresham College. The name of Matthew Gwinne had been handwritten on the back of one of the drawings. Did this mean that the collection was, in part, rare evidence of the early lineage of our scientific establishment? The Schweighardt book was prefaced with an engraving of the Rosicrucian concept of an Invisible College. Robert Boyle, one of the founding fathers of modern chemistry and physics, referred to an Invisible College. It seemed that it might be possible to trace a line back from the Royal Society, through Gresham, to the idea of an Invisible College. Byrom's Journal shows his interest in Rosicrucian thought. That, combined with his interest in Freemasonry, the activities of the Sun Club and his membership of the

Royal Society, made him a suitable keeper of the collection, but although the drawings ended with him, he was most certainly not their originator. Detailed examination of the various watermarks in the paper has proved that conclusively. Some can be placed as early as the beginning of the seventeenth century. Some unmarked paper suggests an even earlier date.

There were other areas of intellectual endeavour which had been recognised, but which, as yet, I had not had time to pursue, in particular architecture. Certain drawings seemed almost intent on pushing investigations into geometry to their limit, while those concerned with architecture were to yield up the most surprising discoveries.

Here, then, is the pedigree of the Byrom Collection, some of the people who created it, the thinkers behind the drawings, what they were seeking and what they achieved.

Jacques Christophe Le Blon (1667–1741)

After leaving England Jacques Christophe Le Blon settled in France, where he attempted to launch his colour printing enterprise a second time, and died in Paris at the age of seventy-four in 1741. His second wife, Catherine, must have died earlier since his four-year-old daughter, Marguerite, was declared sole heir and a guardian was appointed to look after her. The inventory of his goods was comprehensive and included the titles of his colour prints, but it contained no mention of geometrical or mathematical drawings. This confirmed my suspicion that they had been left when he fled his creditors. Left but not abandoned. Once the esoteric nature of some of the drawings became clear, it seemed more likely that they had been carefully deposited with a suitable custodian in England. The final date on the drawings and the year of Le Blon's departure were not a coincidence. Curiously his name still appeared in the rate books for property in Chelsea in 1734.[1]

Le Blon had worked in London for at least thirteen years but where exactly had he lived during this time? The answer to that question, which might lead me back to Byrom and the drawings, lay in an advertisement for his treatise on colour printing, *The Coloritto*. In May 1725 *The Monthly Catalogue*, a register of books in print, tells us that one place where Le Blon's book could be purchased was 'at the Author's Lodgings at the Dial and Bible in the Strand'.[2] The *London Gazette* for 6 June 1721 announced that examples of his work were being sold at 'Mr. Vaillant's Booksellers over against Southampton Street in the Strand'. Roche's map of London for 1746 shows that this was practically opposite the Picture Office, the factory where Le Blon produced his colour prints. The Dial and Bible, a centre of much literary activity, was a bookshop owned by Edmund Curll, a well known bookseller and publisher. It appeared that Jacques

Christophe Le Blon was the lodger of one of the most colourful, not to say notorious, figures of London's literary scene. We shall return to Curll later; for the moment I noted that Vaillant's bookshop was one of Byrom's regular haunts. He cultivated the assistant as a go-between for his own ends and would innocently stay there 'some time looking over the books'.[3] It was an ideal meeting place for him.

Le Blon was a man of evident skill and his patrons had high hopes of the success of his new colour process. One of the shareholders in the Picture Office, the first Earl of Egmont, wrote to his brother in 1721 praising the quality of the pictures on sale. He was delighted to be able to report that the King (George I) 'has ordered likewise one of his rooms to be entirely furnished with them'.[4] The King had granted Le Blon a patent for 'Multiplying Pictures' in 1719, but by 1725 Jacques Christophe was in trouble with his creditors. On 16 March the *London Gazette*, together with other newspapers, announced:

> The persons concerned in the undertaking for Multiplying Pictures by Impressions are desired to meet next Wednesday the 28th of April 1725 at the Runner Taverne . . . at five o'clock precisely.

It was the beginning of the end. On 25 June the *Daily Post* reported the arrangements for distributing the 'moneys and effects belonging to the proprietors of the invention'. Jacques Christophe was nevertheless resilient. That same year he published his treatise on colour reproductions and continued to work on other technical processes. His inventiveness is beyond doubt, and can be judged by a second warrant from George I in March 1727, granting him an exclusive use for fourteen years of his latest technique: 'The Art of Weaving Tapestry in the Loom'. Whatever may have caused the collapse of the earlier venture, Le Blon was still regarded as a man with ideas worth backing.

In order to establish the provenance of the drawings it was necessary to investigate his earlier history. Although, as we have seen, it is generally thought that he came to England in 1718, he first visited this country in 1710, a man of forty-three with a wife almost half his age. Some of the drawings in the collection have on them the date 1707 and could not have originated with Byrom since he was then a youth of seventeen preparing for Cambridge. Other drawings are older still. Did Jacques Christophe have earlier associations with London? His picture factory had been sufficiently close to the French Huguenot Church to suggest a search through the Huguenot Society's records. The 'Returns for Aliens' dating from the mid-sixteenth century showed that 'Le Blonds' had settled in England. Le Blond is a form of spelling used by other branches of Jacques Christophe's family. One entry lists the 'names of those who presented themselves with good evidence to be received into the Church'.[5] Dated 29 January 1568, it includes a George Le Blond. Records show a George Le Blond's descendants living in London, one of whom was later knighted by George III. These two Georges are, I believe, the same man, the begetter of the English Le Blonds. Hitherto it has been assumed that George died in 1576, but it is more likely that he settled as a refugee in this country with two of his sons while his wife fled with three others to Frankfurt. The parents may well have deliberately sought safety from religious persecution in two separate communities rather than risk all in one bid for safety. The massacre on St Bartholomew's Day 1572, which had caused the exodus, cost the lives of two thousand Protestants in Paris alone.

Living in the same Huguenot community at the same time as George Le Blond was a 'James Debraie . . . Picture Maker'.[6] In Frankfurt the Le Blon and De Bry families were closely connected in the same publishing house and engravers' book trade. The two families intermarried. In London we find people with the same names, albeit anglicised, following the same profession, working and living parallel to them. It would be an extraordinary coincidence if they were not related. The evidence points to London's George Le Blond being Michel's grandfather and the great-great-grandfather of Jacques Christophe.

In 1920 C.T. Courtney Lewis wrote a history of a firm of copperplate engravers and printers registered in London as Le Blond and Co. The founder members, brothers Robert and Abraham Le Blond,

> were descended from an old Huguenot stock, whose property in France being confiscated, the family came to London; indeed it was said to be an ancestor of these two who set up in Spitalfields the first silk-weaving machine; they also claimed to be descended from that James Christopher Le Blon, the well known figure, who in the time of Hogarth was the first to print pictures in their natural and proper colours from a series of metal plates, which was the real origin of printing in colours by the three-colour process . . .[7]

Abraham Le Blond, the surviving brother, died at the age of seventy-five in 1894 after the Official Receiver had sold off the assets of the firm, which had gone bankrupt.

The financial collapse recalls the mismanagement of Jacques Christophe's two London enterprises. Was there, perhaps, a fatal flaw in the Le Blon family which emerged at intervals in its history? Or were they simply dedicated artists exploited by artisans and patrons alike? Listed in Abraham's stock in 1895 were 'Cartoons of Raphael'. These were drawn by Jacques Christophe over a hundred and fifty years earlier for his tapestry venture. It looks as if one of Jacques Christophe's kinsmen had purchased them when the tapestry company was sold. They remained with the family until Abraham's assets were liquidated.

The Le Blon family, although based originally on the continent, had clear links with England and these would account for Jacques Christophe's earlier visits to this country. Lord Halifax would have no difficulty in persuading him to settle here. Apart from the security of Halifax's own influence, there would be the pleasures of family connections already comfortably established. In addition Le Blon shared an interest with the greatest English scientist of the day, Sir Isaac Newton, which bore directly on his career and ambitions. Both men had studied the three primary colours blue, yellow and red. Le Blon claimed to be able to reproduce the colouring of an original painting by overprinting them one on top of another. Lord Halifax knew Isaac Newton and would be acquainted with his theories on colour. These may well have been the cause of his initial interest in Jacques Christophe.

Le Blon clearly attracted men of high rank and social stature as his patrons. Among them was Colonel John Guise (1683–1765), an officer in the Grenadier Guards who was highly regarded as an expert on art. He was joined by his cousin, Sir John Guise, the head of the Guises of Elmore, Gloucester, and a friend of George I and the Princess of Wales. In a family memoir[8] Sir John recounts the period when he was able to exercise some influence with the royal house of Hannover. It was at the time when Princess Caroline was distraught because her father-in-law George I ordered her husband, the future George II, to leave the palace of St James after the christening of her son Prince Henry, Duke of Gloucester. There had been a violent disagreement over the choice of godparents which had resulted in a family rift showing the two Georges at their most stubborn and disagreeable. The Princess turned to Sir John for advice and he tactfully recommended submission to the King's 'will and pleasure' in order to bring about a reconciliation between father and son. Caroline obviously came to rely on his advice and friendship, which had commenced in 1717, just before Jacques Christophe arrived in England. It is clear from the memoir that Sir John remained the confidant of George I also.

With two such well-placed patrons as Lord Halifax and Sir John Guise, it is not surprising that Le Blon was introduced to Court circles soon after his arrival. In 1728 a room was set aside in Hampton Court during the time when he was painting the Cartoons of Raphael, once wall hangings in the Vatican, while they were housed in the Cartoon Gallery, an annexe to the palace designed by Sir Christopher Wren. Caroline was no longer Princess of Wales but Queen Consort to George II. Although copies of the Cartoons were finished, only one of these was used to weave a tapestry for Le Blon's new weaving enterprise – the head of Christ taken from the Miraculous Draught of Fishes. A rare specimen of this can be seen in the museum of the Spalding Gentlemen's Society. It was presented to the Society by Sir Richard Manningham (1690–1759), obstetrician, in 1732. The Spalding Society was founded in 1712[9] for gentlemen interested 'in the liberal sciences and in polite learning', a wide enough term to embrace all the areas dealt with in the drawings. Among the members were Sir Isaac Newton, Sir Hans Sloane, Alexander Pope and Dr William Stukeley. Manningham had shares in the weaving factory which Le Blon had set up in Chelsea. Just before the collapse of that venture Le Blon himself was invited to become a member of the Society.

Despite the ultimate failure of his career in England, Jacques Christophe Le Blon was so well thought of that his meeting with Byrom was almost inevitable, and it was through Jacques Christophe that Byrom obtained a large part of his collection. Mutual connections in royal circles, Sir John Guise, or the loosely knit group of freemasons who were members of the Royal Society brought them together. It was James Anderson, who drew up the Constitutions of the Grand Lodge of Freemasons, who translated Le Blon's *Coloritto*. I believe that Jacques Christophe began instructing Byrom in the mysteries of those drawings which are dated 1724 to 1732. Byrom announced the formation of the Cabala Club in 1725 and the last date coincides with the sudden failure of the tapestry weaving enterprise through which thousands of pounds were lost. At about the same time Byrom retired to Manchester suffering from some kind of indisposition, and did not return until December 1734. His absence may account partly for the few drawings retained by Sir Hans Sloane and placed in the Schweighardt scrapbook. Nevertheless Byrom's interest in the drawings had not ceased.

The Mysterious Mr Rose

My attention was caught by an entry in Byrom's journal for Thursday 1 May 1735:

> I went to Sam's coffee house at one o'clock, called upon Mr. Charles Houghton by the way, found Dixon and Graham there, we to Mr ... in Bartholomew Close, where he showed me his engine for cutting and working Egyptian pebbles, and the collection of nine figures and papers of Rose about the cabalistic alchemy etc. very extraordinary, and many curiosities which I think to call some day to look at, Jacob Behmen's three principles; there we parted and I came to Abingdon's.[10]

I was intrigued by the references to 'papers of Rose about the cabalistic alchemy', the 'nine figures' and Jacob Behmen. Each of these had a bearing on the drawings. But who was Mr . . . ? Why the deliberate omission of his name, even in shorthand? Byrom's interest in the Cabala had started at least ten years earlier. Why did he make such a mystery over this particular encounter? The 'papers of Rose' could refer to Rosicrucian material and that recalled the Schweighardt book which had written on the front 'An Account of the Rosicruc. Fraternity . . . with the addition of several prints and miniature paintings by Mr. Rose'. Given the similar contexts there had to be a connection.

I had first come across the name of Mr Rose in connection with Edmund Curll, the infamous landlord of Jacques Christophe Le Blon. Curll was frequently brought before the courts for publishing irreverent and indecent books. In 1716 he was reprimanded with a printer on his knees before the bar of the House of Lords for piratical publishing. His unscrupulousness landed him in prison more than once. Hogarth caricatured him, and Pope, with whom he feuded bitterly for twenty years, pilloried him in *The Dunciad*.

Curll's list of publications did include some important works, but his indifference to authority bordered on arrogance. He did not expect an official complaint when he published *The Nun in Her Smock*, nor to be brought to trial, as he was, towards the end of November 1725. In his defence Curll suggested that the book was 'a satirical piece exposing the intrigues of the Nunes and Fryars by Mr. Samber of New Inne of which we only sold one . . .'[11] Naturally he pleaded Not Guilty, adding:

> This prosecution appears to be malitious for the following reasons –
> in being brought Seven Years after the publication of the first Book
> which will be proved a Physick Book ex professo by Mr Rose – of
> the Coll of Physicky . . . To prove that the Treatise of the use of
> Flogging is a Physicale book – call Dr. Rose.[12]

The year this book was first published was the year that Le Blon settled in London. Could Curll's Mr Rose and his tenant Le Blon be the same person? Jacques Christophe, we know, is associated with Byrom's drawings, some of which have a Rosicrucian content. Two engravings by Michel Le Blon accompanied the Rosicrucian pamphlet by Schweighardt. Rose is an obvious *nom de plume* for anyone connected with the movement, adherents of which were fond of playing on the words 'Rose' and 'Cross'. Jacques Christophe may well have known of a bawdy anti-Catholic satire which amused him as a Protestant whose ancestors had suffered as a result of religious intolerance. A man of his robust temperament would see Curll's book as a harmless squib in 1718, when it appeared under the guise of a medical treatise on the harm of flogging. The later edition was another matter. Re-issued with a more prurient title, *Venus in the Cloister* or *The Nun in Her Smock*, it led to Curll's arrest and imprisonment. Besieged at this time by creditors, it is not surprising Jacques Christophe changed his lodgings. The squib had backfired, and by April 1726 Curll was advertising for a new lodger.

Mr Falkner

It was now necessary to trace the identity of 'Mr . . . in Bartholomew Close'. Moving back through Byrom's Journal from the May entry, I came across this for 21 January 1735:

> thence to the King's Head where there were fourteen of us . . . talked about deciphering. Mr Glover, upon my saying it was impossible to decipher if only the numbers of letters in a word were given, gave me this: 4, 2, 3, 5, 4, 5, which I found out to be 'What do you think this means?' I drank a little more sack negus and ate heartily . . . Young Graham showed me his circles within circles for cutting jewels, said that Falkner in Bartholomew Close had them and other things to sell, and said something of mystical divinity.[13]

Clearly Byrom was playing games with friends over his shorthand, pleased at his success with the numbers and in convivial mood. The important thing is the mention of Falkner, obviously the name he had left blank in the later entry. In January it was safe to mention his name, but by May, in the context of papers of Rose and cabalistic alchemy, it is deliberately omitted. It must be remembered that the journal was a collection of separate notebooks which were put together later. For some reason, in May, Byrom did not want anyone with access to his loose papers and who knew his shorthand to learn Mr . . .'s identity.

It is almost certain that Byrom returned to Bartholomew Close and acquired the cabalistic papers. His observation that they were 'very extraordinary' implies that he would want to place them with his own. Perhaps he was intended to have them. Jacques Christophe Le Blon, alias Mr Rose, had left England hurriedly earlier while Byrom was away. Why did he choose to leave the papers with Falkner? It is obvious that they were not part of the business stock of either of his enterprises. They must have been part of the philosophical archives of his family's engraving and publishing concerns both in Amsterdam and Frankfurt. Who better to leave them with at a time of crisis than a relative, however distant? One of Jacques Christophe's forebears had married a Margaret Falkner. Was it a relative of this woman who was living in Bartholomew Close, engaged in pursuits not unconnected with the family's traditional hermetic interests?

In March 1736 Byrom chose to record the election of Falkner to the Royal Society. Its Minute Book lists his proposers and the reasons for his nomination, which was soon after Byrom's visit to Bartholomew Close. Apart from being an expert on precious stones and fossils, Falkner was 'well versed in most branches of Mathematics'.[14] Two of his proposers, Sloane and Martin Folkes, were present when Byrom announced the idea of a Cabala Club. Sloane had acquired drawings which fitted the description 'cabalistic alchemy' and matched some of Byrom's. Folkes was present when Falkner's extraordinary collection was discussed at the Sun Club in January 1735. The importance of Falkner's papers was not in doubt. Moreover, Byrom's subscription to the Royal Society had not been paid for eight years, but the day after he heard of Falkner's election he went to the Society and accepted a bill for his dues.[15] Falkner's election undoubtedly prompted his renewed interest. It looks as though Falkner was regarded as a source of further material now that Jacques Christophe had departed.

I searched every appropriate record for additional information on Falkner. The Scavenger Rates for Bartholomew Close show that his property was a house, not a shop, and that he lived there from 1734 to 1748. He was also of sufficient standing to serve as a vestryman at St Bartholomew the Great. Curiously the church records do not mention his death. The minutes of the Royal Society contain no further information except that his membership lapsed in 1751. There is no further mention of him in Byrom's journal and no trace of a will. After being the centre of great interest among Byrom's innermost circle he disappears, but the evidence indicated that for a while he had a role in the dissemination of alchemical and cabalistic literature.

Michel Le Blon (1587–1658)

The Le Blons were one branch of a large and influential group of families whose activities as engravers, artists and publishers spanned several generations. The founder of this remarkable dynasty was Theodore de Bry (1528–1598). It was this family blood line, combined with shared and inherited beliefs, which ensured the safe transmission of the drawings. Michel spent his childhood in Frankfurt, the home of Theodore de Bry, but moved in his youth to Amsterdam, where he rapidly acquired a fine reputation as a goldsmith, silversmith and engraver. For fifty years he was a leading figure in artistic circles in Amsterdam and far beyond. In addition he became a successful art dealer whose clients included not only the aristocracy but royalty as well. His blessings were completed

Figure 1: Michel Le Blon, 1587-1658.

by his marriage in 1615 to Margaretta Houtmann. They had six children and their happiness was marred only by the loss of a daughter when she was thirteen.

Michel's talent, combined with his charm, assured his success; his wit and vivacity seem always to have made a great impression on people. Van Dyck's portrait shows both the successful artist and the man of the world. His masterly skill as an engraver survives in books of heraldic devices and coats of arms. A two-volume edition of his heraldry was published by Jan Claes Visscher, and this is of particular relevance to the Byrom Collection. Visscher was responsible for one of the few panoramic views of London which contain the Globe Theatre and other Elizabethan playhouses. Matthaeus Merian, the father-in-law of Michel's brother, drew another. We shall return to these relationships in the next chapter. For his own coat of arms, a cross of St Andrew on a field of silver, Michel chose the motto 'Mourir pour vivre' in keeping with a dominant characteristic – his interest in spiritual and philosophical ideas.

Success as an artist led Michel into the world of diplomacy. From 1618 he was an 'agent for Sweden', though it was not unusual for governments to employ private citizens as unofficial envoys. Such men did not have full diplomatic status but nevertheless played an important part in negotiations between countries. From being employed initially to purchase works of art, Michel was gradually entrusted with other commissions. On Van Dyck's portrait he is described as 'Agent for the Queen of Sweden and the King of Great Britain'.

Michel became an important art dealer.[16] One of his most distinguished and colourful patrons was the Duke of Buckingham, the arrogant favourite of James I. In 1625 Buckingham employed Michel to negotiate the purchase of Rubens's magnificent collection of paintings and statues. Le Blon's commission enabled him to travel to Italy to study the work of Italian painters. His next important English patron was Thomas Howard, Earl of Arundel, a professional diplomat and one of the great English collectors of art. These aristocratic connections stood him in good stead and he became 'ambassador of Sweden to the English court' which entailed frequent visits to England. His diplomatic activities increased further after 1632, though frankly some of them were for espionage. From 1647 to 1649 he lived in Sweden as one of Queen Christina's advisers but then returned home, aged sixty-two, anxious to be with his wife and children. Always conscious of his family ties and their shared beliefs, he visited his father in Frankfurt in 1651, for he was nearing his end. Michel died seven years later at the age of seventy-one.

Michel's association with the drawings is not surprising; he was deeply interested in mysticism, especially the life and work of Jacob Boehme – the same Jacob Behmen mentioned by Byrom in connection with Falkner. Boehme, whose ideas are represented in some of the drawings, was a humble German cobbler who became one of the great religious visionaries of the early seventeenth century with an immense following. In England he attracted the admiration of many, including Sir Isaac Newton and, later, Byrom. Michel Le Blon translated one of his books and belonged to a small group of Dutch followers anxious to learn all they could about him. In 1638 Le Blon met Abraham von Frankenberg, a disciple of Boehme, and in 1642 bought from him the manuscript of Boehme's 'Little Prayer Book' together with some letters. Frankenberg's name also appears on a drawing. In Frankfurt Michel's brother, Christoff, translated some of Boehme's work into French. Michel's personal sympathy with the ideas embodied in part of the Byrom Collection can be seen in his dealings with a Dutch Jew, Menasseh Ben Israel, who possessed a large collection of cabalistic drawings which Le Blon at one time tried to sell to the Queen of Sweden. He also recommended to the Queen a Dutch painter who had to flee the Spanish Netherlands because of his Rosicrucian beliefs.

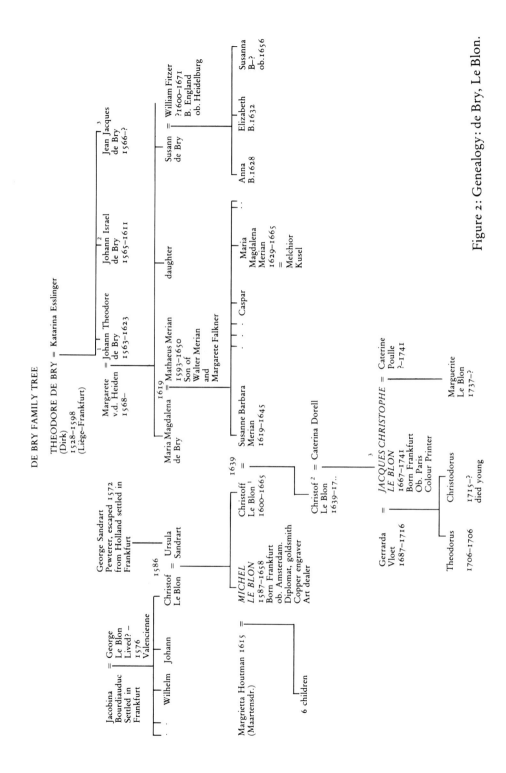

DE BRY FAMILY TREE

Figure 2: Genealogy: de Bry, Le Blon.

44

THIBAULT FAMILY TREE

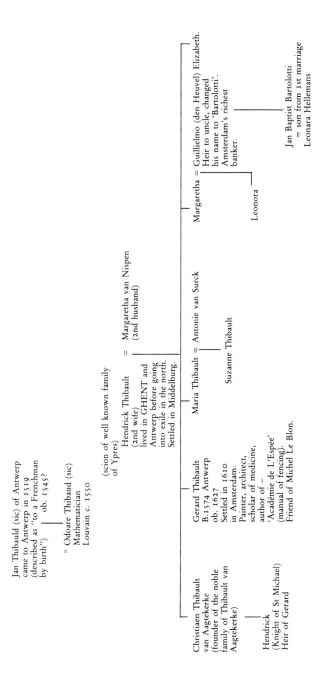

Figure 3: Genealogy: Thibault.

De Bry and Co

Michel and Christoff remained close all their lives. Christoff stayed in Frankfurt, married the daughter of Matthaeus Merian, and through that marriage eventually inherited a half-share in the publishing concern founded by Theodore de Bry. Merian had married Theodore's grand-daughter, Maria Magdalena. Theodore and his two sons, Johann Theodore and Johann Israel, are crucial figures in the pedigree of the Byrom Collection. Each, directly or indirectly, played a part in the evolution of the Elizabethan theatres. Links between the continental and English elements were maintained by different generations of this family. Merian's mother was Margaret Falkner, a putative relative of Jonathan Falkner.

Another link was forged by William Fitzer, an English printer from Worcestershire. In 1624, after completing his apprenticeship with one of the leading booksellers in London,[17] Fitzer made straight for Frankfurt. Within a year he had married the youngest daughter of Johann Theodore, who had died in 1623. Johann Israel had died some years earlier. So the family firm was being carried on by the elderly widow of the founder who was anxious to be relieved of the burden. She obtained permission from the city fathers in Frankfurt to admit Merian as a resident to help her run the business. In 1625 Merian and Fitzer bought the concern jointly and divided the stock equally. Fitzer remained a resident alien in Frankfurt until 1632, when he left because of the Swedish occupation of the city. He moved to Heidelberg and continued publishing under the Frankfurt imprint until much of his stock, including copperplates, was destroyed by fire in 1638. Fortunately Merian's stock, with which the Le Blon family were involved, was not affected by this disaster. In Frankfurt Fitzer had specialised in printing English writers who were long established clients. These included Robert Fludd, a personal friend and another figure in the collection, and William Harvey, the physician who discovered the circulatory system of blood. The de Brys had established a tradition of publishing philosophical, hermetic and mystical texts in handsome editions which were beautifully illustrated. In the process they had accumulated a rich heritage of knowledge from their association with the writers they promoted.

Gerard Thibault

Gerard Thibault has a place in the evolution of ideas connected with the drawings. He commissioned the two engravings for his book in 1615 when fencing had long ceased to be solely a skill required in war. Successive exponents had raised it to an art and an essential accomplishment for the educated gentleman. The first of the 'modern' manuals of fencing was produced in Italy by Camillo Agrippa in 1553. It was no accident that this man was a philosopher, mathematician and architect.

These three disciplines overlap in varying degrees in the work of other personalities connected with the drawings. Two great Spanish masters of fencing, Jeronimo Carranza and Luis Panchero de Navaez, developed the mathematical basis of the art further. In 1600 fencing was taught at the University of Leyden by the Professor of Mathematics. Thibault, a disciple of the Spanish school, was also highly regarded for his skill as a painter, an architect, and for his knowledge of medicine.[18]

He refined his system until about 1611 when he presented himself to the acknowledged Dutch experts for one of their competitions, and took first prize. He was then summoned to demonstrate his skills to Prince Maurice of Nassau. In a series of demonstrations over several days he again emerged triumphant. The sensation this caused fired his ambition to produce the definitive manual on fencing. *L'Académie de L'Espée* took fifteen years to produce and contained forty-six illustrations by sixteen different engravers, but apart from the engravings the text shares several basic assumptions with some of Byrom's drawings. Chief among these is the idea that man is a microcosm of the universe: the harmony and proportion of his physical body reflects the harmony and proportion of the universe. This idea, which gained great currency with the Renaissance, has its origins in the philosophies of Plato and Pythagoras, and was inspired in part by the work of Vitruvius, the Roman writer on architecture. He stated that a man's body with its arms and legs extended fits into a square and a circle. Leonardo da Vinci's famous drawing of this idea was used to illustrate some editions of Vitruvius's *De Architectura*. It was inevitable that other artists and scholars should produce their own versions. Dürer attempted one, Henry Cornelius Agrippa drew another in *De Occulta Philosophia* in 1531, Robert Fludd used yet another in book two of *The Microcosm* in 1619. Yet it is apparent that Michel Le Blon's representation in his 'Zeus' engraving is very close to Leonardo's, much more so than either Agrippa's or Dürer's. It is possible that Le Blon had seen a copy of Leonardo's drawing, perhaps in Cesare Cesariano's illustrated edition of Vitruvius.

I decided to look further into the family of Gerard Thibault for any other links with the Vitruvian tradition. He was the son of a merchant, Henrick, and descended from a well established family in Ypres. Henrick Thibault had lived for some time in Antwerp, where a Jan Thibault had settled in 1519. He was, I believe, Gerard Thibault's great-grandfather. A Frenchman by birth, Jan had a varied and colourful life.[19] He appears to have been something of a charlatan but one who always managed to obtain the most distinguished patrons, including Margaret of Austria, the aunt of the Holy Roman Emperor Charles V. He claimed to be 'doctor in ordinary' to Louis XII of France and 'physician in ordinary and astrologer' to his successor Francis I. How reliable these claims are we cannot now be certain, but, if they are well-founded, he could have been a member of the King's household at Amboise during the time Leonardo was in the French King's service and living in the chateau at Cloux nearby. A subterranean passage connected Leonardo's palace with the King's. Francis used it frequently to visit Leonardo. As physician to Francis, Thibault would have met Leonardo, possibly even attended him as his health failed. He could not have been unaware of the proudest acquisition to the King's household. Jan's acquaintance with Leonardo would have become part of the Thibault family lore and one means of the transmission of Leonardo's Vitruvian ideas to Gerard.

Leonardo da Vinci and Pacioli

Who had inspired Leonardo towards his interest in Vitruvius? At the time he is thought to have done the Vitruvian drawing, he was working at the court of Lodovico, Duke of Milan. In 1494 Leonardo read the *Summa de Arithmetica* of Luca Pacioli, perhaps the greatest mathematician of the Italian Renaissance. This book dealt not only with pure mathematics but also with its application to book-keeping and commerce. Widely read throughout Italy, it so impressed Leonardo that he urged the Duke to bring Pacioli to Milan, where Pacioli lectured on arithmetic, geometry and military tactics. The two men became great friends, so much so that Leonardo collaborated with Pacioli on his other great work, *On Divine Proportion*. This was written between 1496 and 1499 and is devoted to the application of mathematical sciences (arithmetic, geometry and proportion), to architecture, and to a treatise on the regular bodies of geometry. All these have a place in the Byrom Collection. One reason why Pacioli's book is so highly regarded is the series of drawings by Leonardo.

At the time when they were producing the book Aldus Manuzio was founding his printing press in Venice. He was one of the great printers in Europe whose name survives because of his beautiful editions of Greek classics. The 'Aldus' type was especially designed for small editions which could be carried in the pocket and were sold at a modest price. They aroused enormous interest and admiration and played a vital part in the spread of classical culture across Europe. In 1500 Leonardo and Luca spent a month in Venice and it is believed that Leonardo visited Manuzio. This is not surprising for there was a clearly established relationship between the proportions of good architecture and good type.

The subject was a matter of genuine aesthetic concern. Earlier writers, such as Leone Battista Alberti, had considered how best to form Latin capital letters according to laws of proportion. Pacioli took up the idea:

There were minor disagreements between these experts about the precise rules governing the height of vertical strokes relative to their width, and about the exact design of complicated 'round' letters such as G, Q, and R. But all saw the correct formation of letters as an important part of the cosmic mystery of proportion, the key to understanding each and every science known to antiquity . . .[20]

Pacioli added an appendix to *On Divine Proportion* which dealt with the formation of letters. We can see the same fundamental ideas in Pacioli's teachings about printing and architecture, Leonardo's work on anatomy and geometry, and Thibault's manual on fencing techniques. They all stem from Vitruvius's original pronouncement in *De Architectura* that the human form contained the two main figures, namely the perfect circle and the square.

John Dee (1527–1608)

Perhaps the most controversial figure connected with the drawings is the Elizabethan scholar John Dee. His attempt to communicate with angels inevitably damaged his reputation, but his contribution to the drawings and to the cultural life of Elizabethan England cannot be ignored. Among the drawings four reproduce a sign devised by Dee which he called the Monas Hieroglyphica. This was intended as a symbol of a religious truth. Just as today a physicist might reduce a universal law to an equation, so Dee chose to express the complexities of his belief in visual form.

He was one of the leading mathematicians in Europe whose skills were put to the service of Elizabeth's mariner-adventurers to improve the navigation of their ships. As a scholar he amassed a library so renowned that it brought the Queen together with her Privy Council to visit him at Mortlake. His reputation brought him invitations to the courts of two Holy Roman Emperors. He was a pioneer in encouraging the technical and mechanical skills in this country. His Preface to Henry Billingsley's English translation of Euclid emphasised the importance of the application of arithmetic and geometry to a number of arts and skills. Closely based on Vitruvius, it, too, was in the tradition of Leonardo and Pacioli.

Broadly speaking there are two sides to Dee's character: on the one hand there is the scholar and scientist, on the other a searcher after esoteric truth with an impulse to acquire supernatural powers. The drawings of his Monad in the collection are a clear proof of the presence of hermetic thought as opposed to more orthodox piety. This aspect of Dee's work was important to the creators of the drawings. It coincided with some of Byrom's own studies and complemented those concerned with the Cabala.

It was for this reason that I turned my attention once more to Jonathan Falkner and Bartholomew Close. One bundle, MS 4048,[21] of the records for the church of St Bartholomew the Great, now lodged at the Guildhall Library, contains a list of the Rectors and among them was the following entry (figure 4):

David Dee. A.M. 15 June 1587 –

This was followed by

Thos. Westfield. L1.B.18 Dec. 1605 per Depriv. Dee+

The cross after Dee's name referred to a note at the bottom of the page:

He was abused in the street, was sequestered, and forced to flee ... He died 1644.

These two entries brought me up with a jolt. Here was the name Dee; but this time as the name of another ecclesiastic deprived of office at St Bartholomew's in 1605. John Dee had been forced to leave his position as Warden of Christ Church in Manchester the same year. Were these two men related and were their summary departures connected?

John Dee drew up his own family tree which one can study at the British Library. In it he claimed descent from Roderick the Great, an early Prince of Wales, and kinship with Elizabeth I. His grandfather was Bedo Dee, who apparently merited the attention of a genealogist on his own account. H.B. Wilson describes him as 'Bedo Dee the Great, Standard Bearer to Lord de Ferrars at the siege of Tournay, 1513'.[22] He also served in the army of the Holy Roman Emperor Maximilian I. More important, Wilson showed Bedo Dee as the grandfather of David Dee, whom he describes as 'Rector of St Bartholomew's, London where he was buried 3 Febr.1619/20'. Wilson had a different date for Dee's death but a more specific one, including day and month of burial. The significant thing was the relationship. He and John Dee were either brothers or cousins, certainly contemporaries.

Wilson's genealogy fortunately contained the maiden names of several women who had married into the Dee family. This showed that Arthur, a son of John Dee and his third wife Jane Fromond, had married Isabel, the daughter of Edward Prestwich of Hulme near Manchester. I knew this family from my biography of Byrom. A copy of the Byrom family tree confirmed my suspicion. The sister of Isabel, Ellen, had married into the Byroms. This meant that John Dee and Byrom were related by marriage. No doubt Byrom knew this and it added to his interest in Dee. His home in Manchester was cheek by jowl with Dee's residence a century earlier. The two men were far more closely linked than has hitherto been realised.

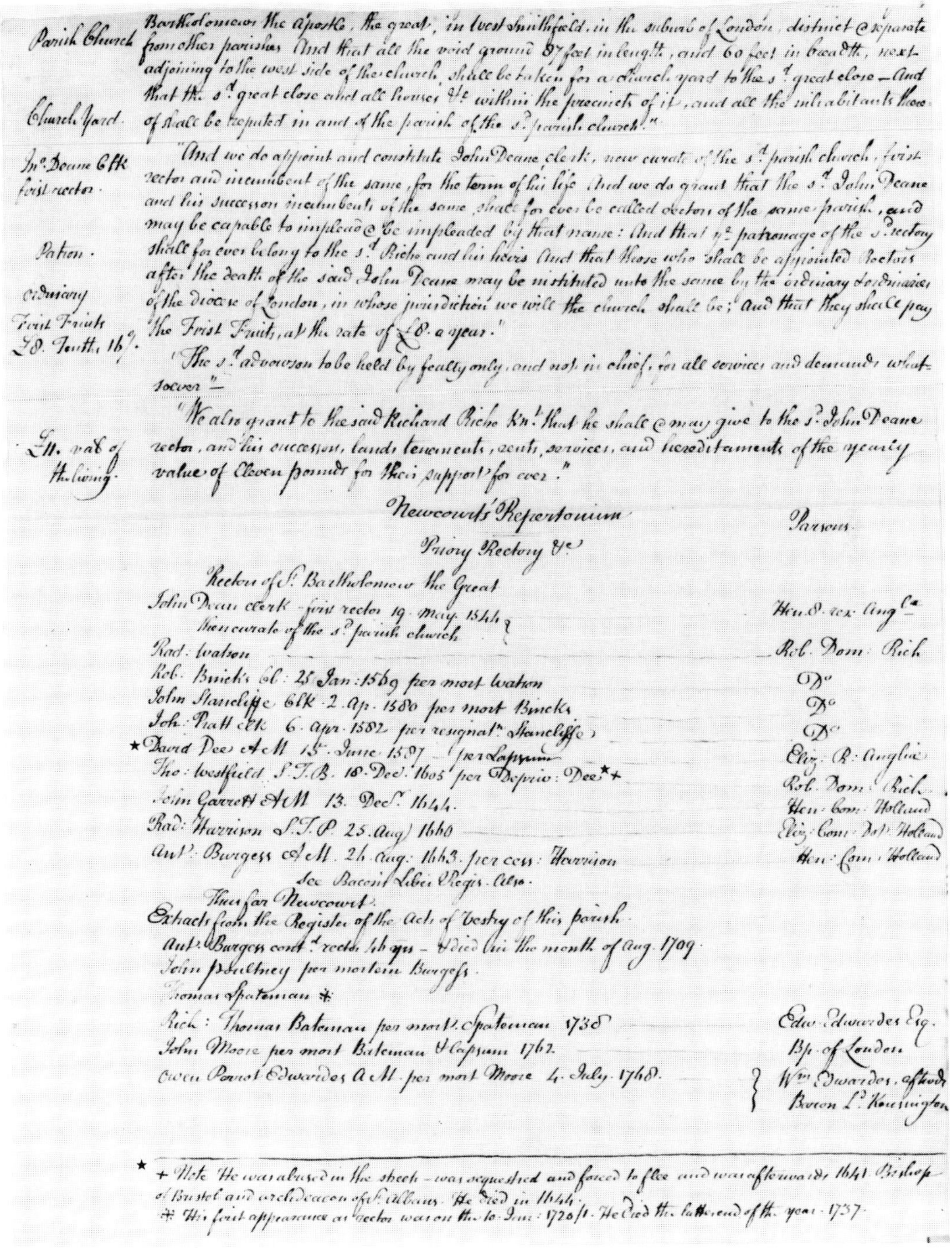

Parish Church Bartholomew the apostle, the great, in west Smithfield, in the suburbs of London, distinct & separate from other parishes And that all the void ground 87 feet in length, and 60 feet in breadth, next adjoining to the west side of the church, shall be taken for a church yard to the s.d great close — And

Church Yard. that the s.d great close and all houses &c within the precincts of it, and all the inhabitants there of shall be reputed in and of the parish of the s.d parish church."

Jn.o Deane Clk first rector. "And we do appoint and constitute John Deane clerk, now curate of the s.d parish church, first rector and incumbent of the same, for the term of his life And we do grant that the s.d John Deane and his succession incumbents of the same, shall for ever be called rector of the same parish, and may be capable to implead & be impleaded by that name: And that y.e patronage of the s.d rectory

Patron. shall for ever belong to the s.d Rich.d and his heirs And that those who shall be appointed Rectors

ordinary after the death of the said John Deane may be instituted unto the same by the ordinary Ordinaries of the diocese of London, in whose jurisdiction we will the church shall be; And that they shall pay

First Fruits L.8. Tenth, 16/9 the First Fruits, at the rate of £8. a year."

"The s.d advowson to be held by fealty only, and not in chief, for all services and demands whatsoever —"

£11. val.e of the living. "We also grant to the said Richard Riche kn.t that he shall & may give to the s.d John Deane rector, and his successors, lands tenements, rents, services, and hereditaments of the yearly value of Eleven pounds for their support for ever."

Newcourt's Repertorium   Patrons.

Priory Rectory &c

Rectors of S.t Bartholomew the Great

John Dean clerk — first rector 19. May. 1544.?   Hen.d rex Ang.ca
    his curate of the s.d parish church.

Rad. Watson   Rob. Dom. Rich.

Rob. Bricks clk. 28 Jan. 1569 per mort Watson   D.o

John Stancliffe clk. 2. Ap. 1580 per mort Bricks   D.o

Joh. Platt clk. 6. Apr. 1582 per resignat. Stancliffe   D.o

★David Dee A.M. 15. June. 1587 — per lapsum   Eliz. R. Anglia

Tho. Westfield S.T.B. 18. Dec.r 1605 per depriv. Dee ★ +   Rob. Dom. Rich.

John Garrett A.M. 13. Dec.r 1644.   Hen. Com. Holland

Rad. Harrison S.T.P. 25. Aug. 1660   Eliz. Com. D.s. Holland

Ant.o Burgess A.M. 26. Aug. 1663. per cess. Harrison   Hen. Com. Holland
            See Bacon's Liber Regis. Also.

            Thus far Newcourt.

Extracts from the Register of the Acts of Vestry of this parish.

Ant.o Burgess cont.d rector 14 y.rs — died in the month of Aug. 1709.

John Poultney per mortem Burgess.

Thomas Spateman ★

Rich. Thomas Bateman per mort. Spateman 1738   Edw. Edwardes Esq.

John Moore per mort Bateman & lapsum 1762.   B.p. of London.

Owen Pownet Edwardes A.M. per mort Moore 4. July. 1768.   } W.m Edwardes, afterw.ds
                                                                 } Baron L.d Kensington

★ + Note. He was abused in the streets — was sequestred and forced to flee and was afterwards 1641 Bishop of Bristol and archdeacon of St Albans. He died in 1644.

⚹ His first appearance as rector was on the 10 June. 1720/1. He died the latter end of the year 1737.

Figure 4: Manuscript from the Church of St Bartholomew the Great, London.

Watermarks and Other Markings

In the summer of 1988 I visited St John's College, Oxford, to discuss the drawings with Howard Colvin, the editor of the authoritative study of the royal palaces in Britain, *The History of the King's Works*. With true academic caution he suggested I should check the drawings card by card for watermarks to establish their authenticity. This may seem an obvious step in hindsight, but I had never felt the need to doubt the genuineness of the material. I knew where the drawings had come from, how they had come to light, and could appreciate why they had lain so long unnoticed. However, I immediately recognised the correctness of Colvin's response and set about establishing the necessary evidence.

Apart from showing that the drawings were not modern forgeries, the watermarks, if there were any, would help to narrow their period of origin. I had often held individual drawings up to the light to examine them, for a number were pierced with holes which form patterns different from the geometrical designs on them. At no time, however, had I seen a watermark. Out of a total of 516 pieces of paper 171 turned out to have a watermark, many of them incomplete and masked by the design of the drawings. Some could easily be missed. Many of the marks were discernible only on close examination with the help of a light box.

Weeks were spent consulting the authorities on English and continental watermarks: Briquet, W.A. Churchill, and Heawood, and a number of interesting facts emerged. One of the earliest English paper

Figure 5: Heraldic design by Michel Le Blon.

mills was established at Osterley in Middlesex between 1574 and 1576 by Sir Thomas Gresham the financier who founded Gresham College. The name Matthew Gwinne, first professor of medicine at Gresham, was handwritten on one piece of paper. The connection might be significant. As I suspected, a great deal of paper was produced which did not contain any watermarks. By 1588 a German, John Spilmann, who became jeweller to Queen Elizabeth, had set up a mill at Dartford. He was granted a monopoly of the collection of rags and paper-making materials in England, but we know from correspondence in connection with this that there were other mills in the country before his: at Osterley, at Cambridge and in Worcestershire. So there is plenty of evidence for the making of paper in this country during Elizabeth's reign, although most English paper was still imported from the continent. Among the 171 drawings with watermarks there are several well established marks. Some

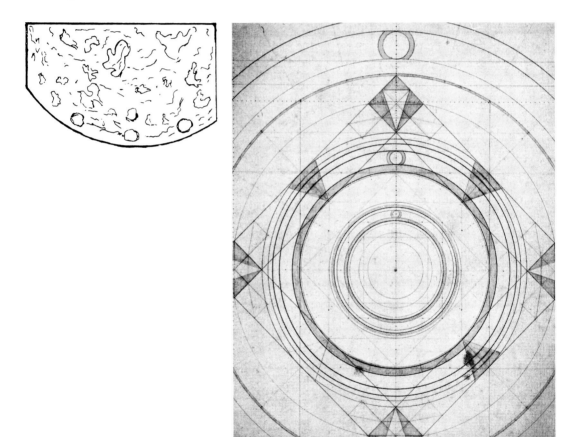

Figure 6: This drawing contains a watermark similar to the border of the heraldic design in figure 5. The initials 'M.L.B.' are on the back.

are clearly Dutch, emanating from Amsterdam with Pro Patria/Garden of Holland motifs. We know too that in Frankfurt Theodore de Bry made his own paper and printed some English commissions on it. Because many of the individual drawings have been cut from larger sheets, some miss the repeat of a watermark altogether. Others have only part – half or less – of a mark on them. Many of these can be identified from comparison with complete examples. Others were drawn on paper which had no watermark apart from a series of parallel lines. One of the drawings which contains the initials of Michel Le Blon has part of a watermark on the top left-hand corner. This resembles a design to be found in Van Der Kellen's catalogue of Le Blon's engravings and helps us date this as pre-1647 (figure 5). The drawing itself is associated with Le Blon's Zeus engraving and is pierced with a symmetrical pattern of dots unrelated to the designs but obviously with some specific purpose (figure 6).

We know that the de Bry family was printing a book on unmarked paper between 1590 and 1602. In the collection there is also a watermark of a fool's cap similar to de Bry's fool's cap from the same period. The earliest date for a known watermark in the collection could be 1600 and the next 1602. The earliest bears the three crescents of Venice (1600) and the next is the de Bry fool's cap. But this does not mean the paper was made in those years: rather it indicates that books containing paper with those watermarks were printed in 1600 and 1602. It has long been accepted that the life of a batch of paper with the identical mark may well have been as much as thirty years. Michel Le Blon could have purchased or used paper made in 1600 when he visited Venice in 1627. It is wise to allow a large margin of time in attributing dates to the *making* of paper as opposed to its *appearance in a book*.

Examples of eighteenth-century publications on unmarked paper tend to be rare, so it is unlikely that Byrom and his contemporaries used it. The absence of watermarks on many drawings, therefore, favours an earlier date. The watermarks we have suggest the seventeenth century or earlier. All the drawings are undoubtedly genuine.

The Handwriting and Other Matters

Most of the drawings, as we have noted, were executed by hand, though some were prints; of these a few were commercial products concerned with mathematical instruments. Many were coloured by hand, predominantly in yellow and gold. Some bear press marks as though they were patterns for printing, which would explain the occasional note on them, 'patterns for the rest'. The material they are written on ranges from coarse card, thick and mottled, to very fine paper. The handwriting presents a variety of styles, as one would expect in a collection which extends from the

Figure 7: Michel Le Blon's lettering styles.

1570s to the 1730s. It is difficult to assign precise dates simply from the script. Some of the calligraphy is very deliberately and beautifully formed, in keeping with the precision of the geometry. It is as much a work of art as the drawings and resembles the lettering illustrated on an engraving by Michel Le Blon (figure 7). Other scripts are bigger, bolder and less carefully formed. English, French, German and Latin comments are written in a variety of cursive styles characteristic of the seventeenth century and taught in such manuals as Martin Billingsley's *The Pen's Excellencie* (1618) and Richard Gething's *Calligraphotechnica* (1642), but changes from the older English script had started before the end of the sixteenth century.

There are a few idiosyncrasies not visible to the reader but which give character to the collection and tell us a little more about their life. The drawings were not designed as works of art. Despite their remarkable workmanship, they were intended to be used, studied, shared. Consequently they carry the humdrum signs of everyday life: coffee stains, grease and occasional scrawls. These last include signs from Byrom's shorthand. Many are pierced with holes of various kinds. Some have rows of pin-pricks around the edges at close regular intervals and are connected with printing. Some were pierced by compass points. One or two of such holes are accidents caused by someone working with one drawing placed inadvertently on top of another. Some larger holes were carefully punched through cards so that they could be hung up. In addition there are series of dots intended as a basis for measure on some drawings and on a specially made ruler. All these are signs of the practical nature of the drawings.

The genealogy of the Byrom Collection has followed a circuitous route because of its diverse components and the range of contributors. In a sense John Dee is the archetypal figure of the pedigree. Broadly speaking, the two sides of his character, which we noted earlier, correspond to the two main strands in the collection: the religious and the scientific, the theoretical and the practical, the esoteric and the orthodox. Apart from Dee, the de Bry family not only helped to spread the ideas, but encouraged the application of some. Michel Le Blon drew a number of the drawings; Jacques Christophe instructed Byrom and his group in their mysteries. They were studied by distinguished men in the late seventeenth and early eighteenth centuries, including Sir Hans Sloane and Robert Boyle. Byrom's friends in the Royal Society and among the freemasons were genuinely interested in using them. They are an important record of a critical time in the transition from pseudo-science to a more scientific approach to understanding our world. They also contain unique archive material of the cultural history of this country, as we shall see in the following chapters.

CHAPTER FOUR

The Globe and the Fortune

TWO DRAWINGS CONTAINED enigmatic references to 'the Globe'. One states briefly 'for Globe: 9: Exact', the other refers to 'the globes uper pt 3:6:9 a rule for itt'. A third drawing, expressing the same ratio 3:6:9 contained the words 'Double size For ye bottom'. Since these cards seemed to be related, the first thing to do was to decide on a meaning for the word 'Globe' consistent with these phrases. Did it refer to the terrestrial globe or to some artefact? Could it even be the name of Shakespeare's theatre? Each explanation was considered at some length.

I felt daunted by the possibility that any drawing might be concerned with an Elizabethan playhouse. The implications of such a find were far-reaching, for until now no drawings of any of the theatres – except a sketch of the Swan and some engravings of London's Bankside – were known to exist. Furthermore a project was already under way on the South Bank of the Thames to reconstruct the Globe theatre. Architects, actors, builders and academics were working together to produce at long last a replica of the playhouse within yards of where Shakespeare's plays were first performed. It was necessary to proceed with caution before even suggesting that any drawings connected with the theatre had by some miracle survived. Money, time and immense personal prestige had been expended in recent years on deciding how best to build the new Globe. It would have been far more convenient to settle for the simpler interpretation that the globe referred to was terrestrial.

Indeed the collection contained prints of the terrestrial globe, so it looked for a moment the most likely explanation. I studied the three drawings within this context only to discover, when I placed them by the side of the navigational ones, that important distinctions emerged: while the navigational drawings were mostly prints, these were not. The others were detailed and complete representations of the terrestrial globe, with precise markings for maritime or astronomical calculations. The two marked 'Globe' were not complete in this way. If they did refer to the planet Earth then they were only cross-sections. There were, moreover, no indications of any spherical shape such as can be seen on other drawings concerned with navigation, no markings of longitude or latitude, no information from which astronomical or geographical bearings could be taken.

I pondered all these points for months before I found myself willing to consider the alternative. Given that the cards were at least 250 years old, it was not impossible for 'the Globe' to refer to a building, and for that building to be the Globe playhouse. The question simply had to be investigated.

I began to take the possibility seriously when I read the argument put forward by Frances Yates in *Theatre of the World*, which I had consulted for information about the de Bry family of publishers who were central to engravings concerned with the drawings. Thus, as so often happens, the pursuit of one clue led to the discovery of another. In *Theatre of the World* Dr Yates traces the origins of the Elizabethan playhouse to the principles of architecture first expounded by the Roman writer Vitruvius at the time of Augustus, and rediscovered with the Renaissance. Yates believed these concepts were later transmitted to Elizabethan England, a theory now held by a number of scholars but still a source of controversy. The opposite school of thought sees the origin of the commercial playhouse in the courtyard of inns or the round arena of bear-baiting houses.

To support her case Dr Yates cited some much debated remarks made by Mrs Hester Thrale, a society hostess and friend of Dr Johnson, who had married a rich Southwark brewer. During the winter the Thrales lived in a house near the brewery in Southwark, and one day Mrs Thrale thought she had seen on the Bankside the 'curious remains of the old Globe playhouse which though hexagonal in form without was round within'.[1] Some scholars have chosen to dismiss Mrs Thrale's account of what she saw. Recent discoveries by archaeologists on the sites of the Globe and the Rose theatres have thrown even greater doubt on her remarks. Yates, writing before those excavations had even been contemplated, set out to determine, if she could, what it was Mrs Thrale saw in the ruins of the tenements her husband demolished in the late eighteenth century. In setting out her case, Dr Yates drew attention to the architectural treatise by Alberti, *De re aedificatoria*, and produced a plan of what she thought was the most likely design of the Globe theatre. To rehearse logically the steps by which she arrived at this design, we must first go back to Vitruvius himself (figure 1) who writes in Chapter 6, Volume V of *De Architectura* of the ideal theatre layout:

> Having fixed upon the principal centre, draw a line of circumference equivalent to what is to be the perimeter at the bottom, and in it inscribe 4 equilateral triangles, at equal distances apart and touching the boundary line of the circle, as astrologers do in a figure of the 12 signs of the zodiac, when they are making computations from the musical harmony of the stars. Taking that one of these triangles whose side is nearest to the scaena, let the front of the scaena be determined by the line where that side cuts off a segment of the circle, and draw, through the centre, a parallel line set off from that position, to separate the platform of the stage from the space of the orchestra ... The sections for spectators in the theatre should be so divided, that the angles of the triangles which run about the circumference of the circle may give directions for the flights of steps between the sections ... The angles which give the directions for the flights of steps, will be seven in number; the other five angles will determine the arrangement of the scene: thus the angle in the middle ought to have the 'royal door' opposite it; ...[2]

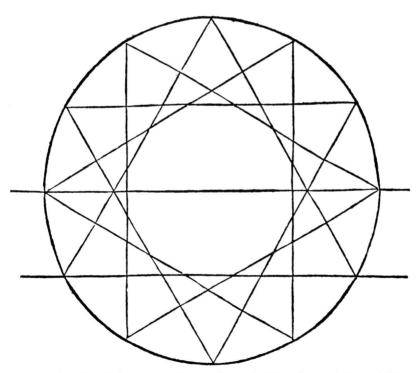

Figure 1: The plan of the Roman theatre from the French translation of Vitruvius.

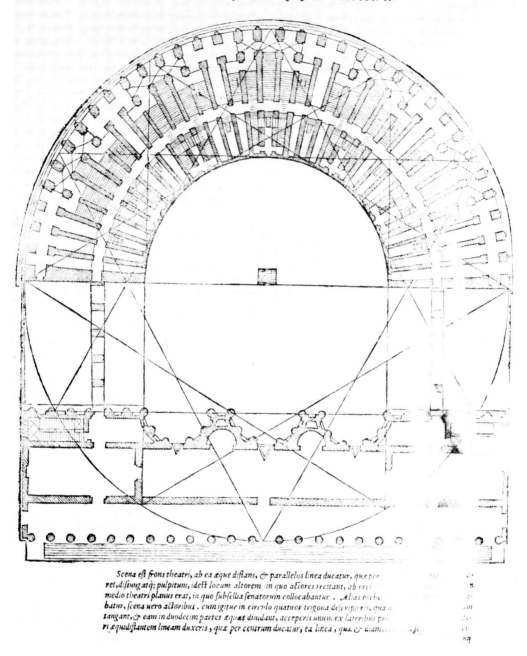

Figure 2: Palladio's plan of the Roman theatre. The geometry is the same as that of many in the Byrom Collection.

This may sound complicated, but Palladio actually designed a Roman theatre in accordance with these instructions which shows clearly the geometric design (figure 2). When in 1485 Leon Battista Alberti published his book *De re aedificatoria* popularising Vitruvius's theories, he added one important touch to the Vitruvian original – an awning painted with stars, spread over the theatre partly to protect the spectators from the elements, partly to help with the acoustics. Renaissance architects, through people like Alberti, were encouraged to employ a number of geometrical shapes in their buildings; the square is an obvious one, but octagonal, hexagonal and a number of other polygonal forms were also advocated. Even though Mrs Thrale's claim to have seen the remains of the Globe are now largely discredited, the outline she described was in keeping with Renaissance precept. Sufficiently so for Dr Yates to adduce the following diagram as a suggested shape of the Globe playhouse (figure 3).

She interpreted the physical shape as follows:

> Within the circle we inscribe four equilateral triangles. The base of one gives the position of the frons scaenae or tiring house wall at the Globe; a line parallel to it on the diameter of the circle gives the position of the front of the stage. Seven of the triangle apices give the positions of seven gangways in the auditorium; the five others would indicate positions of five entrances on to the stage in the frons scaenae.[3]

She continues:

> Hexagon and circle; but there is also a square in this suggested plan. The square represents the stage, or rather the whole stage building, including both tiring house and stage.

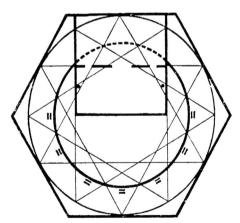

Figure 3: Suggested plan of the Globe theatre, from *Theatre of the World* by Frances Yates.

There were several drawings in the collection which appeared to explore the geometrical layout of a Roman theatre along these lines. Figure 4 is remarkably close to both a French drawing based on Vitruvius (figure 1) and Palladio's version (figure 2). There are differences, of course, but the Byrom drawing is clearly concerned with positioning equilateral triangles inside a circle, and that is in keeping with the Vitruvian formula for constructing a theatre. A theatrical provenance seemed confirmed by the drawing marked 'for Globe: 9: Exact' (figure 5) and the geometrical correspondences between both of these diagrams and Dr Yates's suggested plan for the Globe theatre. In her reconstruction Frances Yates had completed all the equilateral triangles necessary to produce the requisite number of gangways in the auditorium and entrances on stage from the frons scaenae. On figure 5 lines radiate out to the circumference from the centre hinting at a similar function. Moreover, figure 6 refers to the 'globes uper pt' and displays circles which fit precisely into the centre of figure 5. Further connections were indicated by the ratio 3:6:9 which was common to both the 'globes uper pt' and the drawing headed 'Double size For ye bottom' (figure 7). Although all was not yet clear, enough

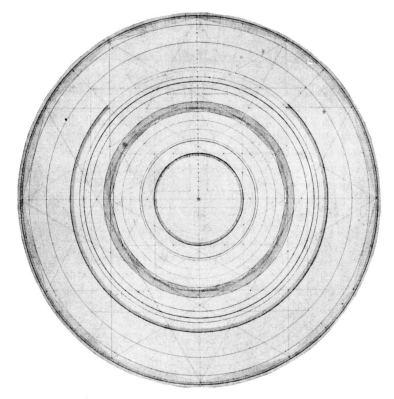

Figure 4: This seems to be a plan of a theatre based on Roman principles with additional details – a typical example from this section of the Collection.

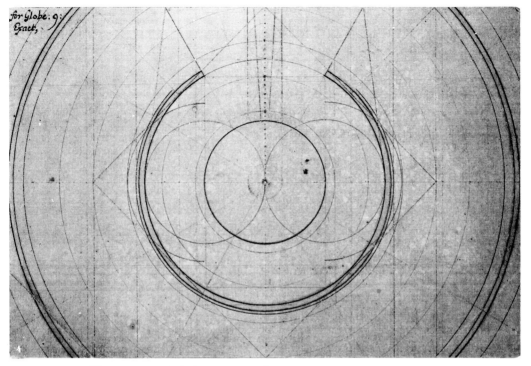

Figure 5: A vital discovery – 'for Globe:9:Exact'.

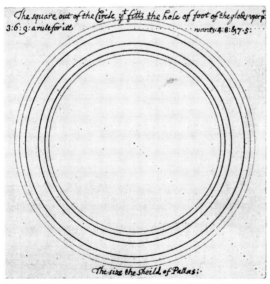

Figure 6: 'A rule for itt – the globes uper pt:' One of the sequence of Globe drawings.

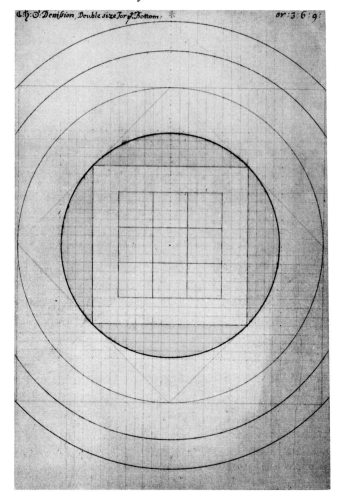

Figure 7: A precise instruction – 'Double size for ye Bottom'.

clues had emerged to link these drawings together in a theatrical context associated with the Globe theatre. One phrase at the bottom of figure 6 – 'the size the sheild [sic] of Pallas' – remained inscrutable and haunted me for months until I finally discovered its meaning and relevance.

The implications of these comparisons led me to consider the relation of the drawing to the Elizabethan theatres in Byrom's day. All the open-air playhouses had vanished from the face of London long before the collection of drawings had come into Byrom's hands. In fact all public theatres had been closed during the Puritan Commonwealth. When they re-opened after the Restoration of Charles II, theatres remained firmly indoors. The old Elizabethan thrust stage had been replaced by the proscenium arch, and the conventions of the indoor theatre, with all its technical devices, became the norm for almost two hundred and fifty years. So if drawings with the word 'Globe' on them did refer to a playhouse, surely they could not be early eighteenth-century sketches by people who had seen the buildings themselves. Moreover they could not be based on Mrs Thrale's dubious observations of some ruins. The last date on the drawings is 1732, and Byrom retired from London in 1750. By that time the drawings would have been locked away in his Manchester home and Mrs Thrale was a child of nine. There is no evidence of any serious investigations into the practical structure of Shakespeare's playhouse as early as this in England. When the plays were performed they were presented within the framework of the eighteenth-century stage and even re-written to suit eighteenth-century taste. Any attempts at authentic interpretations of the plays were more than a century away. So one was forced to consider that these drawings were in some way concerned with the design of Shakespeare's theatres. Unlikely as that might at first seem, on closer consideration facts began to emerge which made it probable.

What evidence is there for what the Globe looked like? All we have to go on are a number of engravings of London's riverside which claim to depict it. They are all different and each is considered faulty in one way or another. I.A. Shapiro, who examined the early engravings of the Bankside theatres in an essay in 1948,[4] demonstrated a series of inconsistencies and inaccuracies which need not concern us; what matters is that some of the engravings show a cylindrical structure and some show the Globe as polygonal. I was especially interested in two of them, one by J.C. Visscher drawn in 1616, the second by Matthaeus Merian. For some time Visscher's engraving has been considered unreliable because Shapiro proved that he had superimposed his own ideas of the playhouses on a panoramic view of the riverside which was out of date by the time he produced his engraving. Merian is said to have based his view of the riverside on Visscher's.

It is probable that Visscher did not visit Southwark or even know London, but that should not lead to wrong conclusions. Visscher and Merian both show the Globe as a polygonal building and this is now the generally accepted view of the outside of the theatre. Exactly how many sides there were to that polygon is still debated, and inaccuracies in the panoramic backgrounds to these two engravings have no bearing on that question. One drawing in the collection which I felt sure was relevant clearly shows an octagonal exterior.

Far more significant is the source of the engraver's knowledge of the playhouse. Matthaeus Merian had married a descendant of Theodore de Bry, and his daughter married a brother of Michel Le Blon, whose initials are on some of the drawings in the collection. These dynastic ties were of great importance in the engraving and publishing world. Merian and

Michel Le Blon were contemporaries, working as artists and engravers, and were the inheritors of the tradition exemplified so brilliantly by their ancestor Theodore de Bry. This relationship between Le Blon and Merian was likely to have a bearing on the theatre drawings. In other words Merian knew from de Bry's family that the Globe was polygonal and indeed eight-sided. As for J.C. Visscher, he too had worked with Michel Le Blon and thus would have been able to discover through him the exact shape of the Bankside theatres. Once I realised this, whether Visscher himself visited London no longer deflected me from thinking his and Merian's views of the Globe were worthy of serious consideration.

A Meeting with Theo Crosby

By a stroke of good luck at about this stage in my work, early in 1989, the project to rebuild the Globe theatre in London had reached a sufficiently advanced stage for two of the academic advisers involved, Andrew Gurr and John Orrell, to publish a book, *Rebuilding Shakespeare's Globe*, in which Professor Gurr expressed the hope that more evidence about the Globe's original design might still come to light:

> It may come from archaeology – digging up some fragments of the original foundations for instance – or from library research turning up some long-lost paper in the way that Dutch Johannes de Witt's drawing of the stage of the Swan playhouse, made on his visit to London in 1596, was found in 1888.

Were Byrom's drawings examples of such evidence? Was this likely? Among its illustrations, Gurr's book contains a drawing by Theo Crosby, the architect responsible for the design of the new replica Globe. He based his plans on knowledge supplied to him by numerous scholars in an attempt to reconstruct the theatre as authentically as possible. In the Byrom Collection I found a drawing (figure 8) very similar to Crosby's setting-out diagram for the new Globe and seemingly made according to the same geometric principles. Now I had isolated from the collection drawings which resembled Dr Yates's theoretical reconstruction and Crosby's basic plan. Guided by Renaissance re-creations of classical theatres based on Vitruvius and Crosby's geometric concept, I began to look for other drawings with similar features. There were several. I thought of speaking to Theo Crosby himself about this altogether unforeseen development.

A great many people had campaigned hard and long to make the idea of a new Globe theatre in London a reality. It had taken an American actor, Sam Wanamaker, to provide sufficient impetus to get the under-taking launched. My admiration for that venture made me feel obliged to put what I had discovered in the hands of these dedicated people. It

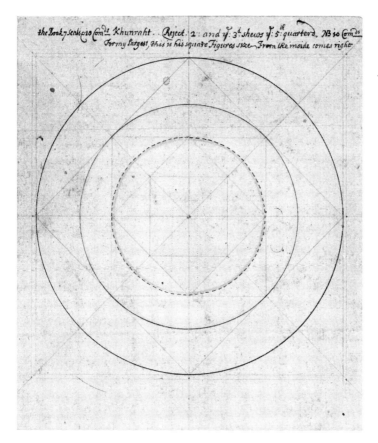

the Book 7 serkspio com: Khunraht . . Reject. 2: and y: 3: shews y: 5: quartered, NB so com:
Formy largest, this is his square Figures size. From the inside comes right

Figures 8 and 8A: Compare the geometrical drawing (above) with the setting-out drawing of the proposed first Globe reconstruction on Bankside (below). The reconstruction shows the stage within the circle of galleries, including the external stair turrets (*drawing by Theo Crosby of Pentagram Design Ltd*).

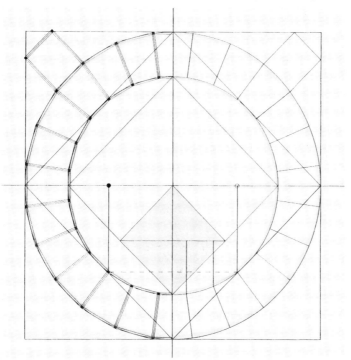

was important that any approach I made should be treated seriously and not be seen as the vagaries of a crank. It was important, too, for me to keep a sense of proportion. The drawings which I had found were part of a greater whole and, while they had to be made public, should not distract from, nor distort the nature of, the collection as an entity.

The Bankside site at this time was beginning to draw a great deal of attention from the media. This made me feel doubly anxious not to appear a sensation seeker, and to ensure that anything which should be in the public domain, or at least at the service of the experts concerned, was made known. For legal reasons I was not at liberty at the time to hand over any of the material entrusted to me, although I could discuss my findings with scholars. So, through an intermediary able to vouch for my credentials, I met Theo Crosby. It would have been difficult to transport the entire collection in security boxes to London at the height of a very hot summer and still ensure their safety, so instead I took a judicious selection possibly connected with the Globe, and others which by now I felt might be concerned with theatres.

The purpose of my visit was to show the drawings to Theo Crosby, and explain they were part of a bigger collection. I was not concerned with getting him to agree with my theories and I made no attempt to explain the pedigree of the drawings. I wanted him to see them and know that someone was working on them. It was up to him to decide how he should receive that news.

His reaction is best summed up by the letter he wrote after my visit. In it he says he was 'much cheered by the sight of the drawings' and went on:

> It is important to publish the drawings as soon as possible. With the discovery of the Rose foundations, and the imminent excavations of the original Globe site, the subject is of great relevance.

I had noticed that Gurr and Orrell do not refer anywhere in their book to Frances Yates's theories about the origin or design of the Globe. This was understandable since Yates came to formulate her ideas almost incidentally in the process of working on the hermetic material to which she devoted so much of her energies. Moreover, she had been unfortunate in placing too great a trust in the accuracy of Mrs Thrale's observations. Much of Yates's finest work lay outside the mainstream of Elizabethan theatre studies. Towards the end of her life[5] she was aware that she did not have time to follow up all the figures who had come to light in the course of her work. Nevertheless she did point out that the whole de Bry/Merian dynasty deserved detailed study because their importance had for so long been overlooked. One member of that dynasty, Michel

Le Blon, was beginning to prove her right. Her work in unravelling the hermetic and mystical contribution to Renaissance thought has been of immense value to later scholars. It was because I recognised something hermetic in the nature of the Byrom material that I turned my attention to her work and was forced to look more closely at one person in particular, John Dee.

Dee had spent part of his later years in Manchester and was related by marriage to the Byroms. Some of the drawings were directly concerned with him. He remains a controversial figure for whom there was no adequate biographer before Charlotte Smith, and whose real worth was revealed for the first time in 1972 by Peter French. As a result, Dee's contribution to the knowledge of his age had been long undervalued or ignored. His disastrous involvement with Edward Kelly, who undoubtedly exploited his pious and credulous side in attempts to communicate with angels, brought him into contempt in the eyes of many scholars. Yet he was a man of enormous gifts and great learning. He was also a man of true vision in his advocacy of the value of applied mathematics. He had a part to play, too, in the story of the Elizabethan theatres, as we shall see later. It is only now that a just assessment of Dee is beginning to emerge.

Theo Crosby's response to the drawings persuaded me to give more attention to that part of the collection which seemed to be concerned with the Globe. This coincided with the announcement that some of the foundations of the Rose theatre had been discovered on an adjacent site on Bankside. I wrote again to Theo Crosby who, amid all the flurry of work, as controversy raged and actors and well-wishers demonstrated in an attempt to save the site from being developed, still found time to send me plans of diagrams showing what had been uncovered. These plans provided further confirmation of what I had seen in some of the drawings. This time in physical form, albeit with broken outlines, the ground plan of the Rose revealed patterns which I could relate not only to architect's reconstructions but also to drawings which I had earmarked as possibly connected with theatres.

Practical Elements

In the collection a number of drawings on thick card looked as if they contained more practical information. One is numbered down the side to provide some kind of measure. Another group mentioned materials used. One heading contains the words 'and the limb of fir fits the ◻ exact from the poyntz from this same root'. A limb of fir could mean either a main section of a tree or an edge or border as for a sextant. Fir is the old Scandinavian name for Scots pine, a timber especially valued in building for its water-resistant properties. It is known that in the construction of the second version of the Globe much of the timber was fir, and the use of fir in building Elizabethan playhouses is confirmed by the surviving contract for the Hope theatre, drawn up by Philip Henslowe in 1613.

The superscription on another card reads:

> to fitt [or fill] out exactly. to fitt within ye ☐ and a thickness of Mr Hd (for the square to fitt the sphere, in wich thickness the glasses is to be fixt without, and a thiner plate within the square to make a rabit for the glass).

This is an instruction to fit glass in a timber frame and the word 'rabit', rabbet or rebate, is the correct term for a groove cut to receive an edge as in a window frame. It is written in a less formal style than others, as if by an artisan. The Mr Hd mentioned is, I believe, Thomas Hood who flourished *c.* 1577 to 1596 as a distinguished mathematician, living in the Minories where he had a shop in which he sold mathematical instruments. This card may be concerned with such an instrument. Alternatively Hood's skills may have been used in the building of the Rose *c.* 1587/89 or even earlier for the Theater. Another feature of the card is the name Khunrath added in a different hand and in different ink at the end of the written note. Khunrath's name also appears on figure 8 which resembles Theo Crosby's setting-out plan for the new Globe. Khunrath was acquainted with Dee and in fact visited him at Bremen on 6 June 1588. (We know this from Dee's own diary.) A few weeks earlier Dee had been paying a visit to Frankfurt, the home of the de Bry family enterprise. Is it possible that among the issues Dee discussed with Khunrath and de Bry was the new theatre, the Rose, then being built in London? Certainly it seemed that Dee, Khunrath and Hood were all part of a network connected with de Bry.

It was now clear that there was a different element in those drawings which I thought were concerned with the geometry of building. Apart from highly conceptualised generalisations and setting-out plans, there were diagrams which dealt with glass and timber. I checked to see if there was evidence of applied skills in any other related areas. I had enough practical experience to be able to recognise the more common joints used in carpentry, but how was I to know what sort of skills were employed in Elizabethan building? Among the drawings was a series of triangles. Some were symbolic, some recalled gable ends, others appeared to be intended for the study of angles and triangles. A number were drawn on sturdier card as if to withstand rougher use than the rest. They were still carefully drawn but not with the customary elegance and may have been intended to instruct or to measure. The series grew in complexity,

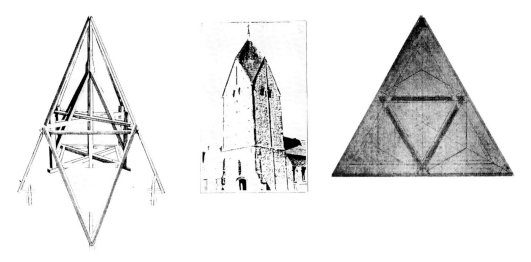

Figure 9: Sompting Parish Church.

but all were designed to show off some aspect of triangular jointing. How was I to assess their true purpose, since this set of drawings was devoid of any writing? I needed guidance from an authority on the history of the carpenter's craft. In his fascinating book *English Historic Carpentry*, Cecil Hewett provides many detailed drawings to illustrate his text, from models of cross-sections of structures to close-ups of every conceivable joint for all manner of buildings. I recognised one of these illustrations immediately; it showed a method of joining three pieces of wood together in what is called a lap dovetail, and it is reproduced clearly in one of the set of triangular drawings which I had thought was some kind of joint. Now I could give it a name and discover when it was used. Turning back to the previous page I saw a more complex illustration which matched one of the more complex triangle drawings. The frame (figure 9), known as Rhenish helm, was used to build a 'square planned and pyramidal spire that rises from the apexes of four gables'.[6]

Hewett had found a rare example of it at the Church of St Mary, Sompting, in Sussex. That particular structure was dated somewhere between 950 and *c.* 1050. The similarity between the geometry of the frame and the drawing can be seen by comparing figures 9 and 9B. It is interesting to note that, although the frame is rare, there are indications that the spire of St Benet's church in Cambridge was also originally of the same type, and that many others have been replaced since first being built. More important still is Hewett's comment on the work at Sompting:

The architectural and structural concept of the Rhenish helm is extraordinary, but its execution in carpentry at Sompting is a work of such assurance and competence, achieved with such economy of means, that it both indicates the work of a master and suggests the previous existence of a tradition of framing such works.[7]

The similarities between Hewett's illustrations and the drawings were so marked that I was forced to stop and consider where the Rhenish helm frame would be used in building the Globe or any other playhouse. So far I had seen drawings which spoke of different levels and a setting-out plan. I turned back to the engravings of London's Bankside in the early seventeenth century. Norden's map of 1600 shows a flag appearing from the roof of the first Globe, but no spire. Visscher's engraving of 1616, however, shows a small tower surmounted by a pyramidal spire, from which the flagpole rises above the Globe. I have argued earlier for more credence to be given to Visscher because of his connection with Le Blon and his access to the de Bry family knowledge of London theatres. Working within the German tradition of carpentry de Bry would have been aware of the Rhenish helm frame, and we should not assume that the tradition of building such frames in England had died out. It is, as Hewett states, soundly designed and of proven durability. 'This system produced a spire that wind pressures have failed to dislodge from the tower.'[8] That is precisely the quality a builder would look for in a theatre too. He would not want his tower blown down upon the tiring house or people below. Merian, also, in his engraving for the Globe shows the same unmistakable pyramidal base for the theatre's flagpole. All these considerations fused together and I found myself examining figure 9B and others similar. Together they formed a group of drawings to which the same principles can be applied, part of a sequence which shows how a roof can be angled – polygonal on the outside and circular within.

The Tiring House

The one conventional architectural drawing in the collection is figure 10. This is clearly a ground plan for a building with a staircase in one corner. A study of the room divisions reveals some unusual features. There are three entrances at the front: A, B, C and two at the rear D and E. The central entrance at the front (B) does not allow entrance to any other area except the staircase and exit (E) out of the building. Two other front entrances (A) and (C) allow admission to the sets of rooms on each side of the main passageway, except for the one at the left-hand rear corner opposite the stairs. That can be entered only at the rear (D). Certainly this ground plan was not consistent with the normal arrangement of rooms in a house. The three front entrances were more in keeping with the frons scaenae of Vitruvius and the tiring house wall in Dr Yates's plan. The tiring house was attached to the Elizabethan theatre

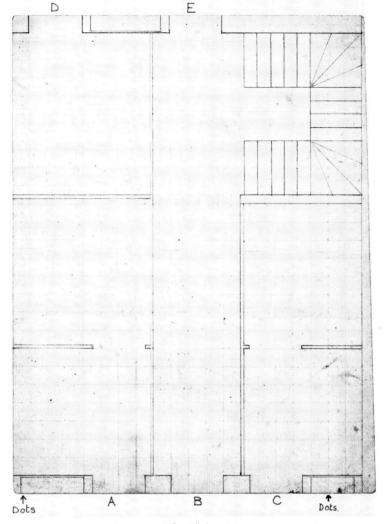

Figure 10: The Tiring House.
The Tiring House ground plan. The underlying scoring of squares is the grid of
measure with dots positioned halfway between the small squares.

at the back of the stage. It contained dressing rooms, storage space, and, above, a gallery for spectators. Was the drawing a possible layout for this part of the theatre?

I examined the card once more, ignoring for the moment the familiar lines which signified wall, doors and stairway. Instead I concentrated on the faintly scored lines underneath the ground plan. These are evenly spaced, vertically and horizontally, to form a pattern of squares over the entire card. Although faint, they became much clearer under a magnifying glass. Once one knew the size of these small squares, one could work out the area of the whole building. There were no words, no numbers, no letters, only a line of dots evenly placed down the left-hand side of the card, dividing each small square by half.

I had in front of me what could be a plan of the tiring house, and I placed alongside it the drawing I thought was a setting-out plan of the Globe theatre (figure 11). Underneath the latter's coloured design were also small squares scored all over the card, and each square was again

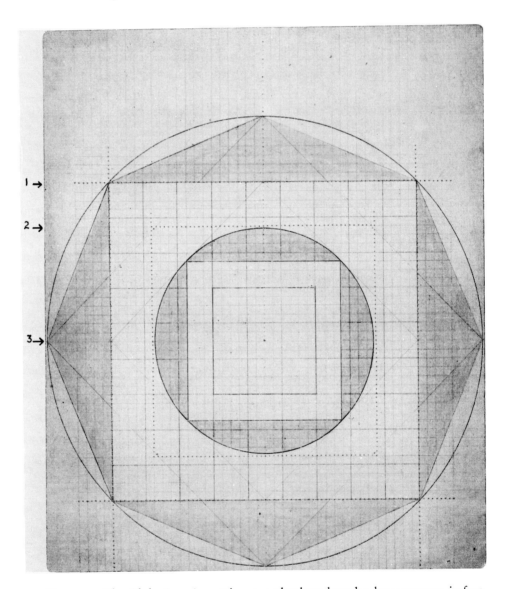

Figure 11: The Globe (1599) – setting-out plan based on the dots measure, in feet.

KEY 1   Line of dots divided by nine squares, each square being subdivided into eight equal parts, or a measure of 72.

2   Line of dots, 53 in all, measure of 52. (Notice the sub-division of the corner dots.

3   Line of dots – vertical, from the centre – 69, a measure of 68.

The reverse side of the card contains further information. See figure 13.

divided by a dot. These were half the size of the small squares on the tiring house card, so I reduced the latter by half and was able to match the two sets of squares exactly. Both drawings could now be fitted on the same grid and studied together. If figure 10 was indeed a plan of a tiring house, there was only one position for it on the setting-out plan. When it was placed in that position, the geometry of the setting-out plan could be seen to extend as far as the back wall of rooms 2 and 4 of the tiring house. Was this neat accommodation a coincidence, or did it confirm that the two drawings should be used together?

The setting-out drawing shows an eight-sided figure the main feature of which is an internal square, the sides of which are evenly divided by seventy-two pin-pricks in groups of eight. I felt sure that these dots, like those on the tiring house card, were some kind of measure. A little further inside the square was a second one made by fifty-two pin-pricks along each side. Positioned within this square is a circle, equidistant from each side, whose diameter is equal to fifty-one of the pin-pricks. If we assume that the minute but regular intervals between each pin-prick is a measure of distance, we can now say we have inside the octagon two squares whose sides measure seventy-two and fifty-two units respectively and a circle whose diameter is fifty-one of the same units. The geometry was beginning to yield up numbers.

It has been necessary to explain these first stages in some detail because it seemed as if I was deciphering a code. It had been comparatively easy to relate the drawings to Vitruvian principles, but none of the scholars I had consulted had recognised the significance of the dots. (At one stage I thought they might have been connected with printing.) One would expect a setting-out plan to indicate measurement by a scale, not dots, lines and circles. But here these have been employed instead, and do make sense when seen as a codified system for storing information.

Once I had broken the code it became possible to apply it to other drawings with similar pin-pricks and to put matching pieces together. At last the drawings began to make sense, not only internally but with each other. I was able to find a place for a small, sturdy, circular card with 'Starrs mall' written on it. It was the same size as the innermost circle of the setting-out plan for the Globe, and as the circle highlighted by dots on the drawing concerned with the 'globes uper pt'. From this it looked as though the 'Starrs mall' was intended to mark out the area of the playhouse open to the sky and stars, including the stage and yard in which the groundlings stood to watch the plays.

The geometry on the front ar.d back of figure 11 contained information from which a classical-style theatre could be set out at ground level. The tiring house plan contained features of a building which could be added to and accommodated within that concept. The geometry also provided the seven gangways for the seated spectators as in Vitruvius. His five entrances to the classical scaenae became the three entrances to the tiring house wall and one each side of the stage giving access to the yard and stairs.

Although this interpretation of the drawings made sense as far as it

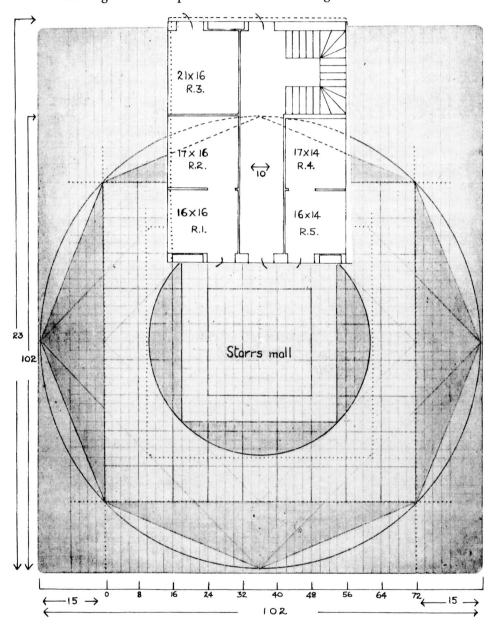

Figure 12: The Globe (1599) – Tiring House in position.
Site required 102 x 122   Tiring house 40 x 54   Starrs mall diameter 51.
All measurements are in feet.   Eight sided building – based on a frame of 72 x 72.

went, one more important feature was missing – an indication of elevation. There was, however, a sequence of drawings so distinctive and complex that I had not yet tried to relate them to any others. At first glance they resembled in outline a flat bottle, each with a different neck (figure 14). Indeed, for convenience I initially referred to them as 'bottle drawings'.

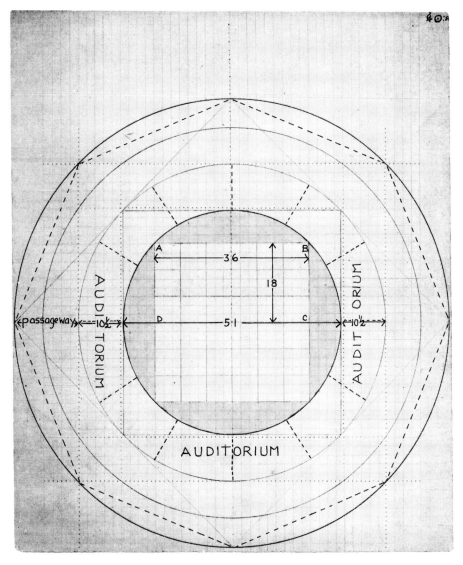

Figure 13: The Globe (1599) – reverse side.
All figures, letters and broken lines have been added to the original drawing.
All measurements are in feet. The rectangle ABCD represents the stage.
The broken line indicates the use of the circle and square as measures for the
outside wall, refer to figure 11. In the Auditorium, the broken lines indicate
the position of gangways.

They also looked a little like pendulums. I considered both explanations in turn only to dismiss them. In the first place, the surface of the 'bottles' was covered with bewildering patterns of circles, lines and dots which were not ornamental and far too complicated for any object as mundane as a bottle. Even the resemblance to an alchemical retort was superficial and still left too much unexplained. Normally the top of a retort is a flat opening which can be blocked either with a stopper or a receiver to draw off any gases produced by substances heated in the bowl. Here each neck ended in a markedly different way. As for a pendulum – this consists of a weight or bob, hung on a fine chain or rod pivoted at the top. The variation in swing, critical for adjusting the mechanism, is the result of varying the length of the pendulum. But the columns in the drawings, apart from being too thick, or too short, and in one instance non-existent, show no allowance for such variations. Again the geometry drawn on the columns is superfluous for a pendulum. Neither could I relate these particular drawings to a device such as an orrery or celestial clock. One thing was certain, the geometry in the base of the figures continued in the columns.

One 'bottle drawing' in particular (figure 16) stood out. It was capped by a triangle. The geometrical patterns on it were very busy and seemed to convey so much information, but not in words or numbers. Almost hidden from the naked eye a line of dots and pin-pricks rose from the centre of the circular base up the column or neck of the card. The presence of these dots made me consider the drawing in relation to the tiring house card, the setting-out plan, and the two cards which referred to the Globe's 'uper pt' and the 'bottom'. By now I had a copy of the contract for the Fortune theatre, which was built to the specifications of the Globe and, therefore, tells us the different levels of the playhouse.

The bottle drawing appeared to have been well used. I could detect the application of a sharp knife at the beginning of the neck and again at the top. At some time the card had been cut at salient points – as if to highlight the outline of what might be a tower. It had been scored deliberately, enabling the drawing to become three-dimensional. Viewed in this way its geometry *combined vertical as well as horizontal features*. I started to measure from the centre of the circle, which according to the setting-out plan marked (in the horizontal plane) the front of the stage. Taking the distance between each dot to represent one foot, I counted eighteen dots up the central column, since according to figure 11 the depth of the stage was eighteen feet. This brought me to where the front of the tiring house would be. From here I calculated the height of the three levels of the playhouse, using the figures laid down in the Fortune contract. The first level is twelve feet high with one foot for foundations and another for the ceiling. Accordingly I counted fourteen dots up the central column to mark off the first level.

I repeated this operation for the second and third levels, allowing each time an extra foot for the floor/ceiling. These calculations completed the measurement of the height of the tiring house and main structure of the theatre at such a clearly defined point in the geometry of the drawing that it emphasised the symmetry of the schema. I could not believe that this conjunction was simply coincidence. The projections above this point mark the height of the towers and the top of the playhouse. At first they appear to make the building too high, until we remember that the schema combines horizontal and vertical planes and we have to deduct the horizontal measure of the depth of the stage (from front to back) to gauge the overall elevation. A detailed account of the towers and this accommodation appears in Appendix One, p.282.

So far I had been able to extract the elevation from the schema; I also wanted to know what it could tell me about the horizontal measurements. Given the Vitruvian principles of the design, one would expect the playhouse to exhibit the ideal of proportion, and this was confirmed by further examination of the schema. The area of the tiring house was 40 by 54 feet according to figure 12, and the length of its front rooms was 16 feet. I measured 16 feet up the central column of dots and found it marked by a circle which leads to the points where the drawing is pulled forward to show the elevation of the tiring house. This distance of 16 feet also shows the point (on the horizontal level) where the floor at the back of the front rooms of the tiring house would drop four feet to ground level with a flight of steps allowing actors access underneath the stage. Since the stage itself stood four feet above ground the drop inside the tiring house is accommodated by the height of the front rooms being eight feet instead of twelve. In this way the external proportions of the building were preserved.

Other horizontal dimensions are contained in the composite schema. For example, in figure 17 I measured the two points A and B and found that the distance between them was the width of the tiring house as shown on the tiring house drawing – 40 feet. I then superimposed the outlines of the octagon from the setting-out plan and the tiring house on the schema. The result showed that the outermost circle on which the octagon is based overlaps and continues the arc CD and binds the geometry of the two separate drawings together. Furthermore, the radius of the outermost circle is double the radius of the Starrs mall circle. I also noted that the arc E–F crosses part of the schema which represented the towers at the top of the building. The 72 rule showed that the combined width of the towers was 28 feet, and that individually the two outer towers measured 7 feet and the central one 14. These repeated examples of the doubling of dimensions showed how closely the proportions were observed through the entire concept.

Despite these conclusions I felt I could not go back to the architectural scholars I had consulted earlier without substantial evidence that my theories were correct. What better proof than to put those theories to the test? I decided to construct a model of the 1599 version of the Globe as I saw it, based on the drawings I had identified with the theatre. I had decoded the rule and measure. I had the builder's contract for the Fortune theatre, one of only two contracts for Elizabethan playhouses that have survived and are available for reference. The Fortune was built in 1600 by Peter Streete,[9] who was also responsible for the Globe. Clear instructions about certain features of the building in the contract link it directly with the Globe and make it a reliable source of information.

It was at this stage that I met Kenneth Peacock, the master model-maker for the School of Architecture at Manchester University, who agreed to construct a model to my specifications. First, however, to acquaint myself with the problems involved I called on my experience as a play producer and made a rough model of my own in cardboard. My brother, who is trained in design, then built a detailed model to scale based entirely on the drawings. Some technical matters concerned with elevation had to be decided by discussion but the result, beautiful in itself, was none the less a model theatre that accurately interpreted my decoding of the measurements in the drawings. Here, it seemed to me, was ample proof that some drawings in the Byrom Collection were indeed concerned with the design of an Elizabethan theatre. If that were not so, I could in no way account for being able to construct so lifelike a model from them.

I was able to select a drawing from the collection which I thought was concerned with steps, but there is no indication on the setting-out plan of the position of any staircases. So these were placed near the main entrances to the theatre at the sides of the stage. Since the corridor behind the auditorium was wide enough for the staircase to contain a return, I decided to include one in the stairs, although they might have been simply steep flights of steps. There must have been some reason why the corridors were so wide; no doubt they contained several entrances to the gangways for ease of movement.

Each level of the auditorium was 10½ feet wide and could hold 4 tiers of benches. If we allow 18 inches per person to sit, this gives a seating capacity of 300 to each floor. Making a generous allowance of 3 feet per person for the groundlings would enable the yard to accommodate 100 spectators comfortably. Thus the design, based on a 72 feet frame and with eight sides as in Visscher's engraving, produced a theatre with a capacity of 1,000 spectators. The one weakness is the sight lines at the third level each side of the thrust stage. Apart from that the sight lines seemed to be good. One advantage of the design was that since the building observed

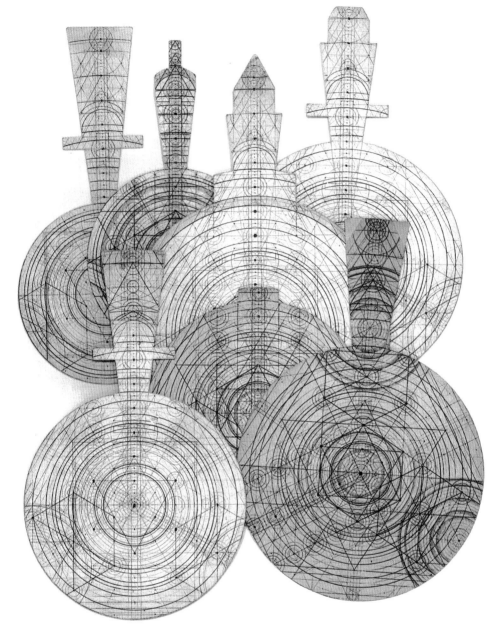

Figure 14: The rich variety of the parametric drawings.

laws of proportion it would be a relatively simple matter to adapt it for larger playhouses.

When I examined the finished model I felt much more confident. Anyone who might wish to postulate some other origin or purpose for the 'theatre' drawings would now have to explain satisfactorily not only an alternative theory but also the coincidence of my application of them so precisely in this way. No longer could it be said that I had been carried

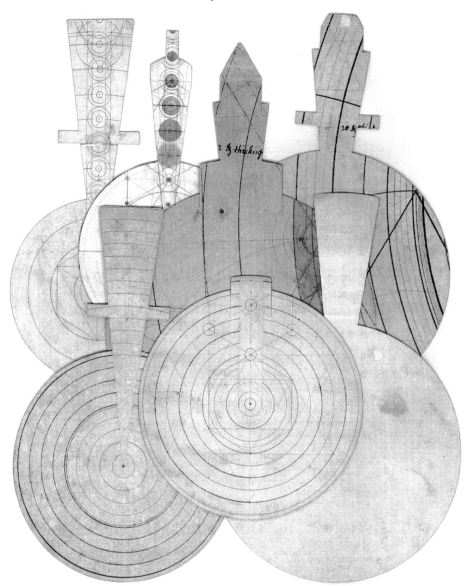

Figure 15: The parametric group in reverse.

away by wishful thinking, or perhaps a misjudgment of the historical evidence, when there before me was a three-dimensional replica of a theatre made directly from instructions in the drawings.

In due course Peacock completed a sequence of models in wood, built to the exact size of drawings I prepared from the originals (figure 20). A fuller account of these models is given in Appendix One, pp.285–7.

I could now turn my attention to decoding the extra information

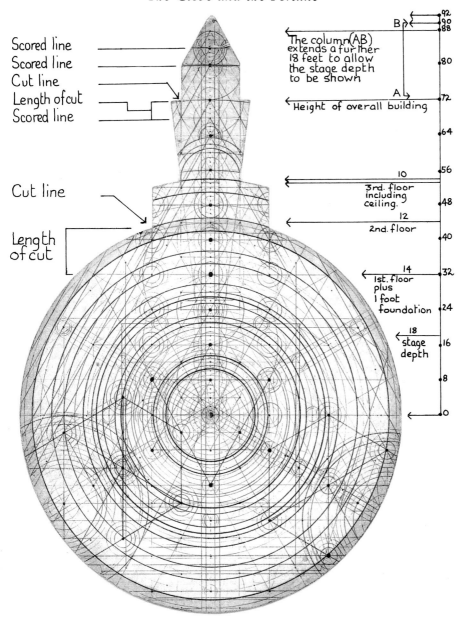

Scored line —————
Scored line —————
Cut line —————
Length of cut —————
Scored line —————

Cut line —————

Length of cut

B
The column (AB) extends a further 18 feet to allow the stage depth to be shown

A
Height of overall building

92
90
88
80
72
64
56
48
40
32
24
16
8
0

10
3rd. floor including ceiling.

12
2nd. floor

14
1st. floor plus 1 foot foundation

18
stage depth

Figure 16: The Globe (1599) – schematic design. The central column contains 'measure of dots'.

included in the myriad patterns of lines and circles contained in the drawings. One of the most unusual features of the collection, one I personally had never encountered before, was the combination in one diagram of both the horizontal and vertical planes. Realising the three-dimensional element in the drawings was as big a step forward in elucidating their mystery as

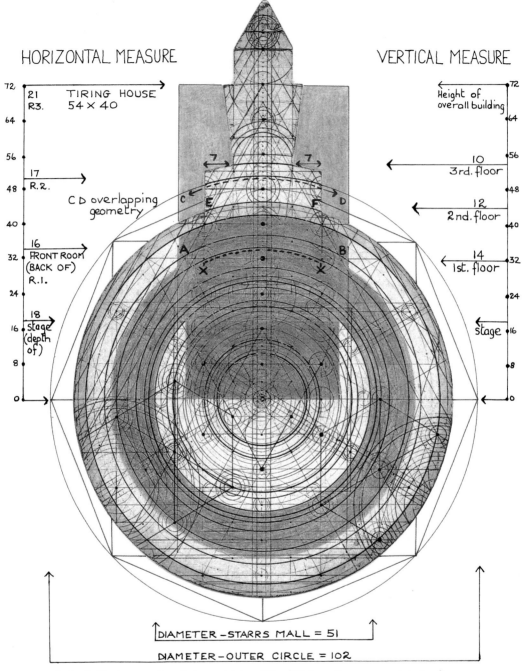

72
21　　TIRING HOUSE
R3.　　54 × 40

64

56
17
R.2.

48
C D overlapping
geometry

40

16
32 FRONT ROOM
(BACK OF)
R.1.

24

18
16 stage
(depth
of)

8

0

Height of
overall building

72

64

10
3rd. floor

56

48

12
2nd. floor

40

14
1st. floor

32

24

stage

16

8

0

7　　　7

C E　　　F D

A　　　　　　B

X　　　X

DIAMETER – STARRS MALL = 51
DIAMETER – OUTER CIRCLE = 102

A to B (between 2 dots) = width of the Tiring House – 40 feet.
E to F – cut out section = width of Towers – overall –28 feet.

Figure 17: The Globe (1599) – schematic design.
Information encoded in figures 10, 11, 12, 13 has been transferred to demonstrate
how all the geometry is contained in the schematic. The dotted line between X and
X highlights the key to this drawing in the Globe sequence.

Figure 18: The Globe model – staircases and seating.

Figure 19: The steps behind Rooms 1 and 5 in the Tiring House at ground level.

the earlier discovery of the '72 measure'! It was a beautifully economical concept and led to one other major development. When I examined the necks of all the other bottle drawings and saw how distinctively different each one was, I was brought suddenly to the realisation that these deliberate distinctions were intended to represent different buildings, different roof lines – different theatres!

One aspect of the model in figure 21 is not derived from the drawings and that is the position of the windows in the outside walls. While the collection does refer to rebates for glass, there is no specific drawing to indicate the placement or frequency of the frames, but because, on completion, the model did look uncannily like the depiction of the Globe in the much-maligned Visscher drawing (figure 22), I allowed myself one piece of artistic licence and based the pattern of the windows on Visscher – rather than leave the walls bare. The final features I should mention concern the gentlemen's rooms in the tiring house and the area above. The number of gentlemen's rooms in the model is the same as that laid down in the contract for the Fortune. Since the Fortune was built as a square version of the Globe, this seemed to be a fair assumption to make. As for the floor above the gentlemen's rooms, that was where the stage machinery for the 'heavens' was kept, namely the winch for lowering and raising celestial figures to and from the stage.

Figure 23 looks like the outline of a winch. It fits neatly on the top of the left-hand half of the ground plan of the tiring house. The obverse of the drawing indicated the position of windows on what would be the outside wall of the tiring house on the left. This may mean that the winch was placed on the left side of the tiring house (stage right), probably with other stage machinery. The winch would of necessity be a fixture, although no doubt it could be moved forward into position to lower actors or objects towards the stage. Faint markings on both sides of the drawing were, I discovered, lines in exactly the same place as the wall divisions on the ground plan of the tiring house. In other words, the room divisions below were to be taken into account when equipping the upper floor with stage machinery. I had already noticed the outside wall on the left-hand side was thicker than the one on the right, thus providing extra support for stress on that side of the building. The drawing was characterised by a roughness not present in the others and looked more like a practical working drawing than an ideal representation. Moreover, the bottom part of the paper had been torn away. For a long time I had puzzled over what this drawing meant. When I discovered that it fitted on the ground plan so well, my question seemed to have been answered. Still the missing portion left a disturbing gap. Had it been simply torn off by accident or had someone ripped this part of the paper in two deliberately?

Some time later I remembered the small sheet of paper inscribed with symbols and a jumble of English words referring to cosmology and cabalism (figure 23).[10] That, too, had a jagged edge. I matched the two sheets and the perforations fitted precisely. I had been studying the two pieces separately in different lines of enquiry and had not connected them earlier. Now, when I matched the join, the addition of this piece provided an extension over the stage area exactly where the canopy would be. This cover provided the actors with some shelter for themselves or their props from bad weather. It would have been painted underneath with the signs of the zodiac and thus represent the 'heavens', and be substantial enough

Figure 20: Model of the Globe theatre made by the model maker of the University of Manchester to the scale of the 'setting-out' drawings.

Figure 21: A more detailed model of the Globe theatre made to scale.

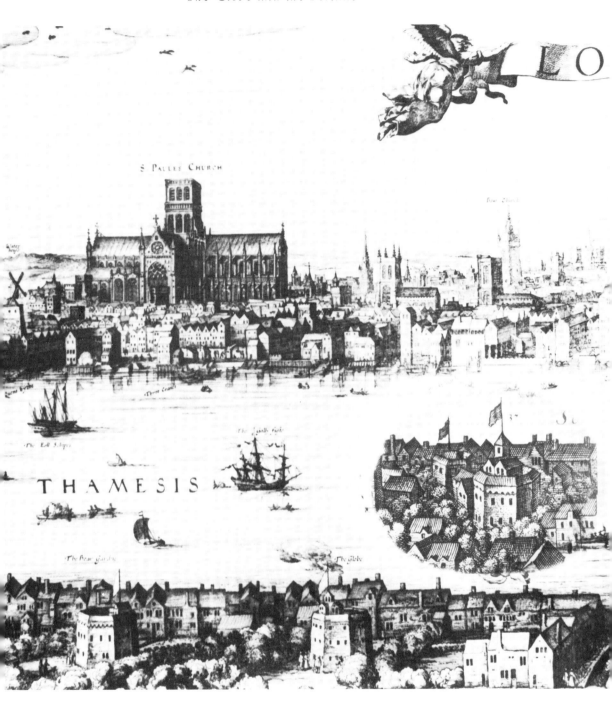

Figure 22: Part of the panoramic view of London from the South Bank showing St Paul's Cathedral and Southwark by J.C. Visscher, 1616. Inset is the view of the Globe by Merian, 1638.

to provide an opening for the gods or a dumb show to descend. The smaller portion of paper with references to the crystalline sphere and the cabala had already exercised my mind greatly, but little did I think when first puzzling over it that I would be able to relate it to part of the Elizabethan playhouse. It began to look as though the representation of the heavens was a much more serious matter than mere pictorial decoration.

I do not claim that the replica I built is correct in every detail. I am aware, for example, that the thatched roof may not have been pitched at precisely the angle I chose (which was the 60 degrees of equilateral triangles). There is in the collection a series of triangular drawings, and I had to select one as a template for the roofing. Whether the angle is right or not, there are drawings to indicate how the timbers for the roof should be laid out. I am happy to be corrected on such details as the degree of slant in the roof, but the general principles of the structure are, I believe, correct. These derive from five main drawings: the setting-out plan, the tiring house ground plan, the 'Starrs mall', the drawing headed 'Double size For ye bottom' and above all the bottle drawing, which held the key to them all.[11]

One other composite drawing in the collection is very similar to that of the Globe, similar but not the same. The differences between the two are minimal but deliberate. The companion to this drawing, which is a

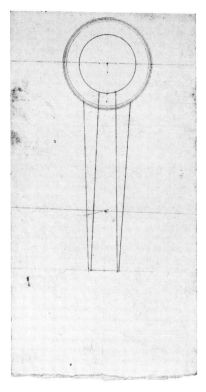

Figure 23: The card is very similar to that used for the architectural ground plan here called 'The Tiring House'. This drawing from the Collection may well have been one of the drawings for the winch which was used to raise and lower properties to the stage. Marks on the drawing seem to indicate work in progress towards the final design in connection with the ground floor plan of the Tiring House. The two drawings were at one time joined together. Were they torn deliberately at some point in their history?

ground plan, is distinctive because of its simplicity. It is devoid of the hermetic content which overlays the geometrical design of other theatre drawings. The presence of these two features, simplicity and similarity, led me to conclude that this was an earlier design for an earlier playhouse, almost one might say a prototype. Since the Globe was preceded by the Theater, and was built from it, this drawing was most probably connected with the Theater, built in 1576.

The Fortune

All the time I was gathering the drawings to build the model of the Globe, I kept referring to the contract for the Fortune theatre. The two playhouses were built within the space of twelve months of each other by the same man. The main difference was that the Fortune was to be built square. So, as I looked for drawings which might be connected with the Globe, my eye began to register others which emphasised a square rather than circular design. I did not separate them off immediately, but as I came to the final stages of the Globe hypothesis, I turned to the sequence of square drawings and the bottle-shaped drawings which I now called parametric because they included both ground plan and elevation in one design. As already mentioned the parametric drawings are in principle the same, but differ in some significant way from each other. Eventually I had to separate those drawings which, because of their square design, might be connected with the Fortune theatre, figure 24.

The Fortune contract specifies that the dimensions of the playhouse should be a frame of 'ffowerscore foote of lawfull assize every waie square'. The theatre was to have a strong foundation of brick, lime and sand one foot above the ground and should contain:

> three Stories in heighth, the first or lower Storie to conteine Twelve foote of lawfull assize in heighth, the second Storie Eleaven foote of lawfull assize in heighth, and the third or vpper Storie to conteine Nyne foote of lawfull assize in heighth; all which Stories shall conteine Twelve foote and a halfe of lawfull assize in breadth througheoute . . .[12]

There were to be gentlemen's rooms and two penny rooms and staircases and divisions:

> as are made and contryved in and to the late erected Plaiehouse on the Banck in the saide parishe of St. Saviour's called the Globe.

Moreover the width of the stage is also specified as 'forty and Three foote of lawfull assize'.

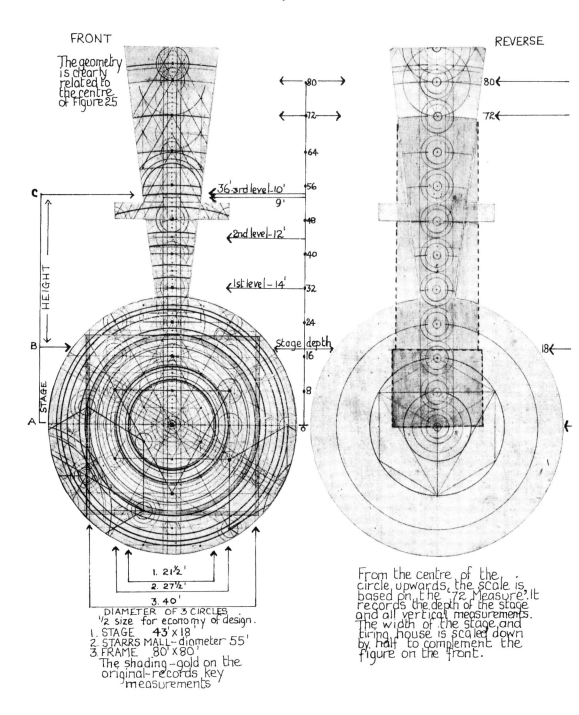

FRONT

The geometry is clearly related to the centre of Figure 25

REVERSE

80
72
64
36' 3rd level - 10'
9'
56
2nd level - 12'
48
40
1st level - 14'
32
24
stage depth
16
8
0

80
72
18

C
HEIGHT
B
STAGE
A

1. 21½'
2. 27½'
3. 40'

DIAMETER OF 3 CIRCLES
½ size for economy of design.
1. STAGE   43' x 18'
2. STARRS MALL - diameter 55'
3. FRAME   80' x 80'
The shading - gold on the original - records key measurements

From the centre of the circle, upwards, the scale is based on the '72 Measure'. It records the depth of the stage and all vertical measurements. The width of the stage and tiring house is scaled down by half to complement the figure on the front.

Figure 24: The Fortune theatre (1600), based on a square of 80 feet.

Like others before me I was able to learn much about the Globe while I noted the measurements laid down for the Fortune. Any plans which had accompanied the original contract had been lost. The drawings I had separated corresponded to the instructions in the contract.

I had the advantage of working with originals and not copies, and so I came to know the shading on the paper and card and their various colours and tints. There is one card (figure 25) which I realised was very similar to the first drawing I had associated with the Globe; the predominant shape on it was square. Taking it out of its folder and placing it alongside the Globe drawing I was surprised by the resemblance. When I placed it on top of the same drawing (which had written on it 'for Globe: 9: Exact') it fitted exactly. The effect was remarkable.

The two cards matched as a pair. The design of the circles on the Globe card complemented the circles on the outside of the square plan on the Fortune card. The lines and colouring continued in one pattern. In other words underlying the measurements in the Globe drawing were some of the chief features of the Fortune. I examined the correspondences more closely. I placed my ruler on the principal square on the Fortune drawing and, sure enough, it measured eighty of the units on the scale derived from the Globe drawing. So the frame was as specified, eighty feet. From that point it became a question of separating off immediately the other drawings which I judged to be connected with this sequence. Again they confirmed other measurements stipulated in the contract. There were drawings which showed that the stage was 43 feet wide; that gave the size of the 'Starrs mall' as 55 feet, and showed clearly that at ground level the auditorium extended 12½ feet.

I have thought carefully before making public the extraordinary find I came across next. I leave it for others to consider and evaluate. It was a discovery in connection with the Fortune drawings and one that has left me both curious and mystified. It happened when I was looking for drawings with an eighty feet square frame.

This particular drawing (figure 26) fitted on that frame. I examined it closely for details of additional information such as doors or entrances. It was then that I discovered some signs or marks in the bottom right-hand corner. The lines were different from those which marked out the square frame. As I looked more closely I could see that some were symbols from Byrom's shorthand. I had not seen them on any other drawings. Perhaps I had been too busy looking at main structural lines but I knew Byrom's shorthand, so I was able to decipher the signs. The shorthand is a phonetic system with symbols allocated to the consonants, and vowels indicated by varying the positions of a dot. This group of consonants consisted of 's', 'p', 'r', and 's'. They could stand for either 'surprise' or 'suppress'. But the omission of any sign for a long vowel meant that it must be 'suppress'.

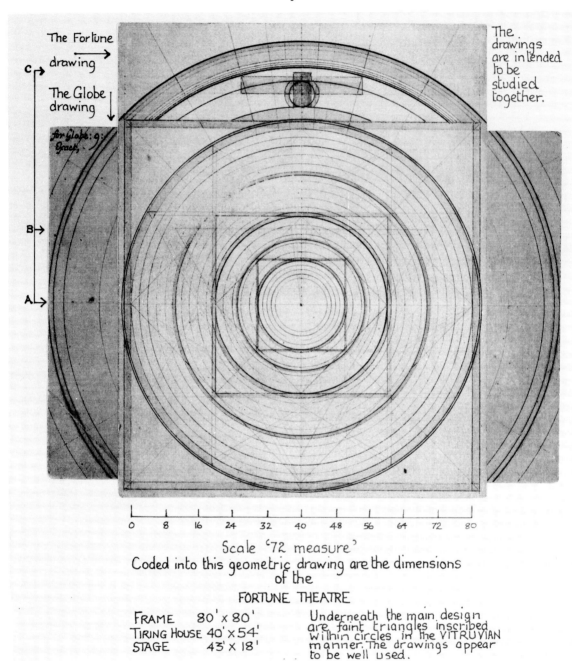

The Fortune drawing →

c →

The Globe drawing ↓

for Globe: g: Grief,

B →

A →

The drawings are intended to be studied together.

| 0 | 8 | 16 | 24 | 32 | 40 | 48 | 56 | 64 | 72 | 80 |

Scale '72 measure'
Coded into this geometric drawing are the dimensions of the

FORTUNE THEATRE

FRAME   80' x 80'
TIRING HOUSE 40' x 54'
STAGE   43' x 18'

Underneath the main design are faint triangles inscribed within circles in the VITRUVIAN manner. The drawings appear to be well used.

Figure 25: The Globe and Fortune theatres – two drawings demonstrating the same geometry. The line BC gives the height of the theatre, as in figure 24.

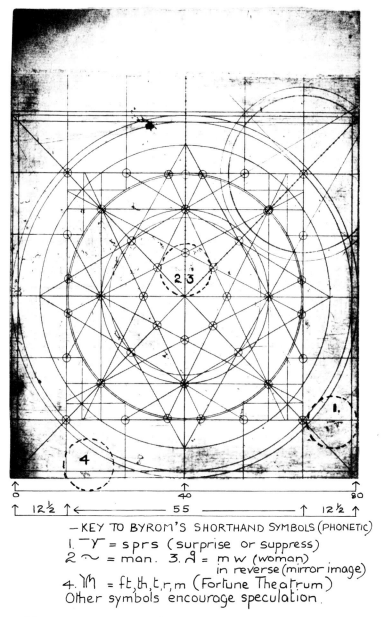

—KEY TO BYROM'S SHORTHAND SYMBOLS (PHONETIC)
1. ⌐Y = s p r s (surprise or suppress)
2. ~ = man. 3. ᕦ = m w (woman)
in reverse (mirror image)
4. ᕟᕅ = ft, th, t, r, m (Fortune Theatrum)
Other symbols encourage speculation.

Figure 26: The Fortune (1600) – scale: '72 measure'. Photography has managed to highlight some shorthand ciphers. The broken circles have been added.

There were several other marks, some less clear than others, but I have not been able to decipher them with any certainty and do not wish to guess at their meaning.

Other symbols were clear enough. In the centre of the stage area on the drawing were the symbols for 'man' and 'woman', although, strangely, the signs for woman were in reverse as though part of a mirror image. Further down towards the bottom on the left-hand side was an even more curious representation. I had been studying the drawing with the help of a light box. Under these conditions I could see a group of signs which seemed to represent the letters 'f', 't', 'th', 'r', and 'm'. They were all invisible to the naked eye but clearly visible under the light box. It appeared that they had been inscribed by an invisible ink. Experiments[13] were made with sophisticated photographic techniques to clarify the symbols but one possible interpretation of these letters might be Fortuna Theatrum, the Fortune Theatre. I must confess to finding this particular discovery perplexing. Why should Byrom write the word 'suppress' in shorthand at the bottom of a piece of paper? Judging by the half-formed signs on the rest of the sheet, I concluded that perhaps he had been doodling while another person was explaining the drawings to him. (Perhaps that person was Jacques Christophe Le Blon.) Byrom might have written down the name of the Fortune theatre as a note to himself, an aide-memoire. The position of the word 'suppress', however, seemed to be more considered, lying outside the main drawing altogether. I can only leave these facts with the reader to puzzle over in turn. Perhaps an answer might emerge elsewhere in the collection. Later research by others might provide another solution. I have looked for other signs of shorthand, and found only isolated symbols, meaningless on their own and unworthy of note. This drawing with shorthand on it is unique.

I paused for a while to review Byrom's own connection with the theatre in early eighteenth-century London. It was not one of the great periods of English drama: the best of the Restoration dramatists were gone, Sheridan and Goldsmith had yet to shine. The most important theatrical events centred on Handel and the rival schools of opera. For a while Byrom had been a regular theatregoer. In 1726 he enjoyed a revival of *The Merry Wives of Windsor* but then he turned his back on the theatre. In 1731 he declared to friends that he was 'against plays'[14] and in 1735 told one that he had made 'a sort of resolution not to go to the opera or playhouse',[15] but that in itself did not seem to explain the word 'suppress'.

CHAPTER FIVE

Elizabethan Theatres – Patrons and Builders

THE DESIGN OF the public playhouse was a new feature in the landscape of London's secular buildings. Earlier versions, such as the theatre built at Red Lion in Whitechapel, are quite different in shape. The new design of the Theater was an extraordinary innovation which in itself seems to argue for a single progenitor for the new sequence of theatres beginning to appear. Since I believed Theodore de Bry to be the man responsible, I examined his career at the time the Theater was built, intrigued that in the same year he was responsible for a detailed engraving of the installation of the Knights of the Garter at Windsor. De Bry must have been in London to carry out that commission and would already be a reputable figure in artistic circles. For generations his family certainly had established an enviable name as goldsmiths on the continent. Moreover, I had to bear in mind that Theodore de Bry was a Huguenot who had been branded as a heretic and forced to flee his native city of Liège.[1] As with so many persecuted families the de Brys did not all choose to seek refuge in the same place. One of them, either Theodore's brother or cousin, James de Bry, settled in London and made a successful career as a picture-maker in the Huguenot community. His home would provide Theodore with his own base during his visit, the equipment he needed, and the space to work on the engravings and any other commissions he might undertake. The youngest of Theodore's three sons was christened Jacques, following the family custom of incorporating the Christian names of forebears. Not much is known about this third son; his absence from the family publishing enterprises in Germany may point to his coming to live with his namesake in England. I did not discover his existence until much later in my researches, when papers in Liège helped to confirm my earlier suspicion of links between the English and continental de Brys.

When eventually I saw a copy of de Bry's engraving of the Garter procession (figure 1), I noticed Robert Dudley, Earl of Leicester standing next to Anthony Browne, first Viscount Montague. The sight of Montague reminded me that Philip Henslowe, the great Elizabethan theatrical entrepreneur, began life as a servant to the bailiff of this man, whose London home, Montague House, was in Southwark. In fact it was Henslowe's duties with the Montagues which led him to settle in Southwark before 1577. He did better than marry the boss's daughter; he married the bailiff's widow, and the property which came with his wife set Henslowe up in his career. Later on he went one better and married his step-daughter to his theatrical partner, the actor Edward Alleyn, but at the outset of his new career, when the Theater was being built, Henslowe was negotiating the sale of timber. He eventually owned and managed the Rose theatre, became involved in the Swan, and, in partnership with Edward Alleyn, built the Fortune. Later he was responsible for the Hope theatre.

Henslowe managed to be sufficiently successful to obtain some minor posts at court: he became Groom of the Royal Chamber in 1593 and Sewer of the Chamber in 1603. Energetic, and with a keen eye for the main chance, he certainly profited from his humble start in the Montague household.

Leicester had his own connection with the theatre companies. As early as 1572 James Burbage, the co-owner and builder of the Theater, had petitioned the Earl to allow his company the protection of his patronage. Leicester was so close to the Queen and so powerful that two years later Burbage's company obtained a royal licence to perform, the first company of adult players to be so honoured.[2]

It is, I suppose, for his relationship with Elizabeth that Leicester is most remembered today. His intrigues were not distinguished with the success which can turn an ambitious man into a great statesman. Indeed he made no permanent contribution to the advancement of Elizabeth's reign. Rather it is Leicester the man who has survived in popular imagination. He was strikingly handsome, tall, accomplished and, above all, dedicated to his own self-advancement. The rumours of murder, poison and intrigue which were forever at his heels make him a character worthy of any Jacobean play. His fame, power and wealth were derived from his hold on the affections of Elizabeth, a relationship he both valued and abused. Yet, with all his faults, Leicester had an acute and questioning mind. He had been carefully educated by his father with a succession of private tutors, one of whom was John Dee. He could read Latin and Italian with ease and had a natural aptitude for mathematics and a real interest in science. It should not surprise us that a man whose life was filled with pomp, extravagance and the manipulation of his fellow men was drawn instinctively to drama, and took a genuine and active interest in its promotion. His involvement was not that of a mere dilettante; from early on in his career he was aware of the political capital to be made out of dramatic presentations.

Leicester won the gratitude and undying loyalty of the Inner Temple for taking its side in a dispute with the Middle Temple. He used his influence with the Queen to gain a decision in favour of the Inner Temple, and in recognition the lawyers declared they would never take part in a legal action against him. Furthermore, they made a very handsome return by choosing Leicester as the Christmas Prince for their Revels at the Inner Temple in the winter of 1561/2. The form of these festivities included some play-like presentation, allegorical and heavily symbolic, ending usually in a masque dance. In this instance the allegory was politically slanted to support Leicester's own ambitions.[3]

The name chosen for the Christmas Prince was Pallaphilos, the friend or lover of wisdom. Pallas was the Greek goddess Pallas Athene, goddess of wisdom, but the name was also intended to hint at Elizabeth herself in her role as Queen. The story for these particular Christmas celebrations was taken from a strange book, *The Accedens of Armory*, by Gerard Legh. It was first published at the end of 1562 and sets out to tell the history of heraldry from its beginning to the Elizabethan day. At one point Legh digresses to tell the Greek legend of how Pallas had helped Perseus kill the Gorgon, Medusa, with the aid of a shield she gave him. Legh reminds us that this shield was kept in the city of Troy, and so long as it remained there the city was invincible. This was intended as an elaborate compliment to Leicester who in his role in the Revels is regarded as a second Perseus with the shield of Pallas. He is essential for the safety of Elizabeth's kingdom. In a metaphorical sense he becomes the shield of Pallas, in the real sense the defender of Elizabeth.

I recalled seeing the phrase the 'Sheild of Pallas' on one of the drawings connected with the Globe. I knew the myth, but still it puzzled me. Legh combines the myth with a second tale of a man named Desire who falls in love with Lady Bewty. After various trials he is allowed by the goddess Pallas to marry Lady Bewty, who in the allegory stands for Elizabeth – as woman, not Queen. Desire is Robert Dudley, the man who loves her for herself. This story, too, was acted out by the lawyers of the Temple and was a neat way of saying that Leicester was truly in love with Elizabeth. When Desire proves himself worthy of Lady Bewty, Leicester is proving himself worthy of his sovereign. In other words the lawyers are championing his claim as a suitor for the Queen's hand. This is their return for his help in the dispute with the Middle Temple.

Figure 1: An engraving of the procession of the Knights of The Garter
taken from Elias Ashmole's *Order of The Garter*.

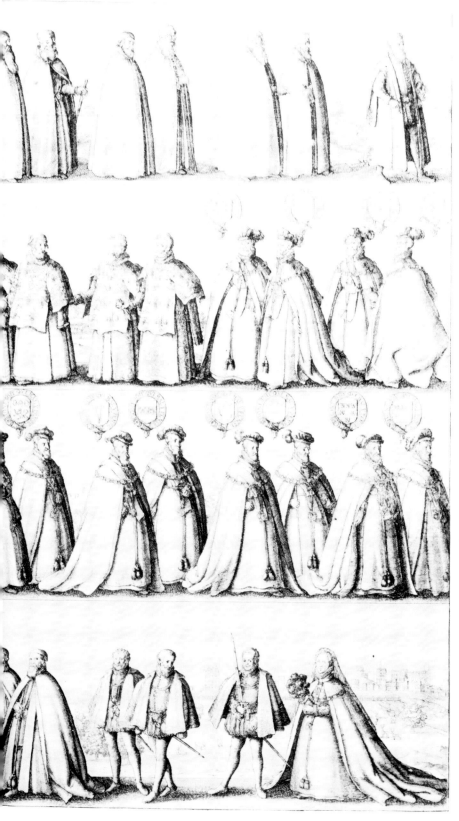

Viscount Montague and the Earl of Leicester can be identified by the coats of arms in the second line fifth and sixth from the left.

These Christmas Revels were linked with performances of the play *Gorboduc* at the Inner Temple in January 1562, and later at court before the Queen. Written by two lawyers from the Inner Temple, Thomas Sackville (cousin to Elizabeth) and Thomas Norton, the play was concerned with the problem which bedevilled Elizabeth's reign, the question of the succession. The allegory of Desire and Lady Bewty offered one solution by supporting obliquely the idea of a marriage between Leicester and the Queen. The play showed the dangers of leaving a kingdom ill-prepared for succession. (The King divides his kingdom unwisely.) At the end of *Gorboduc* the authors suggest that succession should be settled by the sovereign acting in concert with Parliament. Thus the Queen, while watching the play, was subtly offered a formula not a nominee to solve her dilemma.

What is important for our purposes is to realise that Leicester, together with his friends at the Inner Temple, made good use of drama and allegory to promote his interests and, although the form of the Christmas Revels may now be outmoded, in its day it was vital enough to make a telling case. Moreover Leicester, in his role as Christmas Prince, would be expected to round off the Revels and lead the customary dance. When the celebrations and the play were repeated at Court, Leicester would step forward to beg the Queen to lead the dance with him. It must have been a most apt and effective climax.

This was not just an incidental use of drama by Leicester. In his official capacity as Governor of the Inner Temple he attended other entertainments put on by the Templars and presented to the Queen. Leicester's relationship with the lawyers and actors of the Inner Temple shows his involvement in drama in a new light. It also helps to explain in a different way his readiness to be a patron for Burbage's players and the seriousness with which he took that role.

His association with Burbage extended over several years before the building of the Theater. The first mention of his company of players is in 1571. The following year 'the Acte for the punishment of Vagabondes' sorted out the better actors from the riff-raff, and it was necessary for Burbage and his fellow actors to become members of the Earl's official household and so enjoy his protection under the law. Leicester's Men performed at Court at Christmas in 1574 and 1575, enabling Dudley to satisfy the Queen's delight in theatrical entertainment and continue his public wooing. Indeed, in the summer of 1575 Burbage and his actors took part in the memorable extravaganza which Leicester prepared for the Queen at Kenilworth. The castle had been a gift from his devoted sovereign, so no expense was spared by her loyal subject in returning his thanks. Fourteen earls and seventeen barons together with their wives, foreign ambassadors and privy councillors were invited to enjoy the festivities.[4] Leicester commissioned a young poet, George

Gascoine, to write a fresh play around the character of Desire taken from the Inner Temple Revels. This new play, *Zabeta and Deepdesire*, shows Leicester still paying court in public to the Queen. The following year the Theater opened as the first permanent home for Leicester's Men. It is hard to imagine Dudley not being actively interested in the playhouse which was to be the home of the players who served him so well.

Eventually the full significance of the phrase 'The size the Sheild of Pallas' dawned upon me. Gerard Legh had alluded to Leicester as the shield of Pallas in the narrative of his book, and it was used in the dramatisation for the Christmas Revels at the Inner Temple. The book itself, *The Accedens of Armory*, is an extraordinary confection, detailed, discursive, erudite, fanciful and obscure. To the perplexed modern reader it shows the total seriousness with which heraldry was treated in the Elizabethan age. We can see from it that Legh had studied mediaeval views of natural science, dabbled in alchemy and knew something of the Cabala. The Hebrew Cabala has long been concerned with number, and before we dismiss a superstitious reverence for number, we should recall the importance of number symbolism in our own culture, often inherited from the Bible: the twelve tribes of Israel, the twelve apostles of Jesus, the twelve days of Christmas . . . Even to increasingly secular ears such numbers still have resonances. Which of us is happy to be thirteenth at table?

It should not surprise us then that number, inextricably part of geometry, should carry symbolic significances in architecture. The 'size the Sheild of Pallas' belongs to that convention. The reference is twofold: to a person and to a place. The person here is the Queen's protector, her shield, Leicester. The place is part of the theatre with whose design he had been intimately concerned. When the time came to rebuild the Theater as the Globe both Leicester (Burbage's patron) and de Bry (the designer) were commemorated in the new playhouse. Leicester was fifty-one[5] when the Theater was originally built; he died before the Globe was opened. The diameter of the 'Starrs mall', that part incorporating the yard and the stage, was fifty-one feet. The card containing the reference to the 'Globe's Uper Pt' also had 'The size the Sheild of Pallas' written on it. Now that I understood the reference to Leicester, it was clear the 'Globe' referred to a playhouse and not anything else. The specification reminds us of Leicester's initial contribution to the innovative design of the new series of playhouses on Bankside. His closeness to the Queen, his role as her defender, which Legh had made so clear in the Christmas Revels, were two reasons why James Burbage had petitioned him so humbly to become patron to his own company of players, and that special relationship between the two had brought Burbage the additional reward of the first royal licence.

The playhouse before the Theater had been at the Sign of the Red Lion, and had been built by John Brayne.[6] He appears to have been a grocer turned impresario, for he later engaged in the construction of the Theater as joint partner with James Burbage, himself a joiner turned actor. Nine years elapsed between the building at the Red Lion and the Theater and the design is so radically different that it raises a number of questions. The men responsible for the actual construction of the Theater were undoubtedly Elizabethan carpenters, supervised by characters such as Brayne, Burbage, Streete and, later, Henslowe; the ideas for its design – the intellectual origins – came from a different level in society altogether.

For me the figure of John Dee emerges as the most likely channel for the dissemination of the sophisticated theories behind the circular playhouses of the Bankside. The polygonal shape of the Theater arises from a geometric plan. Dee was the leading mathematician in this country at the time, with an international reputation and international contacts. He was court astrologer to Queen Elizabeth and, as such, fixed the appropriate day for her coronation. She had promised him her protection to allow him to pursue his studies. He had been tutor to Leicester and to his nephew, Philip Sidney. He settled at Mortlake in 1570 and stayed there until 1583, his house becoming a centre of study rather like Manuzio's academy in Venice. His library was one of the greatest in the country and contained no less than five editions of Vitruvius and two of Alberti's famous treatise on architecture. Peter French gives some idea of the rich resources for learning Dee had at his disposal.

> His catalogue reveals a library that was universal in scope, a collection in which antiquarians, geographers, practical scientists, architects, theologians, even physicians could find the most recent works on their subject . . .[7]

It is not surprising that Elizabeth and her court travelled to Mortlake to visit the man she called her 'old philosopher'. Leicester and Sidney were frequent visitors. Even the cautious Burghley had some regard for the unorthodox Dr Dee.

Through Dee, Leicester and Sidney were introduced not only to the world of science and mathematics but also to the hermetic and cabalistic tradition. The name of the new playhouse seems to be almost a symbolic declaration, the Theater, linking the revolutionary design with classical precedents in Greece and Rome. It is quite clear that the design of the forerunner of Shakespeare's Globe was not simply the result of functional constraints.

It is known that when a dispute arose over the land on which it was standing, the Theater was dismantled and moved piece by piece to a new site in Southwark where it became the Globe. It is known, too, that it was not unusual for some Elizabethan houses to be built in such a way that they could be taken apart and moved. John Orrell has argued convincingly that from the start the Theater was probably planned as a moveable structure,[8] though so detailed a geometrical design would have required careful direction from a small group of people advised by one creative thinker. I believe that person to be Theodore de Bry. We have already seen that he was in England completing an engraving of the Garter ceremony at Windsor in 1576, the year the Theater was built. He also spent some time in the capital in 1587 and 1588. In 1587 de Bry engraved the thirty-four plates for Sir Philip Sidney's elaborate funeral procession and became interested in the great explorations of the Tudor mariners. Thomas Hariot, one of the original settlers in the new colony of Virginia, published his account *The Briefe and True Reporte of the new found land of Virginia* while de Bry was still in London. De Bry was so impressed that on his return to Frankfurt he produced a magnificently illustrated edition with his own engravings based on John White's watercolours.[9] This period in London was a turning point in de Bry's career, for it marked the end of his work as a goldsmith. Henceforth he concentrated on engraving and publishing.

Today we may wonder why a goldsmith should even be considered as a possible progenitor of a series of theatre designs. We have become too confined in our horizons by increasing specialisation arising from the growth of knowledge, especially in the sciences. It was not so in Elizabethan times. Professions were not so rigidly defined as they are now; the man who rebuilt St Paul's was a professor of astronomy before he turned to architecture, just as earlier the man who painted the ceiling of the Sistine Chapel was first and foremost a sculptor. In de Bry's case, as I myself discovered, his connection with the guild and craft of goldsmiths was very relevant to his interest in architecture.

During one of my intermittent visits to the Science Museum to research the mathematical instrument makers connected with the Byrom Collection, I came across *Gothick Design Techniques* by Lon R. Shelby, which contains translations of some pamphlets written by two late medi-aeval masons, Conrad Roriczer of Regensburg and Hans Schmuttermayer of Nuremberg.[10] These claimed to reveal 'secrets of the medieval masons'. Roriczer and Schmuttermayer had published papers on certain techniques used by masons in 1486–88. In addition Roriczer drew attention to the importance of geometry in the work of a mason and describes how to arrive at an elevation from the ground plan. Since I believe my parametric drawings were composed of both the elevations and setting-out plans I was naturally intrigued. Here was printed confirmation that my interpretations were on the right lines.

Of equal importance was the discovery that Schmuttermayer was himself a goldsmith, like de Bry; what is more, a goldsmith fully conversant with the design techniques of masons. Shelby shows that, despite the organisation of the various crafts into guilds, techniques and practices were not all kept compartmentalised, distinct and separate. De Bry as a goldsmith from a family of goldsmiths would have known this, and no doubt knew the writings of his fellow-goldsmith Schmuttermayer. He had lived for several years in Strasbourg, the home of German Masonry, where the first lodge was founded for the men building the city's cathedral. In short, de Bry would automatically have acquired practical technical knowledge as a goldsmith which he could put to good use when it came to designing the theatres. In addition he knew all about the Vitruvian theoretical tradition. His sons even published a book on architecture when they had access to all his material. Theodore de Bry, then, working with John Dee, is the most likely candidate as the originator of the theatre designs. Dee himself was the intermediary with Leicester, his patron and former pupil.

Theodore de Bry
and As You Like It

When the Globe theatre was built it was not just Leicester whose memory was honoured. De Bry's contribution was also commemorated by the first performance of a new comedy by Shakespeare, *As You Like It*, in 1599, shortly after the Globe was opened. It may even have been the first play to be performed there.

Towards the end of her book *Theatre of the World* Frances Yates turns her attention to the use of the idea of the theatre as a symbol of the cosmic setting within which man plays out the scenes of his life. Philosophers and preachers were familiar with the belief that this world is a moral testing place where man is sorely tried before he can attain perfection or paradise. The Old Testament contains a good example of this in the Book of Job. The analogy with a theatre in which an actor plays out a part before an audience sitting in judgment is not so very far away. In the end the metaphor of man playing out a tragic role became a commonplace of Elizabethan and Jacobean playwrights. Theodore de Bry gave expression to a similar view of life in a series of engravings, inviting Jean Jacques Boissard to write poems and prose commentaries to accompany them and to elaborate on the moral behind each engraving. The result was a book entitled *The Theatre of Human Life* which was published in 1596 by de Bry when he was sixty-eight.

The first plate in the book is an allegorical illustration of its title (figure 2). It shows a man's life as a tragic spectacle played out as if in a theatre, with an audience watching the miseries that beset him. The

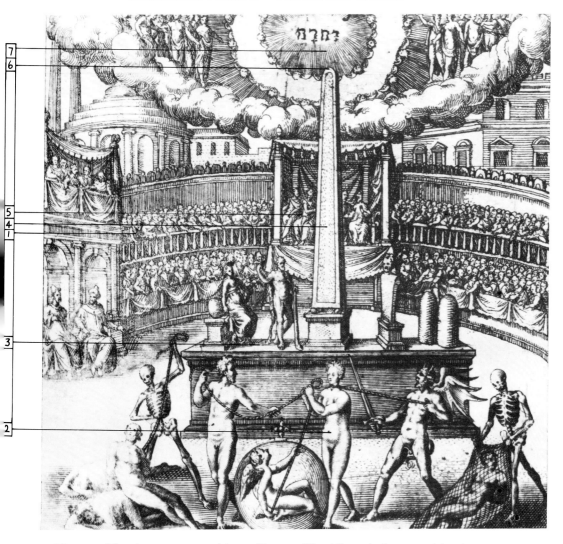

Figure 2: The theatre as an emblem of human life. Allegorical composition by
Theodore de Bry. (Compare this with figure 4.)

theatre depicted seems to combine aspects of the Roman amphitheatre,
as can be seen from the central obelisk which rises from an island in
the middle of the arena. Behind this, in the centre of the tiered ranks
of the audience, is placed a royal box; to the left are special seats for
distinguished guests. The picture is heavily symbolic. The obelisk rises
up towards the heavens where in the clouds we can see the name of
the Godhead surrounded by a heavenly choir. No doubt this represents
man's goal, the heaven far removed from the hell on earth. 'Why this is
Hell, nor am I out of it!'[11] is the sentiment of the scene acted out in the
foreground by a man and a woman ensnared by devils. The audience is

the rest of the human race being made aware of the true nature of life. The heavenly choir is composed of those who have survived the temptations of this world and been taken up into eternity. Yates links this scene with the famous speech of Jaques in *As You Like It*.

> All the world's a stage
> And all the men and women merely players:
> They have their exits and their entrances;
> And one man in his time plays many parts,
> His acts being seven ages . . .[12]

The connection is unmistakable since the verse Boissard wrote to accompany the first plate begins 'The life of man is like a circus or a great theatre', and, in the prose commentary which follows, Boissard lists the seven ages of man. That is important, because Boissard wrote the commentaries at the request of de Bry, after consultation and after de Bry had finished the engravings. The idea of the seven ages came from de Bry not Boissard. However, I do not claim that this is the first time that the idea was expressed. Jaques's speech in *As You Like It* is clearly related to this theme. It should be remembered, too, that Jaques is a character added to the story which Shakespeare had borrowed from Thomas Lodge.[13] It is significant that the play was first performed at the Globe theatre, whose motto was 'Totus mundus agit histrionem', the Latin equivalent of the first line of Jaques's speech.

After reading once more that speech various elements of the puzzle suddenly fell into place. The speech and the engraving coalesced and reminded me of a drawing in the collection (figure 4). This, I realised, was a geometrical representation of the de Bry engraving and its message. It also pointed towards the connection between Theodore de Bry, Shakespeare, and the Globe. De Bry had drawn a portrait of himself the year before, which is reproduced as figure 3. It shows the haunting face of a man who has within him stores of accumulated wisdom and is now waiting for the final revelations of death. The eye is still bright, the left hand rests calmly on a skull, the right hand still holds the artist's dividers which he had used so skilfully all his life. It is a masterly work. Jaques's speech about the world being a stage could be seen as Shakespeare's tribute to this man who designed his theatre.

In 1983 the editor of the *Hermetic Journal*, Adam McLean, drew attention to an important feature in the work of alchemical and Rosicrucian engravers of the sixteenth and seventeenth centuries. That feature is the presence in certain symbolic diagrams of an 'underlying geometric skeleton structure upon which the symbols are arrayed'. He had come to the conclusion that

The engravers of that period, de Bry, Matthieu Merian, Lucas Jennis may well have worked a complex geometric message as well as a symbolic one into their beautifully executed engravings. I consider that this discovery is of great importance and hope that some of my correspondents might have the intention to follow up in detail this aspect with regard to other engravings. There may well be a whole layer of meaning that we are at present unaware of woven into these ancient emblems.[14]

We know that geometry together with number was seen by some philosophers, notably Plato, as an ideal means of conveying philosophical thought. Thus, while an emblematic picture can convey through its symbols a hidden meaning, the underlying geometry of the picture as a whole can also demonstrate its truth. In the illustration for his book *The Theatre of Human Life*, de Bry shows one level of meaning through the emblems in the engraving; the rest of the story is told through the inner geometry and the introduction of the number seven, indicated here by the seven ages of man and the seven celestial spheres.

It was at a critical juncture in the early stages of my investigations, when I was wondering whether I should proceed with the work or not,

Figure 3: Theodore de Bry, 1597.

that I picked out figure 4 as my favourite. It was now clear that this was one of those 'underlying geometric skeleton structures' mentioned by McLean.

It was about this time I looked into Cesare Cesariano's 1521 illustrated edition of Vitruvius. Book One includes a diagram showing the geometrical structure of the front of Milan Cathedral (figure 5), with the triangular elevation rising from a circular ground plan. It uses the same principles employed in the parametric drawings. The façade of the Cathedral in the design was welcome proof of the existence of such composite drawings outside the Byrom Collection. Such an impeccable precedent gave me confidence to address the remaining parametric drawings concerned with theatres in the collection.

The Rose

The Rose theatre is one of two Elizabethan playhouses for which some physical evidence now exists. To date it is the only one which has been excavated extensively. The finds at the site of the Globe, although important, have been very limited in comparison. Fortunately, by the time the archaeologists from the Museum of London, who were responsible for the excavations at the Rose, had begun their work, I was fully immersed in my analysis of the theatre drawings. Of course I was aware of these activities through reports in the press, but at the beginning of December 1988 I thought that the connection between the drawings and the theatres was confined to the Globe. I followed the developments at the Rose site as an interesting side issue to my concern with the Globe.

It was a little later, probably July 1989, that I first considered whether the collection might also contain drawings of the Rose. In February archaeologists had discovered the external wall of the playhouse, and when Theo Crosby sent me a plan of their findings, the similarities seemed clear. The circular outline of the foundations that had been unearthed resembled the layout of my circular drawings (of which there were several apart from those for the Globe and Fortune theatres). I separated off a sequence of drawings which I felt could be attributed to the Rose theatre. In doing so I realised there were still others concerned with additional theatres built on Bankside during the heyday of the Elizabethan and Jacobean public playhouses, but first, what could be gleaned about the Rose sequence? While the Fortune contract helps to establish a measure of confirmation for the Globe drawings, the Rose sequence needs to be examined in the light of the information gathered from the excavations.

The Rose theatre, built before the Globe or the Fortune, opened in 1587. It is said that the actors' company which spent most of its time at the Rose became worried about competition from the Globe when it was

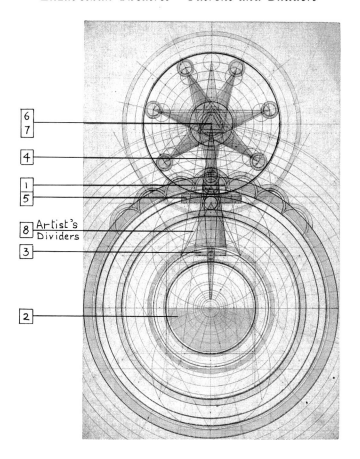

Figure 4: 'The Theatre of Human Life', a geometric representation of the engraving by Theodore de Bry.

KEY 1   Audience watching the miseries of the life of man from the galleries of a theatre. Seven Ages of Man represented by seven scallops.

2   The miseries of the life of man, the temptations of the flesh, sin, death and Satan.

3   Allusion to Circus (Alberti influence).

4   Central goal of the circus in the form of an obelisk.

5   Royal Box.

6   Winning post in the race of life.

7   Godhead △ and seven celestial spheres surrounding the Godhead.

Frances Yates's interpretation of de Bry's emblem has been translated to this drawing, 1 to 7.

erected practically opposite. So they moved north across the Thames to the Fortune when that theatre opened. Thus the Rose and Fortune are linked by this company. Since the Globe and the Rose were so close, concern over a fall in takings was understandable. The Rose had been built by

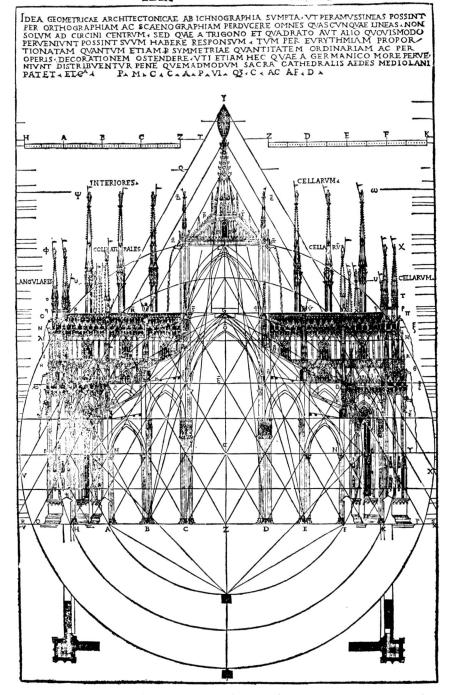

Figure 5: Milan Cathedral – a parametric drawing from Cesare Cesariano's edition of Vitruvius, 1521.

a carpenter, John Griggs, and the financier was Philip Henslowe, later concerned with building the Fortune.

What was it that made me group the Rose theatre drawings together? Even within the general similarity of all the theatre drawings they seemed to be distinctive. From figure 7 it appears that the Rose had twelve sides. I began, therefore, separating off all the twelve-sided drawings, some of which are tinted rose pink. When I studied the archaeological plans of the Rose, I noticed the entrance to the theatre had been placed at the southern end of the site. Examining figure 6, I saw what appears to be an entrance indicated by a small but distinct circle, tinted pink (A) in approximately the same position. A concentric circle (B) just within the drawing contains a break opposite the pink circle, seeming to confirm the position of an entrance. This may seem a very easy deduction to make, but by now I was aware of how the slightest variations in a drawing were used to indicate different features in design. Another variation separating the Rose drawings from the rest was a marked difference in the representation of the towers of the tiring house, the shape of which has always been a matter of conjecture. The neck of the drawings contains the elevation of the tiring house, as with the other theatre drawings, and reveals the shape of those towers (D). Judging from this, the towers resembled cupolas or small domes.

Henslowe acquired the site in 1585, but before that there were, it seems, other properties on it. A widow, Thomasin Symonds, had owned a 'messuage or tenement called the Little Rose with two gardens to the same adjoining'[15] in the parish of St Saviour, Southwark.

According to Henslowe's lease the size of the plot was 'in length and breadth square every way four score and fourteen foot of lawfull assize little more or less'.[16] The same indenture talks of the 'playhouse now in framing and shortly to be erected and set up'. This is somewhat ambiguous. Does it mean that the building of the playhouse had already started? Or that the frame for it was being prepared elsewhere ready to be brought to the Rose site and be set up?

The size of the plot made me ponder; 'four score and fourteen foot' adds up to ninety-four feet – a plot of ninety-four feet square. I calculated from figure 7 that this design would have occupied an area 84 feet by 114 feet, far too large to go into a plot 94 feet square 'more or less' as given in the indenture. When I discussed the site some time later with archaeologists from the Museum of London, it was clear that, according to their findings, the area of the theatre did not extend at all as far as 114 feet in any direction. Yet I felt sure this drawing was connected with the Rose. I must admit I was perplexed, but closer inspection of another drawing (figure 8) revealed it had been heavily scored in various places by some sharp implement. Markings across the drawings had prevented me from

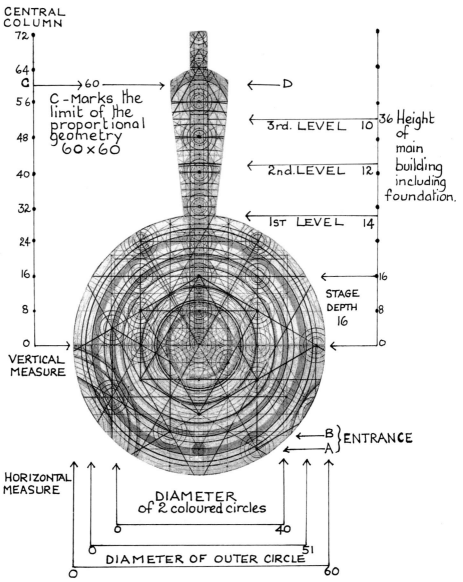

CENTRAL
COLUMN
72

64
C

56

C – Marks the
limit of the
proportional
geometry
60 × 60

48

40

32

24

16

8

0

VERTICAL
MEASURE

← 60 →

← D

3rd. LEVEL   10   36 Height
of
main
building
including
foundation.

2nd. LEVEL   12

1ST LEVEL   14

16

STAGE
DEPTH
16   8

0

B } ENTRANCE
A }

HORIZONTAL
MEASURE

DIAMETER
of 2 coloured circles

0   40

0   51
DIAMETER OF OUTER CIRCLE

0   60

Inner of the two coloured circles shows 'Starrs mall'
to be 40 feet. Larger circle shows a 'Starrs mall'
diameter of 51 feet. Diameter–60, shows limit of the
auditorium. The entrance is shown by the pink circle
and the break in the coloured circle immediately above
it. All colouring is as the original.

Figure 6: The Rose theatre (1587) – a modified schematic. The reverse side of this
figure gives extra details.

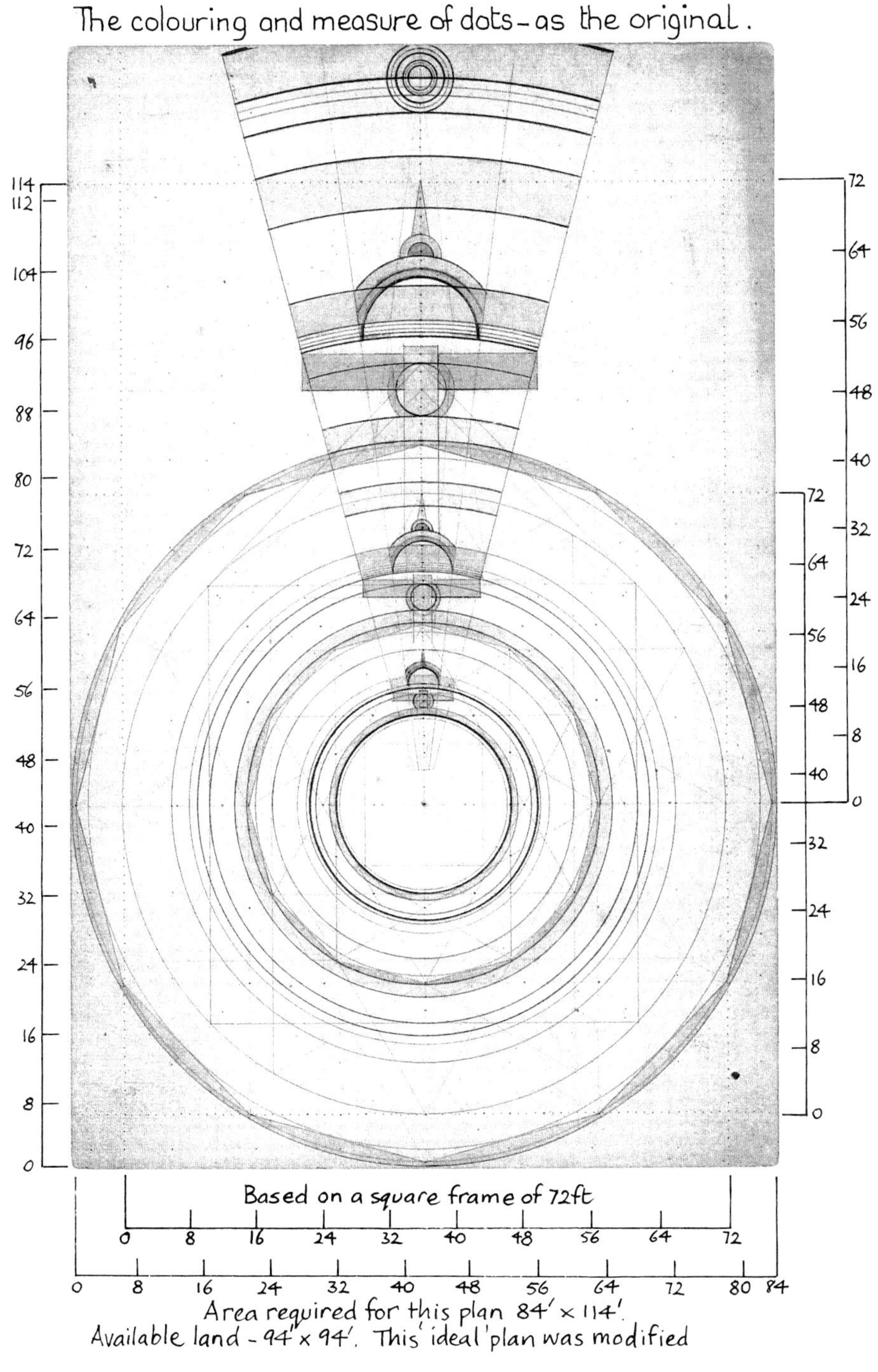
The colouring and measure of dots - as the original.
114
112
104
96
88
80
72
64
56
48
40
32
24
16
8
0
72
64
56
48
40
32
24
16
8
0
72
64
56
48
40
32
24
16
8
0
Based on a square frame of 72ft
0 8 16 24 32 40 48 56 64 72
0 8 16 24 32 40 48 56 64 72 80 84
Area required for this plan 84' x 114'.
Available land - 94' x 94'. This 'ideal' plan was modified

Figure 7: The Rose theatre (1587) – the ideal.

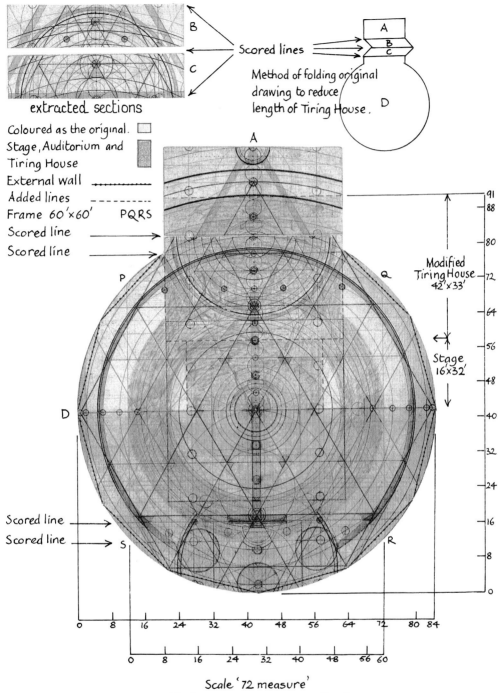

B

C

Scored lines

extracted sections

Method of folding original
drawing to reduce
length of Tiring House.

A
B
C

D

Coloured as the original. ☐
Stage, Auditorium and
Tiring House   ▨
External wall   · · · · · · · · ·
Added lines   - - - - - - - -
Frame 60'x60'   PQRS
Scored line   ———→
Scored line   ———————→

A

P   Q

D

S   R

Scored line ———————→
Scored line ———————→

91
88
80

Modified
Tiring House
42'x33'   72

64

56

Stage
16'x32'   48

40

32

24

16

8

0

0   8   16   24   32   40   48   56   64   72   80 84

0   8   16   24   32   40   48   56 60

Scale '72 measure'
Minimum area required 84'x91'

Note-width of Tiring House is shown as 42'
    - on other drawings 40'

Figure 8: The Rose (modified).

114

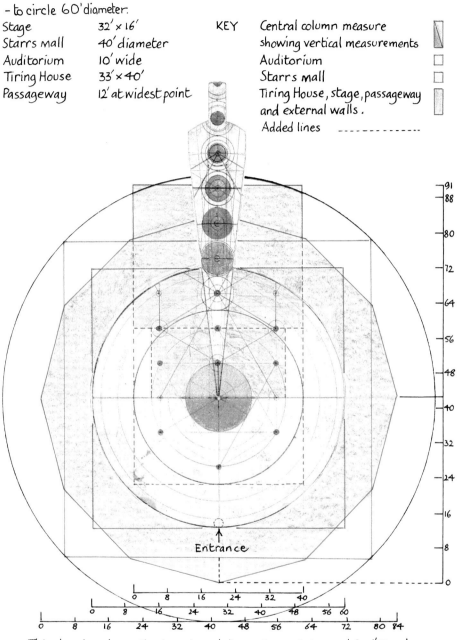

- to circle 60' diameter.

Stage   32' × 16'
Starrs mall   40' diameter
Auditorium   10' wide
Tiring House   33' × 40'
Passageway   12' at widest point

KEY   Central column measure
       showing vertical measurements
       Auditorium
       Starrs mall
       Tiring House, stage, passageway
       and external walls.
       Added lines   _ _ _ _ _ _ _ _ _ _

Entrance

This drawing shows the layout and dimensions of the modified 'Rose'.
Information from collated geometric drawings Figs. 6, 7 and 8.

Figure 9: The Rose based on a twelve-sided figure, the reverse side of figure 6.

noting this earlier. When the drawing was held up for examination, it became obvious that it could be folded along the scored lines, and when this was done, the area covered was reduced. I folded the drawing in the places marked and noted the possible permutations in the shape of the overall plan.

In this way I was able to work out three alternative sizes for the Rose theatre. There were other possible variations, but these I dismissed because it was immediately obvious, from the aerial photographs of the site and the archaeologists' map, that these variants were truncated in such a way as to contradict the physical evidence. The three possibilities were, first, a theatre 84 feet by 111 feet; second, a theatre 84 feet by 106 feet; and third, a theatre 84 feet by 91 feet. This last would obviously fit into a plot 94 feet square. Moreover, it was the most in keeping with the findings on the site.

What appears to have happened is that the 'ideal' drawing of the Rose was adapted to the physical constraints of the site by reducing the depth of the tiring house by 20 feet. I should emphasise that I had worked out my measurements independently of the archaeological plan and according to the '72 measure' which I had already decoded. The principal measurements of the Rose theatre based on this drawing are as follows: the 'Starrs mall', or yard, had a diameter of 40 feet and the seating in the galleries extended for 10 feet. This meant that the distance from the centre of the front of the stage to the back wall of the auditorium was 30 feet, giving an overall diameter to the auditorium of 60 feet. These measurements tallied with those on figure 9, which had been drawn and coloured by hand on the back of figure 6. Perhaps they had been placed back to back to show how one had evolved from the other. The relationship between these two drawings seemed to be evidence of designs working towards a final version of the Rose.

This design created a very wide corridor on the outside of the auditorium. Why was more space not given to the auditorium itself rather than the passageway round it? The original diameter of the main circle of the structure had been kept at 72 feet, and the widest point of the twelve-sided polygon based on that circle was 84 feet as originally planned. But the auditorium had been reduced. When I considered the severe limitations of the outside site, I had to agree that a wide corridor would have been very useful. The theatre had been squashed into the plot; it had even been built off-centre on the site, presumably to accommodate existing buildings, with the main entrance placed to avoid blocking access to adjoining property. These constraints would make a wide corridor a useful feature for movement, waiting, and possibly staircases.

It is the design of the tiring house which appears to have been modified most owing to the shortage of space. The designer eliminated one room from each side of the passage in the standard design (see p. 73). This would have left two rooms at the front and a central entrance, with, at the back, a storage space to the left and a staircase on the right to the gentlemen's rooms and balcony. It also looks as if the gentlemen's room above would have been in an almost continuous line with the galleries. The size of the stage seems to have been 32 feet in width and 16 feet deep. This is a wide stage in proportion to the 'Starrs mall'. Performances at the Rose would have been even more 'in the round' than we have realised. The thrust of the stage would only allow four feet each side for the groundlings to stand, but at its widest point, in front of the stage, that area became 20 feet. Apart from that we should note the shape of the towers as indicated on the drawings.

I superimposed the outline of the theatre (as shown in figure 9) on the top of an accurate ground plan of the archaeological finds at the Rose, reduced to the scale of the '72 measure'. The remarkable correspondence between the two is shown in figure 10. One can even see a drain uncovered by archaeologists travelling at an angle under room 'A' of the tiring house, the return of the stairs, and out at the back of the building. This would seem to have been a sensible arrangement. An aerial photograph of the site bears out the similarity between the drawing and the finds. There were modifications to the Rose after it opened, but none of the drawings in the collection is concerned with those changes.

One company of actors which performed at the Rose was Lord Pembroke's Men. His presence as a patron may have indirectly influenced the design of the theatre. Henry Herbert, the second earl, is an interesting figure. He was a very good friend and strong supporter of Robert Dudley, and had been an ally of Dudley's father in his attempt to put Lady Jane Grey on the throne in preference to Mary and Elizabeth. (His first wife had been Lady Jane Grey's sister.) This early association with the father was bound to dictate Herbert's relationship with the son. Like all the Herbert family, Henry was a cultivated man and close to Sir Philip Sidney, whose sister, Mary, was his third wife. His private secretary was Arthur Massinger, father of the playwright Philip Massinger, and he became the patron of a company of players in 1589, maintaining his interest in them until his death in 1602. He and Mary had two sons, William and Philip, both of whom continued the family interest in literature and the theatre. They were the 'incomparable pair of brethren' to whom the first folio of Shakespeare's works was dedicated.

I had noticed that Henslowe first negotiated the lease for the Rose in 1585. In October the following year Sir Philip Sidney died while still in the prime of life and his funeral in London was a magnificent occasion, on the scale of a state funeral. As we have seen, Theodore de Bry engraved plates of the procession. Mary Sidney, one of the most intelligent and best

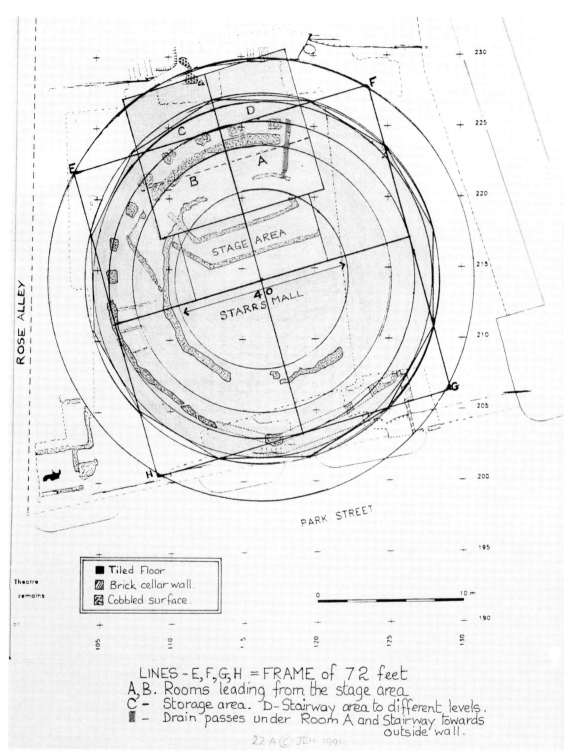

Figure 10: Archaeological map of the Rose site. Superimposed in the setting-out plan of the Rose theatre – figure 9.

Figure 11: Rose theatre. The archaeological remains.

educated women of her day, lost her mother and father in the same year as her brother, and this triple blow led her to devote her energies to the promotion of literature. The great Pembroke house at Wilton became a centre of Elizabethan culture. Mary was the patroness of many leading poets, including Spenser, Donne and Ben Jonson. She also set about shaping her brother's major literary work, *Arcadia*.

Philip Sidney had a great hold on the imagination and affection of many of his contemporaries. He represented the complete ideal of the Elizabethan courtier, scholar and soldier. He was highly accomplished and his death was a devastating blow to people at all levels of society. The great Queen herself was overwhelmed. Sidney's intellectual interests had been so wide that they had brought him into friendly contact with people beyond the narrow confines of the court. Fulke Greville claimed: 'There was not an approved painter, skilful engineer, excellent musician or any other artificer of fame that made not himself known to him.'[17] Like his sister, he was especially fond of the company of men of letters. He also took a great interest in drama and was actively concerned in the welfare of his uncle's players, Leicester's Men. In 1582 he was happy to be godfather to a son of Richard Tarleton, one of the great clowns and famous for his extempore wit. Moreover, he made a lasting contribution to the cause of drama when he defended it from its detractors in his *Apology for Poetry*. When I reflected on these aspects of Sidney's career I could not believe that his death would have gone unmarked in some way by the theatre he had championed. With both his uncle and his brother-in-law patrons of companies of players that would have been unthinkable.

When Theodore de Bry came to England to work on the plates of the funeral, he worked from sketches by Thomas Lant who had been a personal servant of Sidney and was a herald and a draughtsman. Like Gerard Legh, Lant would have been steeped in allegory and symbolism. He was also the same age as Sidney. I believe that Lant also worked with de Bry on the drawings for the theatres. Sidney died at the age of thirty-two, and that is commemorated in the width of the stage at the Rose as a gesture to the man who had proclaimed the value of drama in his *Apology*. We have already seen the allusion to Leicester, the Shield of Pallas, in the building of the Globe, and Shakespeare's tribute to de Bry in the speech from *As You Like It*. Such emblematic conceits appealed to the Elizabethan mind. Their presence in the dimensions of Elizabethan playhouses should not surprise us.

The Hope and the Swan

There are three Elizabethan theatres for which there are no drawings in the Byrom Collection: the Red Lion at Stepney, the Curtain, and Newington Butts. The Red Lion playhouse dates from nine years before the Theater and, therefore, before the involvement of Theodore de Bry. It was no doubt a substantial structure, but, as one of the earliest theatres, still experimental in design. Its shape remains uncertain. The Curtain, according to witnesses, was round, and this may be a further indication that classical theories about playhouses were beginning to reach Elizabethan builders. I could not trace any record of its builder in the year after the Theater. Little is known of Newington Butts. First mentioned in

1580, it takes its name from some archery butts near to what was then the village of Newington.

I did find drawings which could be attributed, I felt, to three other playhouses, and I had three more parametric drawings to help in distinguishing them. These were the Bear Garden, the Hope and the Swan. The Bear Garden and Hope are closely connected because the Hope replaced the Bear Garden, although not on exactly the same spot. The baiting of animals was a popular sport in Shakespeare's day, and bulls, bears and horses had been sacrificed for this gruesome entertainment since the beginning of the sixteenth century. It is known that the Bear Garden was in use in 1594, and that in 1598 Henslowe, together with Alleyn, had applied unsuccessfully for the Mastership of the Royal Game of Bears and Bulls and Mastiff. They were determined to get the monopoly of the 'sport' and finally purchased the office in 1604. Seven years later Alleyn sold his interest to Henslowe, who then took a new partner, Jacob Meade. In 1613 these two men demolished the Bear Garden and replaced it with the Hope. The contract for the Hope has survived and makes clear that, uniquely, it was designed for a dual purpose: for both plays and baitings.

Gilbert Katherens, the builder, was required to construct a 'fitt and convenient Tyre house and a stage to be carried or taken awaie'.[18] For this purpose the stage had to be on trestles, so that when both stage and tiring house were removed an arena was left for the baitings. When I came to examine the parametric drawings which I had identified with the Hope, I could see on one (figure 12) incisions around the area of the tiring house to indicate the arrangement. This is another double-sided drawing like those to be found in the Rose and Fortune sets. One side contains the prototype for the theatres, the other the details specific to the Hope. The most striking feature here is the absence of the neck from the drawings to indicate that the tiring house, as stipulated, was not included in the usual form. It emphasises the circularity of the arena or auditorium. The presence of the Hope drawing in the collection helps to confirm the nature of the parametric drawings as a composite design for playhouses.

The Swan, built in 1595, became the home of the Earl of Pembroke's Men. The contract for the Hope frequently refers to the Swan as its model. The Hope was to be built 'of such large compass, fforme, widenes and height as the Plaie house called the Swan'.[19] To judge from the drawings, the Swan's frame was based on a square of 80 feet. The distance between the outside walls at their widest point is 112 feet. Also, according to the drawings it had twelve sides, which seems to be the same number depicted by Visscher in his 1616 engraving. The tiring house fitted into two of these sides, giving the appearance of ten sides. The Swan is probably the best known of all the Elizabethan theatres because of a sketch by a Dutchman,

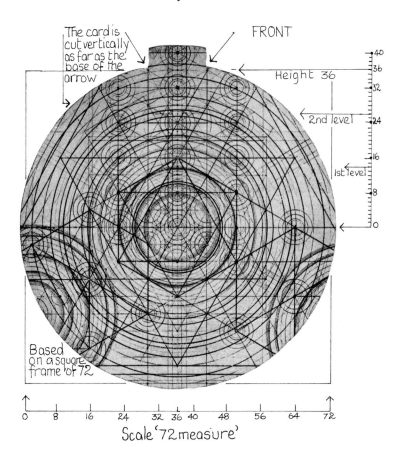

The card is
cut vertically
as far as the
base of the
arrow

FRONT

Height 36

2nd level

1st level

Based
on a square
frame of 72

Scale '72 measure'

Figure 12: The Hope, 1614. The central column is a measure of height.

Johannes de Witt. According to him, it was the largest of all the theatres and its capacity he calculated at three thousand. When de Witt drew his sketch he interpreted the features of the playhouse in terms of the classical Vitruvian amphitheatre. He was especially impressed by the beauty of the decoration, with the wooden pillars cleverly painted to look like marble.

For all its magnificence the Swan had a chequered history. In 1597 Pembroke's Men performed a play called *The Isle of Dogs* which was written by several playwrights including Thomas Nashe and Ben Jonson. The civic authorities were highly incensed by its 'seditious and slanderous matter'.[20] Jonson was sent to prison, the other writers took cover. Worse, the Privy Council ordered the closure and destruction of all the theatres on Bankside. Somehow they gained a reprieve, but the Swan seems never to have recovered. In 1602 one Richard Venner played a hoax on the public by

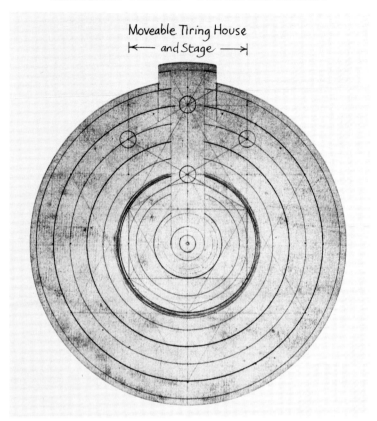

Figure 13: The reverse side of the Hope Theatre drawing in figure 12. The theatre was designed as closely to the Swan as possible but seems to have been slightly smaller in its overall area. Other drawings in the collection show it to be a twelve-sided structure based on a frame of 72 and built in principle as an arena. This drawing is quite different from the rest of the schematic drawings, the central column has all but disappeared. It demonstrates clearly that the collection contains the specific demands of the individual theatres.

selling tickets for a performance which never took place, and the audience vented its anger on the furnishings. Other companies, such as the Lady Elizabeth's Men or Prince Charles's Men, used the theatre, but it slips out of history and appears to have closed around 1637. The presence of these drawings in the collection again leads to the conclusion that the overall design was the responsibility of the de Bry family, although I would suggest that, at this time, it would be Michel Le Blon who supervised the building of the Hope and the second Globe after the first version of the Globe burned down in 1613.[21]

The Fortune, also destroyed by fire, was rebuilt in 1623. Shortly after it was opened all the theatres were closed because of the death of James I. A severe outbreak of plague soon closed them again, so the beginning of the Fortune's second phase was, to say the least, uncertain. None the less there was a significant visit from the King and Queen of Bohemia's company in 1626. The Queen of Bohemia, Elizabeth Stuart, was the daughter of James I, and her husband was Frederick of the Palatinate, the 'Winter King', who was forced into exile after the defeat in 1620 of his attempt to establish his claim to the throne of Bohemia. He had been the hope of the Protestant princes of Europe against the ambitions of the Catholic Habsburgs.

Abandoned by James I, they were now living in exile in the Hague, dependent on a somewhat irregular pension from England, although at the outset their marriage had been celebrated with extravagant splendour in London. Elizabeth's route from Holland to Heidelberg was treated as a triumphal progress. The first of her husband's cities to welcome her was Oppenheim, now the home of Johann Theodore de Bry, the son of Theodore de Bry who had recently moved the family business there and engraved and printed many of the lavish scenes of welcome. During their brief reign from 1613 to 1619 Johann printed scores of books on philosophical and hermetic subjects, all beautifully illustrated. The marriage of Frederick and Elizabeth had a wide and profound impact on artists, writers and thinkers. The appearance of their company of actors at the Fortune in 1626 was an appropriate, if sad reminder that they were once the focus of a strong Protestant cultural movement of which the de Brys, father and sons, were part.

The year Johann Theodore engraved the scenes of welcome for Elizabeth, his kinsman, Michel Le Blon, would have been playing a part in supervising the designs of the Hope and the reconstruction of the Globe, and through him the drawings would have returned to the de Bry family. After the death of his father and brother Johann Theodore produced one book on architecture in 1613. It may well be that he intended to use the theatre drawings as the basis for a second book but this was prevented by his own death in 1623. Any further work on the theatre designs would then fall to Michel Le Blon. Many features in the collection establish a personal association between him and the drawings. Then came the division of the family firm between the two inheritors, the Merians and Fitzers. Judging from the publication dates, it looks as if the bulk of the hermetic titles remained with the descendants of Susanne Merian – in other words, the Le Blons. In this way the drawings would reach her grandson Jacques Christophe Le Blon. He could have brought them to England either before or after they became part of the collection. Alternatively they might have remained here, passing from keeper to keeper, until they reached John Byrom, who included them with the others as source material for study at his Cabala Club. After

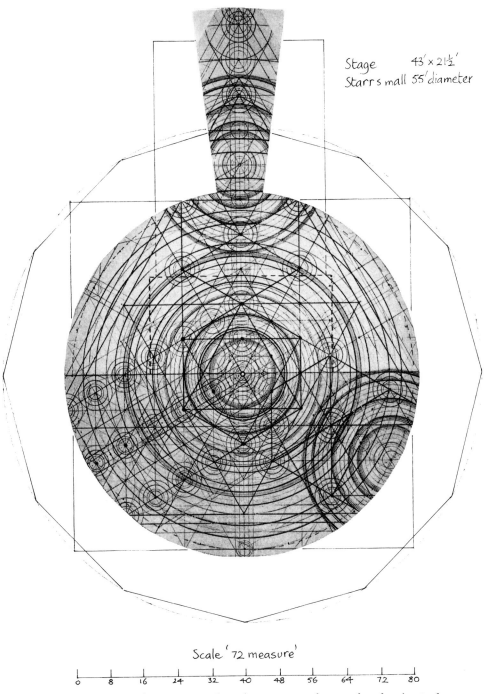

Stage 43' x 21½'
Starr s mall 55' diameter

Scale '72 measure'

0   8   16   24   32   40   48   56   64   72   80

Figure 14: The Swan theatre, 1595, based on a square frame of 80 feet by 80 feet, as was the Fortune theatre. The Swan's outer walls had 12 sides, the Tiring House cutting into two of those sides, so that in actual appearance it would appear as ten-sided. Katherens, the builder, had been asked to model the Hope on the Swan and there is a clause in the contract for the Hope which stipulates a building of 'such large compasse, fforme, widenes and height as the Plaie house called the Swan.'

125

such a lapse of time it is not possible to be certain how they reached Byrom.

Although the theatres spanned a period of some seventy years, the drawings I was studying display a unifying bond in their initial conception. Anyone looking at the design of the Elizabethan playhouses is struck by their extraordinary, unique and totally organised structure. They were conceived as totalities. There does not seem to have been anything like a development through trial and error once the Theater sprang fully formed from the soil of Shoreditch. Even with one departure from circle to square in the design of the Fortune, these buildings all display a coherent, confident, geometric unity. They speak of a consummate awareness of what the designers were about right from the start. To me this suggests the Vitruvian tradition through its Renaissance advocates. Only minor additions appear to the general plan. The Rose, for example, was the first to develop the protruding heavens over the stage, and this was incorporated into the Globe and the Fortune, but it was an integrated addition and can be traced back to Alberti's treatise. The mind which produced such sophisticated architectural concepts was well-versed in the classical tradition and able to translate his ideas in a simple way in order that they could be applied by an Elizabethan carpenter.

It should be emphasised that nearly all the theatre drawings are on paper without watermarks, and, in the case of the parametric drawings, on card too thick for them. Nor is it possible to use carbon dating procedures to assess their age. The playhouses opened, flourished and closed between 1574 and 1642. Bearing this in mind, together with the wide margin which has to be allowed for any particular batch of watermarked paper, it is difficult to date the drawings with precision. Furthermore, the quality of the paper varies in colour and texture. However, apart from those drawings which are obviously prints, all are originals in the sense that each was individually drawn in pen or ink and often finely incised by some sharp cutting tool.

The evidence of the handwriting is not as clear-cut as one would wish. While many examples of Elizabethan script are markedly different from that on the theatre drawings, many others are not. The handwriting of John Dee, for example, changed several times. Certainly the more formal script on many drawings is similar to that displayed on some of Michel Le Blon's alphabets and his signature on the 1613 Zeus engraving for Thibault. It also resembles the lettering on Visscher's 1616 engraving of the Bankside.

The silence of the parametric drawings, the total absence of language and number made the recognition of their function difficult. All of them are evidently concerned with the same general concept which dictated the distinctive shape common to all, but with significant variations. The two closest to each other are those I attributed to the Theater and the Globe respectively, and, since one was built from the other, this is not altogether surprising. The detail of the individual geometry on the parametric cards is quite specific, as can be seen from the back as well as the front (figures 14 and 15, Chapter 4). Such detail would be difficult to recall if the drawings were later than the theatres themselves. I find it hard to believe that once the theatres had disappeared from the London landscape anyone in the later seventeenth or early eighteenth centuries would be able to reconstruct the concept of their design. Despite the absence of watermarks, I would suggest that the parametric drawings are contemporary with the theatres.

Furthermore, the drawing headed 'for Globe: 9: Exact' and the square plan of the Fortune which fit so neatly together share, underneath their own patterns, features common to the Vitruvian geometry for setting out theatres. This would seem to link the name 'Globe' with Vitruvius. The surface of the Fortune drawing shows it has been well used. Since the Fortune was closely modelled on the Globe, one would expect the two drawings to be related and their geometry to be complementary to each other. These two drawings are a pair and should always be considered together. In the same way each parametric drawing has a cluster of other diagrams which are concerned with details related to it.

Yet another question raised by the theatre drawings is who originally owned them. Was it Theodore de Bry, the man who I believe was responsible for the classical concept of the theatres, or someone like John Dee, who championed the same ideas and helped to see them take shape in lath and plaster? The quick succession of theatres meant that the Vitruvian principles and cabalistic ideas continued with other artists such as Michel Le Blon who also had the understanding and was ready to serve men of like mind. In this way, either deliberately or incidentally, the theatre drawings became a repository for information about the playhouses. Other drawings, connected with sacred buildings already in existence, suggest the same thing: a store of knowledge kept for reference and study. There are also drawings concerned with buildings that have not been discussed. How many were created by Byrom's Cabala Club it is difficult, after all these years, to say, but in my view he had the use of the earlier material for him and his friends to explore.

I myself have not come across any other drawings of a similar nature, nor have I met anyone else who has. Yet there may well be others in private collections or even national archives which have been put aside because of the absence of any key or clue such as the '72 measure'. The absence of physical evidence may make some scholars and academics reluctant to reconsider the origin of the Elizabethan playhouses, for the symbols of the geometry have survived the buildings which were their explanation.

Their enigma combined with their remarkable visual power recalls the masonic poem *The Palace* by Rudyard Kipling:

> I read in the razed foundations the heart of that builder's
> heart.
> As he had risen and pleaded, so did I understand
> The form of the dream he had followed in the face of the thing
> he had planned.
> ....
> All I had wrought I abandoned to the faith of the faithless
> years,
> Only I cut on the timber – only I carved on the stone:
> *"After me cometh a Builder. Tell him I, too, have known!"*

John Byrom's interest was in the whole collection of drawings. Those concerned with the theatre, exciting as they are, form part of a much larger body of material, unified by common ideas and beliefs. One area reflects another, one discipline leads into another. While correlating all the theatre drawings, I became very much aware of the unifying thoughts within the whole group and in particular a close connection between these drawings and designs for certain churches.

CHAPTER SIX

*S*acred Geometry

THE DRAWINGS CONNECTED with sacred buildings are concerned with the principles of a concept including the main dimensions. They do not contain detailed features of design. Since these churches and chapels observe the laws of proportion, once the scale of a particular drawing has been decoded, not only the overall size but certain internal features, such as the position and dimensions of the nave, choir and high altar emerge, and can be verified with the building itself and other existing data. The drawings were produced centuries after these structures were built, and the purpose of the statistical information in them was, I suspect, for verification and identification. There is one notable addition to these drawings: the concept and scale are worked out in conjunction with cabalistic ideas. Often these take the form of a Tree of Life – sometimes more than one – carefully superimposed on the geometry. Sufficient measurements have been encoded in the drawings to show how meaningful the cabalistic element is.

In searching to identify the ecclesiastical drawings, I studied many conventional ground plans drawn by architects, some including illustrations of internal geometry. I had been introduced to the extrapolations of sacred geometry from buildings in the work of Keith Critchlow, Robert Lawlor and Nigel Pennick. I studied Renaissance expositions of Vitruvius. The drawings in the Byrom Collection seem to contain elements of all three and more besides. It is this which make them so rare, if not unique.

My main measure in decoding the drawings was the rule of 72 units which was a universal measure and could be adapted to both English and continental units – feet, yards or metres. In the case of the playhouses the basic unit was a foot, as I knew from the Fortune contract. For other buildings it could be different, so I made my own rulers and graph paper and with these I was able to explore the collection.

Several drawings seemed to be connected with towers. Already I had come across examples of geometric figures which resembled wood jointing used at St Mary's Church at Sompting and which I thought had been employed in building the towers on the Globe's tiring house. From this it was not too great a leap to consider that some of the drawings might be concerned with church steeples.

The similarity I saw between the geometry in drawings and illustrations of the Rhenish helm construction showed a continental influence in the collection. Sompting Church, although Saxon in origin, was given in 1154 to the Knights Templar, who added to and altered the fabric. Certain masons involved in this church appeared to share a common tradition with the makers of the Byrom Collection. As I learned more about the early years of Theodore de Bry as a goldsmith and of the links between German goldsmiths and masons, parts of that tradition became clear. The cabalism I had detected in many of the drawings was not simply a feature of Jewish, or even Christian mystical thought, but had become part of a tradition of building. It was evidently an element which interested the men who produced the sequence of six-pointed stars I came to connect with places of worship. The first of these drawings (figure 1) bears no watermark, no date, no writing. There is, however, a close companion to it based on the same frame, with the same measurements and with the same symbolic colouring, which has the watermark of three crescent moons. The colour and textures of the two cards are identical and they could have been cut from the same sheet. According to Heawood, the Venice watermark of three crescent moons was in use in 1600, so if we allow the acknowledged thirty year margin, drawings could date from the 1570s. Theodore de Bry was in England completing his engraving of the Procession of the Knights of the Garter at Windsor in 1576 and at the same time, I believe, working on the initial concept of the Theater. As the exponent of cabalistic and sacred geometry which was to be embodied in the playhouse designs he may well have produced these two drawings to demonstrate how the same tradition had been employed in building churches. De Bry's patrons would regard this as a precious store of information, showing the age and importance of the tradition of building. Hence these cards and their companions were carefully preserved for con-templation and instruction. This method of building would be a highly guarded secret, linking as it does the hermetic and Vitruvian ideas. John Dee, steeped in hermeticism and the most likely intermediary between de Bry and his patron Leicester, would have encouraged that secrecy. (Dee's own writings, when he chose, were clouded by cryptic utterance and symbolism.) This probably accounts for the absence of any means of easy identification on the drawings. The information was in code known only to initiates.

In his book *The Mysteries of King's College*, Nigel Pennick sets out to explain the inner geometry of the chapel. My interest was first caught by the design on the front cover of his book and even more by illustrations in the text. There for all to see was a ground plan of the chapel and, superimposed on it, the geometry of the design. The similarity of this geometry to that in one of the drawings was unmistakable. Although the Byrom drawings are more complex, Pennick's interpretation of the chapel complemented the precise and elegant patterns of the collection.

It was not simply the visual correspondences which impressed me; I was confronted by a surprising similarity between some of the mathematics which Pennick had worked out and that which I had decoded from the Globe drawings. Moreover, he had found a cabalistic element in the dimensions of the chapel. I had already begun to suspect there were drawings of churches in the collection, so I followed up the visual comparison by a mathematical analysis of figure 1 to see if it did in fact correspond to the chapel. Other drawings emerged in this process from the collection and figures 1 to 3 are in my opinion concerned with King's College Chapel.

King's College was founded by Henry VI in 1441 and dedicated to St Nicholas of Bari, the patron saint of scholars. Later Henry decided to enlarge the college and make it the biggest in Cambridge and to link it with its sister foundation, Eton. So a new chapel was built and rededicated with the college to Our Lady and St Nicholas. Today King's is no longer linked exclusively with Eton, and has long been established as one of the leading colleges in the university, numbering in its long line of distinguished scholars such celebrated names as John Maynard Keynes, Rupert Brooke and E.M. Forster. The foundation stone of the new chapel was laid by the King in July 1446. Four years later Henry was admitted to the craft of Freemasonry. During the first phase of construction, which lasted until the death of Henry VI, the Master Mason was Reginald Ely.

At that time the King's Master Mason was simply his employer's agent. He ran no financial risk from the undertaking, which was just as well considering the length of time it took to complete the project. Henry VI came to the throne when he was still only nine months old. The regency of his uncles and cousins saw the country riven with dispute and in constant conflict with France. Henry was deposed, restored, and for a while lost his sanity. Work on the college proceeded slowly through the reigns of four more kings. Indeed, apart from the chapel, the college was never completed according to Henry VI's intentions. Even so it is one of the last great Gothic structures built in this country. In it the mysteries of the Gothic mason's craft were fully exemplified.

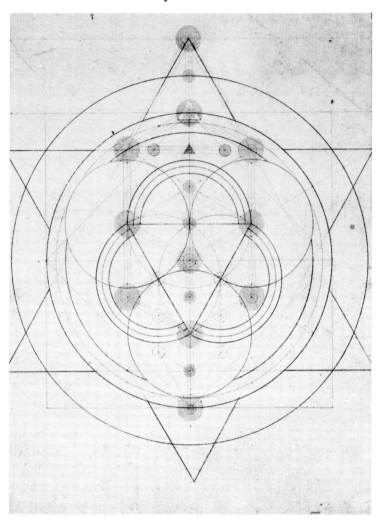

Figure 1: King's College Chapel, without the key. This drawing has no
watermark. Some lines have faded with age and have been re-drawn for clarity.
A vertical strip of the surface extending from the circle surrounded by four dots to
the circle above and passing through the blue triangle has been deliberately pared
away. This highlights the triangle when the card is held against the light.

As Nigel Pennick makes clear, a place of worship, whether church or
chapel, was not constructed like any secular edifice.[1] At the time King's
chapel was built the laws of sacred geometry were still part of the Gothic
tradition, and the freemasons were fully conversant with the mysteries.
The laws of geometry can be seen in the structure of organic objects
and dictate every form of human habitation from the Indian wig-wam
to the Palladian mansion. The basic shapes – whether circle, square or

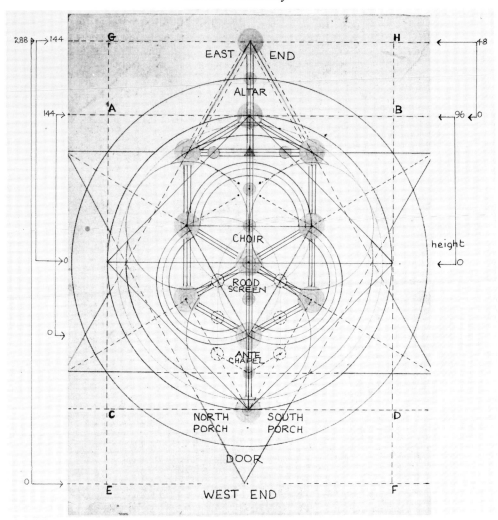

Figure 1A: King's College Chapel. The overall Ad Triangulum geometry, combined with the Tree of Life. The measurements are based on a grid of ABCD, 192 x 192ft, and EFGH, 288 x 192ft. The central column from the radius point for the outer circle is the vertical measure giving the height. From Centre Circle to Centre Circle measures 24 feet.

triangle – were believed to have innate properties that reflected universal laws. Their appeal was not just intellectual or aesthetic but spiritual, even psychological. The circle, for example, is regular, complete and unbroken; its continuous line became symbolic of infinity and totality. It is not surprising that over the centuries such a shape has been endowed with mystical importance. The square is another deceptively simple shape associated with qualities valued by men, in this instance stability and rigidity. The Egyptian pyramid was constructed on a square ground plan. The Temple of Solomon was built around a sequence of squares. From the square grew up a system of construction known as 'ad quadratum', where one square is laid out on top of another at an angle of 45 degrees to produce an octagon. Its most sophisticated form can be found in the great Romanesque and Gothic Cathedrals of Europe. The triangle, too, is a figure with symbolic associations which had been used in the design and construction of buildings, although to a lesser degree than the square. The discovery by the Greeks of the Pythagorean triangle was an important influence here. The sides of this triangle are related as 3:4:5, and thus form an arithmetical progression. We just accept this now as a fact, but once it was endowed with a special significance. No other right-angled triangle can be constructed with this property. When Cesare Cesariano published his lavish edition of Vitruvius he chose a diagram of Pythagorean triangles to illustrate the importance of symmetry. For the Christian the triangle embodies the Trinity; to others, an equilateral triangle with the apex facing upwards can stand for the active or male principle, and with the apex facing down it represents the passive or female principle. A combination of two such equilateral triangles in a hexagram may symbolise the integration of both active and passive, male and female. King's College Chapel is one outstanding example of a church designed on a series of triangular interconnections.

Figure 1 is the ground plan of the building in purely geometric terms. Clearly delineated is the Tree of Life extending from the west window to the east and indicating the crucial position of the 'Non-Sefirah' Daat by a small circle surrounded by four dots. This is placed most aptly below the high altar. According to Jewish teaching, Daat is where the Absolute may enter into existence, it represents Knowledge that comes direct from God.[2] Where better should that become manifest for a Christian cabalist than before the high altar, which witnessed daily the miracle of the Word made Flesh again in the bread and wine of Holy Communion? The companion drawing, with the watermark, shows it in the same position.

On the back of figure 1 is a second, much simpler drawing showing clearly the system of circles used to set out the dimensions of the chapel (figure 2). The background of the card, like that of the theatre drawings, is divided up into a grid. The next illustration (figure 3) is a simplified version of figure 2 leaving out the Tree of Life that enables the reader to see more clearly the similarity to the layout of King's. Pennick told me that since none of the original plans of the chapel had survived he had reconstructed the ground plan from his own measurements and then superimposed the inner geometry on to this scheme. It was that inner geometry which coincided with the Byrom drawings. Even more curious is the fact that when Pennick's interpretation of the ground plan is reproduced on the same scale as the grid on figure 2 it again shows similarities to the Byrom drawing. Even the position of the high altar can be calculated. It was all very puzzling. No other church in England had been constructed to the design of King's College Chapel, though something similar to it appears in the cathedral at Albi, built a century before, in the south of France at a spot notorious for the Cathar heresy. How the design of the cathedral had come to be copied and adapted to a college chapel is another of the mysteries of this extraordinary building.

Another small detail intrigued me. The stained glass windows were added to King's chapel after the completion of the stone work. One of the team of glaziers engaged on the windows after 1526 was a certain Symon Symondes from Westminster, who worked with a partner from a colony of glaziers in Southwark. It was another Symonds, Ralph Symonds, who was listed as the owner of the site of the Rose in Southwark in 1546, and of the Fortune around 1552. A second Ralph Symonds, also from Westminster, was a master mason. He was summoned to Cambridge to build the two great Elizabethan foundations Emmanuel and Sidney Sussex on which he laboured from 1584 to 1604.[3] If they were related, it would exemplify how a family with a tradition of skills and crafts could spread its influence even then.

The fabric of the chapel walls was completed as King Henry VI had wished, but with the coming of the Reformation much of the overall concept for the chapel was lost. Elizabeth tore out the high altar and with it probably the foundation stone laid long since by Henry VI. When foundations were dug for a new altar in 1770 it was found to be missing and has never been recovered.

The fate of the chapel at Emmanuel was characteristic of the new age. Hitherto it had been the custom to build churches with the altar to the east, so that congregations would stand to recite the creed facing east. Sir Walter Mildmay, founder of Emmanuel College, was a strong Protestant and, in a fit of religious zeal, he turned the original chapel into the college hall and the college hall into the chapel, so flouting the old catholic tradition as yet another example of superstition. The notorious puritan William Dowsing visited King's to view the glory of the stained glass and saw only 'a thousand superstitious pictures'.[4] He noted it in his diary as an idolatry to be dealt with, but by a miracle, probably in the form of a small bribe, the windows were spared.

The history of King's chapel served to heighten the importance of this set of drawings in the collection. Here were signs of that inner geometry which had been devised to underpin the massive structure that soars effortlessly above as you enter the chapel. Henry VI had been absolutely precise in his dimensions for the chapel, and despite all the turbulence of the Wars of the Roses, despite the succession of four

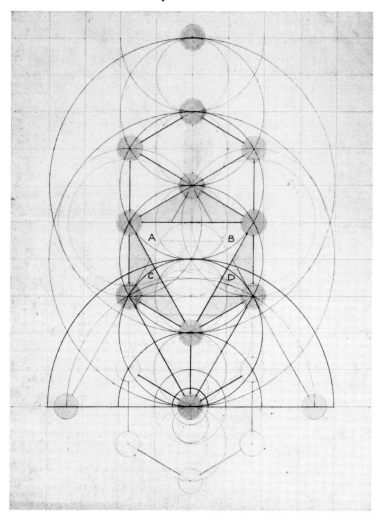

Figure 2: King's College Chapel, without the key. This is the reverse of figure 1. The internal width of the chapel is clearly shown by the two lines A-B, C-D. These are positioned on the rood-screen and in the choir respectively. The measurement is constructed on the 24 feet square grid.

more monarchs before the task was done, those dimensions were adhered to. They had a sacred significance. The chapel was not simply intended as an architectural wonder, it was also to be a re-creation in stone, wood and glass of the divine order which lay at the heart of the faith to be celebrated there daily. That faith was denounced, the ritual transformed, the high altar ripped out, but fortunately the chapel survived. The scholars and fellows may have entertained Elizabeth I in the ante-chapel on a Sunday with a bawdy play by Plautus, a custom of public performances which has since continued the process of de-mystification, but the founder's original

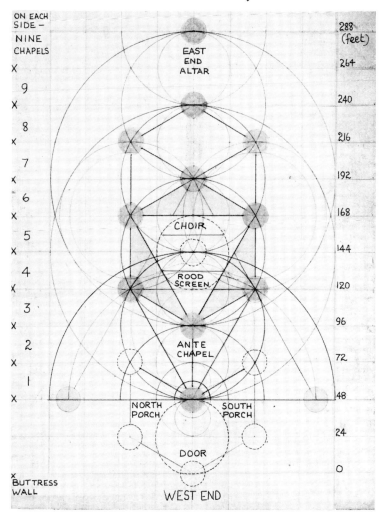

ON EACH
SIDE –
NINE
CHAPELS

X

9

X

8

X

7

X

6

X

5

X

4

X

3

X

2

X

1

X

X
BUTTRESS
WALL

EAST
END
ALTAR

CHOIR

ROOD
SCREEN

ANTE
CHAPEL

NORTH
PORCH

SOUTH
PORCH

DOOR

WEST END

288
(feet)

264

240

216

192

168

144

120

96

72

48

24

0

Figure 2A: King's College Chapel. A geometrical ground plan to scale. The Tree of Life in position demonstrates the Cabalistic properties. The ground plan is shown on a grid measuring 12 x 8 squares. Each square represents 24 x 24 feet. Total area covered 288 x 192 feet. According to the will of intent by Henry VI – 1447/8 – the length of the Chapel was to be 288 feet. The internal width 40 feet. Centre columns based on 6 circles – radius 24 feet.

intention had been the opposite: to create a house of God imbued with His spirit wherever eye turned or hand touched.

In sorting out the alternative designs for the roofs and towers of the tiring house of the theatres I had become accustomed to the ways in which the sides on the elevations in the parametric drawings had been cut to indicate different structures. One was shaped like a church with a steeple, or rather *part* of a church with a steeple. It seemed to me that I was

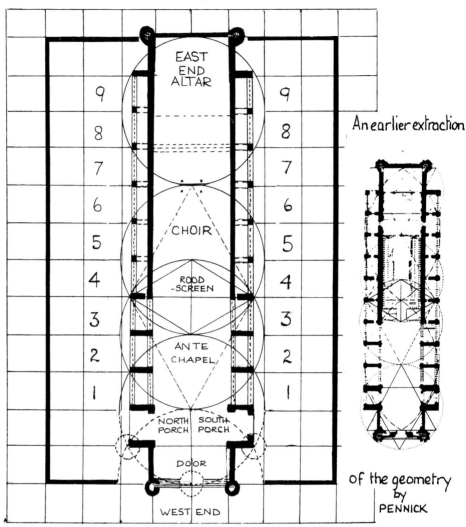

EAST
END
ALTAR

9   9
8   8
7   7
6   6

CHOIR

5   5

ROOD
-SCREEN

4   4
3   3

ANTE
CHAPEL

2   2
1   1

NORTH SOUTH
PORCH PORCH

DOOR

WEST END

An earlier extraction

of the geometry
by
PENNICK

J. Willis Clark: The Architectural History of the University of Cambridge Ch. X.
Dimensions derived from the Will of Intent and the Accounts.
Width "within the respondes" = 40 feet, Length = 289 feet, the length
of the Antechapel = 120 feet, total height = 94 feet.
N. Pennick: The Mysteries of King's College Chapel.
" The whole length of the chapel is based upon six 24 foot radius circles."
(288 ft.)

The measurements should be checked against those in figs. 1A and 2A.
Whoever was responsible for the drawings had detailed knowledge of the
dimensions of the Chapel.

Figure 3: An extraction of geometry from figures 1A and 2A superimposed on the
ground plan.

looking not at a conventionally shaped church, but at a round one. This narrowed the field of possibilities considerably. Even so, where was I to start looking for its location? Since the theatre drawings were of playhouses in England, I began with the assumption that the ecclesiastic drawings were most probably connected with places of worship in the British Isles. Perhaps the best known of the early round churches in England are those in Cambridge (St Sepulchre's) and London (the Temple Church) while two others, both Templar churches, are in Northampton and Little Maplestead in Essex. The next logical step was to check the possibility of a connection between the drawing and any of these churches. This became imperative in the light of the discovery of the King's College sequence of drawings.

The round churches pre-date the college chapel and, of course, the playhouses. Clearly this card (figure 5) with drawings on both sides was not contemporary with its subject, unlike the theatre drawings, but certainly, like the King's College Chapel drawings, it showed the basic geometry of the structure, and with my '72 measure' I was able to work out dimensions of a possible ground plan. My next step was to visit the surviving early round churches in England and I started with the Temple, London.

The Temple Church London

The Temple Church takes its name from the Knights Templar who built it originally in 1185, though for centuries it has been associated with the Inner and Middle Temple and the Inns of Court. Figure 5 is, I believe, a representation of this church, with a circular base and a conical upper storey in keeping with the design of the first part of the Temple, called the Round. The body or choir of the church was added later, in 1240. What we see today at the Temple is a building restored after suffering severe damage in an air raid in 1941. However, much of the early fabric survived and the dimensions have remained the same through the centuries.

A small scaled ground plan in the church guide book showed the diameter of the Round to be between sixty and sixty-five feet, dependent on whether one allowed for the thickness of the wall. This correlated with the diameter of the circular section at the base of the drawing which I had already measured. Here was an encouraging start. It looked as if this circular section might be a representation of the ground plan of the Round. Using the same method by which I had discovered the level of the upper galleries in the theatre drawings, I was able to decipher two levels within what I took to be the elevation. When you look at the Round today you see a low battlemented roof reminiscent of a fort. The conical roof was destroyed during the war, but before 1941 the church had been surmounted by a two-tier roofline comprising an outer

Figure 4: King's College Chapel. View from the front court.

ring covering the triforium and an inner ring with a roof like a candle snuffer.[5]

The solution was unfortunately too neat. I had not allowed for the vagaries of time. I discovered that the conical roof had been erected in 1862, and that date was too late for the drawing. Then I learned that the 1862 roof had replaced an earlier version of the battlemented roof dating from the eighteenth century, but the shape of this roof did not agree either with the drawing. The roof of the Round must have been a different shape even before then, something more akin to the conical roof of 1862. Either that, or the drawing was of another church altogether. The building history of the Temple was fragmentary and I needed more facts.

Accordingly I approached the former Surveyor to the Middle Temple, Geoffrey Parr, who allowed me access to plans and engravings still in the possession of the Middle Temple. These drawings were orthodox in their draftsmanship; none displayed the techniques of the Byrom drawings, and none went back beyond the beginning of the nineteenth century. Next I visited the library of the Order of St John in Clerkenwell, since that Order had once owned much of the Temple site in London. The librarian showed me a ground plan and prints of earlier engravings of the Temple and, in addition, suggested I would probably discover more at the Guildhall Library. There I saw a much earlier view of the Temple, dated 1720, and to my delight it displayed the Round with a roof that matched the elevation of my drawing. Small and distant though the church is in the engraving, the shape is clear. Earlier engravings from *c.* 1550 and 1671 confirmed what the outside of the Round looked like before the series of alterations started in the eighteenth century. During my visit to the surveyor's office I measured the internal diameter of the Round. It corresponded with the diameter I had calculated from the drawing.

I could not leave the matter there. What was this drawing doing in the collection? Who had made it? This was not an ordinary church, not the normal shape of the English parish church: had it been included because of its shape, or was there some other explanation? There had to be a thread linking these different buildings, playhouses and churches. In the hope of finding an answer I decided to look at the history of the people who had built the Temple Church.

The Round had been modelled on the Church of the Holy Sepulchre in Jerusalem which marks the site of Christ's tomb. This, one of the most sacred places in Christendom, had been buried under layers of soil to make way for a temple to the Goddess Aphrodite during the Roman occupation of Palestine. Later the Emperor Constantine uncovered the site around the year AD 326 and vowed to build a church worthy of the place and of himself. At first he left the actual burial place exposed for pilgrims to see and, in front of it, erected a magnificent Basilica. This was to be the most important church in Jerusalem, and it was completed by AD 335. Meanwhile it was decided to enclose the tomb in another building, circular in shape. This was the Rotunda, the model for the Round.[6]

After Constantine's empire fell into decline, seventh-century Palestine became a province of Islam and for four hundred years Jerusalem remained under Muslim rule. In 1009 orders were given for the complete destruction of the Holy Sepulchre. The tomb itself was all but smashed to pieces, but enough of the Rotunda's exterior wall survived for a later emperor to make an accurate reconstruction in 1048. The Basilica of Constantine was not rebuilt but remained a field of rubble. In 1099 the first Crusade ended with the freeing of Jerusalem and the crusaders found the reconstructed Rotunda much as it is today. Wishing to include the site of Calvary, they built their own Church of the Holy Sepulchre on the courtyard site of the Basilica and joined it to the Rotunda. The galleries in the crusaders' church were placed on the same level as those of the Rotunda, so making one continuous floor. This new building was completed in 1149 and still stands today.

The Knights Templar played a large part in protecting this church. Formed in 1118 as a religious military order to guard pilgrims to the Holy

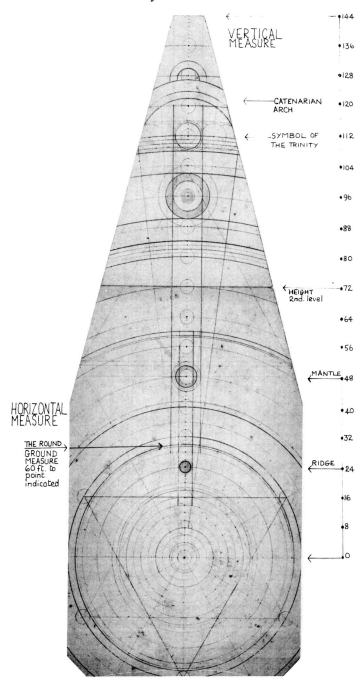

VERTICAL
MEASURE

←————CATENARIAN
ARCH

←——SYMBOL OF
THE TRINITY

←HEIGHT
2nd. level

HORIZONTAL
MEASURE

THE ROUND→
GROUND
MEASURE
60 ft. to
point
indicated

←MANTLE

RIDGE←

•144

•136

•128

•120

•112

•104

•96

•88

•80

•72

•64

•56

•48

•40

•32

•24

•16

•8

•0

Figure 5: The Temple Church (Round) plan.

Sepulchre, they were housed near the site of the Temple of Solomon and from this they took their name. Even today the Knights of the Temple of Solomon have a strong hold on popular imagination though in the wake of tales of the warrior knights' bravery and success went rumours of greed, corruption, immorality and heresy. Rumour gave way to accusation. The downfall of the Templars was even more spectacular than their rise. The King of France, Philippe le Bel, arrested all the Templars in his kingdom in one swift swoop. Under torture many knights confessed to the charges levelled against them and the Pope, who owed his throne to Philippe, was compelled to pursue the order with rigour. Trials followed all over Europe and the pattern was the same in England. Reluctantly at first and then under pressure Edward II ordered the arrests and interrogations. Finally, in 1312, the Knights Templar were suppressed and the Pope ordered that their lands and property should be given to the other great military order of the church, the Knights Hospitaller of St John.

Edward protested that the Pope had no powers to dispose of property in England without the consent of Parliament. Almost as if to make his point, he gave the Temple in London with the church and all its buildings to Aymer de Valence, Earl of Pembroke. The Temple lands extended from Aldwych along part of Fleet Street all the way down to the banks of the river Thames. So the headquarters of Europe's most prestigious military society was a very handsome gift for any man to receive. The Knights had accordingly built on a grand scale. There were monastic cells, cloisters, a council chamber and two refectories all linked to the splendid church. Along the riverside there was plenty of open space for the monks to walk and the knights to train.

In due course Edward's cousin, the Earl of Lancaster, forced the King to revoke his gift to Pembroke and give the Temple site to him. It was then that the doctors of common law obtained a lease from Lancaster for part of the property where they might retreat from Westminster to study law with their students. This was the beginning of the famous inns of court centred on the two old refectories of the knights and their serving brothers. Over the years the law students and their teachers became accustomed to dining in the separate halls and these eventually became formalised into the Inner and Middle Temple. Meanwhile, during the successive changes of ownership, the Hospitallers of St John were still trying to get their hands on the property which the Pope had declared should be theirs.

Although the Knights Templar had been suppressed, the round church remained a monument to their past importance. Buried within lay some of the most distinguished Templars, notably three Earls of Pembroke, William Mareschal and his two sons William and Gilbert.[7] William the elder was a man of singular honour and great skill in an age distinguished by treachery and dissension. He accompanied King John to Runnymede

and persuaded him to sign Magna Carta. He was also a loyal and coura-
geous protector of the boy king Henry III. His son, William, married the
sister of Henry III, and waged a successful campaign against the unruly
Welsh, finally defeating Prince Llewelyn in a decisive victory. Gilbert
Mareschal married the daughter of the King of Scotland; because of his
services in the crusades he was buried in the Temple Church.

The Round was one of several churches built by the Templars in
this country, though before that they had taken over St Mary's, the
strange church at Sompting, in 1154. Curiously enough, that was one of
the dates marked on an enigmatic triangular card.[8] It was also the date
when Henry II succeeded to the throne. He would almost certainly have
been present at the consecration of the Round. Was there, I wondered,
some connection here which was eluding me?

I turned back to the drawing (figure 5) which was the first I had
sought to identify with the Temple Church. I had been able to decipher
the two levels of the original buildings, which corresponded to the two
levels inside the Rotunda in Jerusalem, and also to relate the dimensions of
the Round to the circular base in figure 9. I now checked that drawing for
a watermark, but there was none. I noticed that a motif in the centre of the
circle was partly shaded black. This was unusual. To my recollection only
one other card had been tinted black to any degree. Here, prominently,
was a small black circle with a little white T-shaped cross in the centre,
set against a mixture of amber, gold and a little pink. Or was that pink
the residue of faded red? I thought this might be a Templar symbol. The
original banner of the Templars, the Beauséant, had been partly black and
partly white. Later, in the reign of King Stephen, it was changed to a red
cross on a white ground.

I was aware that in the eighteenth century the freemasons had begun
to claim an association with the Knights Templar and to have inherited part
of those doctrines which the Templars are said to have learned in the East.
The charge of heresy arose from suspicion of such doctrines. It was hardly
surprising that during the crusades the Order had gained some insight into
the culture and beliefs of the people around them. They fought with the
Saracen and learned his language and with it acquired some knowledge of
his sciences. They lived among the Jews and likewise absorbed elements
of Judaic culture, particularly the Cabala. Over the centuries stories have
persisted of a secret body of doctrine, known to at least an inner group,
if not to all knights, and handed on even after their suppression. Many
esoteric groups claimed to have inherited some of this wisdom. (I do not
include the present Catholic order of Knights Templar, which is not in
any way associated with the masonic Knights Templar.)

Was the T-shaped cross a clue of some sort? Tau is the Greek
equivalent of the letter T, and the Tau cross, I knew, was a masonic

Figure 6: The Temple Church, showing the conical roof of the Round as it was in 1862.

Figure 7: The Temple Church showing the battlemented roof, restored after 1941.

Figure 8: The Temple, 1720.

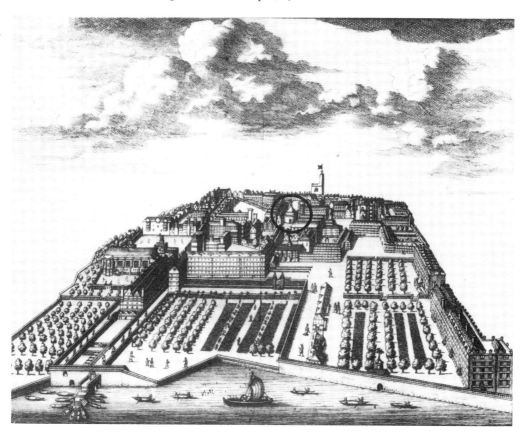

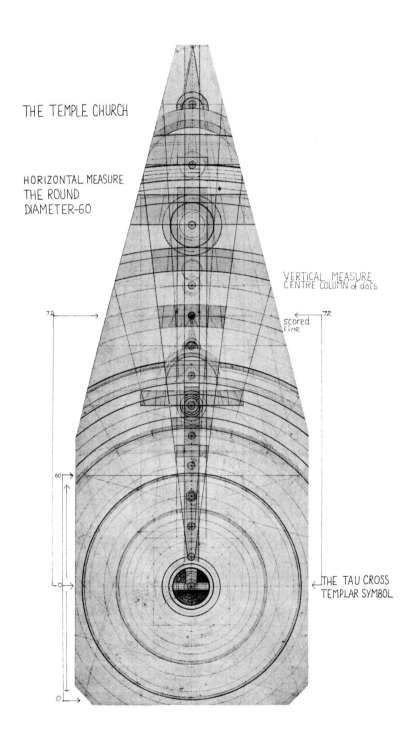

THE TEMPLE CHURCH

HORIZONTAL MEASURE
THE ROUND
DIAMETER-60

VERTICAL MEASURE
CENTRE COLUMN of dots

scored
line

THE TAU CROSS
TEMPLAR SYMBOL

Figure 9: Reverse of figure 5.

146

symbol of long standing. Moreover, it resembled the T-shaped motif in the centre of figure 9. The Tau Cross is the same as the sign which Moses commanded the Israelites to paint on their doorposts when God punished the Egyptians with plague. It was clear that it has been an important symbol in several cultures over the centuries. Was its presence on the drawing a confirmation of some Templar element in the collection?

I raised these questions with the Reverend Neville Barker Cryer, Secretary of the Quatuor Coronati Lodge and Provincial Prior of the Knights Templar of Yorkshire, North and East Ridings. He was able to confirm that the Beauséant banner had been divided into black and white in the same fashion. This particular circle had two black segments above the Tau, but these might have been shaded in to highlight the symbol, which was undoubtedly a Tau. He also reminded me that the symbol on the apron of an Installed Master Mason may be either a level or inverted Tau. After studying the drawing for a while he pointed out that, if viewed down the plan of the church from the east end towards the west, the Tau represented the true form of the cross on which Christ was crucified. What we think of as the top of the upright post is simply the projection to bear the plaque of the inscription I.N.R.I. above. This would mean that there was a very ancient and accurate sign of the cross on what I believed to be a drawing of the Round.

When he examined the reverse of figure 9 (figure 5) he found further evidence of Templar symbolism. Towards the top of the elevation could be seen three overlapping circles. These, Mr Cryer felt, were symbols of the Trinity, belief in which was an essential requirement in the Templar Order. Just above these circles were three small contiguous circles in a line. If we interpret this part of the design as the east end of the building, then that would be an appropriate place to find such a symbol, for it represented the three leading figures in the Templar Chapter when it sat in session – a tradition still observed today in the Chapter of the Royal Arch. In the Chapter the three figures sit as if in the form of a Catenarian arch, and on the drawing in question the three circles appear to be under a Catenarian arch. In the light of these observations a Templar element in the collection seemed undeniable.

I now knew the collection so well that I could recognise that this particular card, from its texture and colour and the gradation of the tints employed, resembled one of the cards with drawings of the Rose theatre plan. It looked as if both had been drawn at about the same time and probably by the same artist. One family of the Earls of Pembroke had been connected with the Temple Church, and later Pembrokes were connected with the Elizabethan theatres. So were Philip Sidney and the Earl of Leicester. Was there still more to unravel about Leicester's connection with the Temple?

Part of the old Temple site in London had been known as the Outward Temple. A property on this site had been used by the Bishops of Exeter and had become known as Exeter House. It was on the north bank of the Thames a little upstream from Southwark. Leicester, casting around for somewhere large enough to accommodate his growing ambition and importance, thought Exeter House would be ideal and leased it from the owners. Unfortunately, the Spanish Ambassador had already taken up residence there and had to be re-housed. He seems to have been shunted rather unceremoniously across the river to the Bishop of Winchester's palace in Southwark. Neither the ambassador nor the Bishop found the move to their liking, but in the end Leicester won the day. With typical arrogance he obtained an order from the Queen's Council (of which he was a member) which enabled him not only to move the Bishop out of his residence but also to fix the ambassador's rent. Thus Exeter House became Leicester House and Dudley transformed it into one of the most imposing palaces in London. When I discovered some of the interests, in addition to drama, which Leicester pursued in this house, I had a strange feeling almost of déjà-vu, for navigation, fortification, astronomy and the compass were also topics featured to some degree or other in the Byrom Collection.

Certain people and their activities kept reappearing during my search. By the time Leicester was installed in Leicester House, the Inns of Court had grown into a small university, rather like Oxford and Cambridge. They had their own life and their own customs, with both Inner and Middle Temple students sharing the Temple Church. Like any other student body they developed their own calendar of celebrations. From the grosser pastimes of indoor blood sports, when a cat and a fox would be let loose in a hall to be hunted by a pack of hounds, these entertainments became more sophisticated, formalised and sumptuous enough for royalty to attend. Masques were a favourite pastime, and, as we saw with the revels in Leicester's honour, the Inns of Court played a direct part in the development of drama. Shakespeare's *Comedy of Errors* was performed at Grays Inn Hall in 1594 and *Twelfth Night* was written for one of the annual festivities at the Middle Temple. It seemed strangely appropriate that the Inner Temple's 'chief governour' should dispense his patronage from an old Templar site, turning it once again into a centre of so much intellectual activity and influence.

The Temple of Solomon

There were among the mass of drawings a number concerned with the regular bodies of geometry, those solids which so fascinated Plato and Pythagoras and which have continued to exercise the minds of later philosophers down the centuries. Some were small and theoretical but others seemed to be working drawings used to examine the properties of solids. One of the latter stood out from all the rest by virtue of its size. It was far larger than any other drawing in the collection and consisted of a thick piece of card with elaborate geometric designs on both front and back. Two Trees of Life were distinctly drawn on one side. The card had been carefully cut and lightly but deliberately scored so that it could be neatly folded into the shape of a flat square. When I first came upon it, it was folded in this way, and, when I opened it out, I found myself staring at a cross of imposing dimensions. When I looked closer I realised the cross shape, while significant in itself, was also intended to be folded into a cube. The versatility of this card and its markings demanded the closest study (see figure 10).

In the philosophical dialogue *Timaeus*, Plato set out to establish that the four basic elements which form the world are earth, fire, air and water. These became associated with four of the five regular solids, and it was the cube which was linked symbolically with earth. Upon these associations all sorts of mystical and philosophical concepts have been built. From the Tree of Life drawings on the side of my large cube I was aware that it had been made not simply for a mathematical but also a philosophical purpose. For some time I studied the group of drawings centred on solids, especially the large cube, hoping that somehow the lettering on the diagrams would yield a clue to their mystery, but, as often happens, enlightenment came in an unexpected, almost absurdly simple way.

It occurred during one of my regular forays into the British Library when, as a break from studying books, I would visit the art shops and antiquarian booksellers nearby, constantly on the look-out for new material that might help. On this particular day I ventured into the Rudolf Steiner Bookshop and found a pile of papers fanned out on a display table. They were photocopies of typed sheets and on the top of one I recognised the outline of some geometric drawings which resembled one of the cube drawings in the collection. The paper had been written by Keith Critchlow and was in fact a worksheet with a detailed analysis of the dimensions of the Temple of Solomon. It contained a specification of the Holy of Holies, twenty cubits by twenty cubits by twenty cubits, proportionately drawn and to the same scale as one in the collection. I had other drawings with the 'Ark of the Covenant' and other Old Testament references written on them. Remembering that the latest date on any drawing in the collection was 1732, I looked for watermarks on the large cube drawing, but found none. The card used for the cube was thick and heavy and that may account for the absence of a watermark. The smaller paper drawings of solids were too small to throw up any details. It was necessary, therefore, to take stock, and, as a matter of routine, I

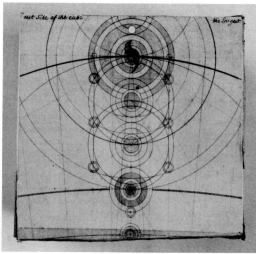

Figure 10: Cube of Space, with detail of Tree of Life.

checked back to Byrom and his closest associates in the first part of the
eighteenth century, looking for any connection with Solomon's Temple.
It would have been easy to relate the drawing simply to the emergence of
the Grand Lodge of Freemasons and their preoccupation with the Temple,
but that, I felt, would have been insufficient. The freshly constituted Grand
Lodge and the people connected with it were only part of the world of the
drawings, not central to it. However, certain facts emerged which need to
be recorded.

According to an entry in William Stukeley's diary, Lord Pembroke
visited him at his home in December 1720, 'to see my drawings of
Solomon's Temple'.[9] Both these men knew Byrom. Stukeley maintained
an interest in the Temple for years. Six years later he recorded a visit he
made to his friend Sir Isaac Newton, President of the Royal Society:

> We had some discourse about Solomon's Temple of which he had
> formerly made the plan; He says that it was older than any great
> heathen temple . . . that Sosostris from hence made his temples in
> Egypt, one in each Nomus, and that from thence the Greeks made
> theirs and borrowed their religion.[10]

Newton in this conversation was evidently drawing on his *Chronology
of Ancient Kingdoms Amended*. Stukeley, like Byrom, was a freemason.
However, the interest in the Temple was not confined to a few antiquarians
or intellectuals with specialised interests. It was shared sufficiently by the
public at large for the London *Daily Courant* to advertise in 1729 that
there was

to be seen at the Royal Exchange Every Day the model of the Temple of Solomon with all its Porches, Walls, Gates, Chambers, and Holy Vessels, the great Altar of the Burnt Offering, The Molten Sea, the Lavers, the Sanctum Sanctorum; with the Ark of the Covenant, the Mercy Seat and Golden Cherubims, the Altar of Incense, the Candlestick, Tables of Shewbread, with the two famous Pillars, called Joachim and Boas. Within the model are 2,000 Chambers and Windows, and Pillars 7,000; the model is 13 foot high and 80 foot round.[11]

I have not been able to find any reference in Byrom's own Journals to him visiting the exhibition, but, since they were so heavily edited, this is not in itself conclusive. Certainly this was not the first evidence of public interest in the Temple. There had been an earlier exhibition in London of another model in 1675. It is obvious from the announcement in the *Courant* that curiosity was not confined to the dimensions of the building alone or its appearance, but included the contents. The precise purpose of some of these remains obscure even today. The 1675 model was exhibited for a second time thirty years later, so clearly the interest was sustained. This may in part be accounted for by the birth and spread of Freemasonry, but that alone could not account for interest among the public at large.

When I examined this group of drawings again I saw that the geometry continued to include the Tree of Life, and in this they resembled those of the chapel at King's and the Temple. There were no elevations and no plans of models, which seemed to indicate that Byrom was not concerned with the exhibitions in London. The intricacy of the patterns on the drawings of the Holy of Holies, and the presence yet again of such a figure as the Tree of Life, pointed rather to the conclusion that this set of drawings belonged to parts of the collection that appeared to be intended as visual aids for teaching and study. Perhaps they were connected with the work that went on in Byrom's Cabala Club, which he had started in 1725. Public discussion of the nature of Solomon's Temple was current at this time.

When the largest of this set of drawings was unfolded, it displayed the properties of the Holy of Holies laid out in the form of a cross. It could also be folded up into a cube. The presence of other drawings entitled The Ark, Moses Mount and The Book of Seales suggested that here was a working kit of geometric drawings which set out to demonstrate, or rediscover, the mystical qualities of the mathematics. The cross, the paramount Christian symbol, became the basic ground plan for most churches – in keeping with the ancient belief that the temple is in some mysterious way the body of God. This can be seen in early representations

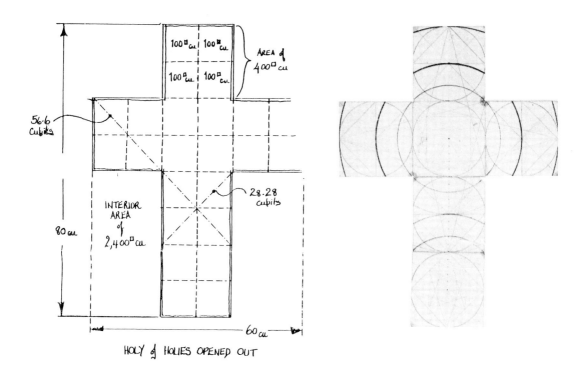

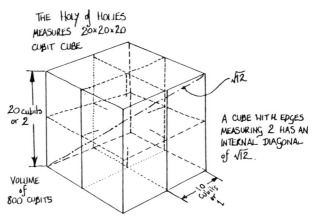

Figure 11: The dimensions and proportions of Solomon's Temple, as seen in a geometric drawing in the Byrom Collection and in drawings from the Keith Critchlow worksheet.

of man with arms outstretched superimposed on to the cruciform ground plan of a church. Folded up the cross becomes a 'cosmic cube' built on a square ground plan whose four sides represent the four directions, North, South, East and West with the square as a microcosm of the earth.

Some of the drawings connected with the Temple group seemed from the colour and texture of the card to be earlier than others, especially the large cube. Moreover, the dimensions of the cube, measured on a modern ruler, proved to be 13 cm × 13 cm × 13 cm. The dimensions of the Holy of Holies according to I Kings Chapter 5 are 20 cubits by 20 cubits by 20 cubits. (13 cm are the equivalent of 1/82 of 20 cubits.) This meant that the volume of Byrom's large cube was a reduction of the Holy of Holies by a factor of 82^3. The detailed calculation of these numbers is dealt with in the notes.[12]

What was the cause of the fascination with the Temple of Solomon in the first place? Even with the growth of the experimental sciences and the accompanying secularisation of thought, the Christian faith was still important to most people in Byrom's day and the only proper basis for morality. The Bible was still regarded as the word of God, and the story of the Jewish race, as told in the Old Testament, was seen as a preparation for the coming of Jesus to save the world. Central to that Old Testament narrative was the building of the Temple.

Solomon's Temple was in fact the first permanent home of the God who had brought the Jews out of bondage. Hitherto He had 'resided' in the Tabernacle, or Tent, which Israelites carried through the desert on the journey to the Promised Land. The dwelling place of the Almighty was the Ark of the Covenant, a wooden chest covered by a lid, the Mercy Seat, on which the God of Israel, Yahweh or Jehovah, would descend in a cloud when He so chose. The Temple building itself was comparatively modest for, unlike a Christian church, the Jewish Temple did not attempt to house the faithful. Their place of worship was the open forecourt, and that was large.

The Temple building was a rectangle of sixty cubits by twenty cubits with a flat roof. The first chamber was the ulam or porch; this had double doors which led into the hekal or holy place, where the implements for the rituals were kept. Beyond this lay the debir or Holy of Holies. Here were kept the Ark and the Mercy Seat. In keeping with the Old Testament teaching that Jehovah was the God that dwelt in darkness, this room was left unlit except for the one day in the year when it was entered by the High Priest; and in obedience to the commandments of Moses there were no idols within the Temple. The building of the Temple was a momentous event in the history of the Jewish race. It meant that henceforward Jerusalem would be the Holy City. The Ark was the most ancient symbol of their religion, supposed to contain the ten commandments and other laws given by God to Moses after his vigil on Mount Sinai.

This Temple stood from 960 to 587 BC, when it was destroyed by the Babylonian King, Nebuchadnezzar. Jerusalem was burned and the Jews were led into captivity in Babylon. The Ark itself was lost for ever. Twice again the Temple was rebuilt, first on a smaller scale and then much more grandly by Herod the Great. His was the Temple Jesus knew and spoke

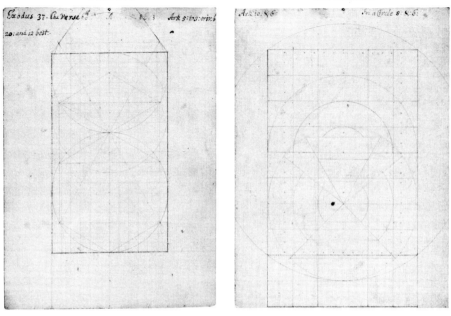

Figure 12: The Mercy Seat of the Ark. According to Exodus 37, verse 6, 'two cubits and a half was the length thereof, and one cubit and a half the breadth thereof'. In the Jerusalem Bible a cubit is given as 21 inches. The length of the Ark is therefore 52½ inches and the breadth 31½ inches. The front of this drawing shows these dimensions in the proportion 5 to 3 drawn on a grid of 20 squares by 12 squares. The reverse side shows the same figure drawn in outline by dots on a larger grid of 8 to 6.

of, where the Holy of Holies housed a simple slab to commemorate the Ark, and the tablets of Moses were replaced by written parchments, the Torah or Scroll of the Law. After the Jewish revolt in AD 66 this building too was destroyed by fire during the final assault on the city by the Romans under Titus, son of the Emperor Vespasian. The destruction of the Temple and Jerusalem was in effect the end of the Jewish state.

The craftsmen who had built Solomon's Temple were Phoenicians, who for generations had continued to use skills practised in Egypt by their forebears. The Jews themselves had not acquired any building skills because of their nomadic destiny. Solomon's version was part of a much bigger complex embracing a magnificent new palace for his Egyptian wife, daughter of the Pharaoh, so, whatever the outside of the Temple looked like, the interior would certainly have been decorated with symbolic motifs which showed their origins. For example, on each side of the Ark there stood a cherub, ten cubits high and with a wing-span of ten cubits. These are thought to have been modelled on the winged sphinxes which guard Egyptian temples. Both the decoration and the dimensions were

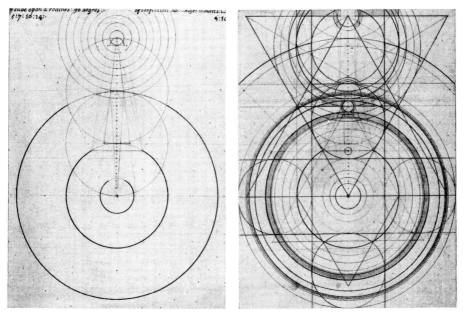

Figure 13: Moses Mount. The incomplete letters suggest that the card has been cut at some time since it was drawn. Many of the heavy lines on the card have been scored to enable it to be folded into various shapes. In Exodus 34, verse 4, 'Moses rose up early in the morning, and went up unto Mount Sinai, as the Lord had commanded him, and took in his hand the two tablets of stone.'

meant to have symbolic significance, even to the extent of the Holy of Holies being constructed as a perfect cube.

I tried to put myself in the place of a seventeenth- or eighteenth-century student of these drawings. There seemed no doubt that the mathematics and its symbolism were the reason why this set of drawings had been included in the Byrom Collection. They extended the study of sacred buildings even further back in time from King's College Chapel and the Temple Church to Solomon's Temple. The measurements on each set had to be related to the prime source. In the case of Solomon's Temple that was the Bible and, as we have seen, those figures correspond proportionately to the measurements on the drawings.

The Dome of the Rock

It was clear that I had not yet reached the end of the trail. There was some other link between Solomon's Temple and the drawings still to be uncovered. Gradually I realised what it was. Nobody knows exactly where Solomon built his Temple, though it has always been associated with the

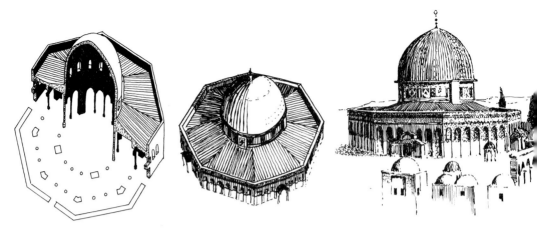

Figures 14, 15 and 16: The Dome of the Rock – in cross section showing the geometric base, from above, and in external elevation.

rock on which Abraham offered to sacrifice his son Isaac in obedience to God. According to one tradition that rock lay in the court at the front and was used for an altar. According to another the rock was inside the Holy of Holies. It is now impossible to establish which, if either, of those versions is true, but given the rock's associations with God's covenant with Abraham its importance to the Jews is understandable.

At the same time, the site is a place of prime importance for Muslims. According to Islamic tradition, the rock is the place where Mohammed talked with Abraham, Solomon, Jesus and other prophets, and from where he ascended into the Seventh Heaven and was shown all the delights of Paradise. After conversing with Allah, who gave him his commands for the faithful, he then returned to the rock. From there he was miraculously carried back through the night to Mecca. The Caliph Abd al-Malik decided to build a shrine to shelter the rock because of its importance. The building was begun in AD 687 and finished within four years. By this time all traces of both Solomon's Temple and that of Herod the Great had long since disappeared. The land around the new shrine, the Dome of the Rock, had been levelled by Herod so that the mosque rose in resplendent glory above the city. Its design had been deliberately modelled on the Church of the Holy Sepulchre. In both there was a sacred rock surrounded by a circular building, a Rotunda; the roof in each case was a huge dome.

What I found most surprising was that the dimensions of both church and mosque are remarkably similar. In both the height of the supporting base is equal to its diameter, and that in turn is all but equal to the height of the dome. There is, however, one major difference. The Dome of the Rock is built on an octagonal ground plan. This idea was taken by the Muslim builders from Roman precedent. The design (figures 14, 15 and 16) is derived from two staggered squares in a central circle. The sides of these squares produce intersections from which an octagon can be drawn. The sides of this octagon in turn can be extended to produce two larger, staggered squares. These are then circumscribed by another circle. Within this circle a large octagon can be drawn with its sides parallel to the inner one. These are in effect the outside walls of the Mosque. Such a command of geometry and proportion has evidently Platonic and Pythagorean origins. It can be traced back to the Byzantine empires, the Greek temples and theatres, and the Egyptian pyramids. One of our foremost authorities on Muslim architecture, Professor K.A.C. Cresswell has said of the Dome of the Rock:

> Under a scheme whereby the size of every part is related to every other part in some definite proportion . . . a building instead of being a collection of odd notes becomes a harmonious chord in stones, a sort of living crystal . . . Some of the ratios involved . . . are fundamentals in time and space, they go right down to the very basis of our nature and of the physical universe in which we live and move.[13]

When I came across this statement it seemed to reaffirm the value of at least some of the insights Byrom and his friends were seeking from the 'architectural' drawings in the collection.

When the crusaders recaptured Jerusalem in 1099 they deliberately desecrated the Islamic mosques. The Dome of the Rock was 'Christianised' and named the Templum Domini, the Temple of the Lord. Guides fabricated a new history for it as the centre of Christ's ministry. Similarly the nearby Mosque of Al-Aqsa was renamed the Temple of Solomon. This in fact was completely inaccurate – one more example of man's readiness to deface public monuments and rewrite the past. Part of Al-Aksa mosque became the palace of the Kings of Jerusalem. The rest of it was given to the Knights Templar for their headquarters, adjoining buildings became their arsenal and store – and so the Dome of the Rock, in its new guise as The Temple of the Lord, became the mother church of the Templars. It appeared on the seal of the Grand Master and on their armorial bearings. It is not surprising that worshipping daily in this polygonal temple the warrior monks should be so moved by its profound synthesis of space and time that they strove to emulate it in their own churches throughout Europe.

As I thought on this I felt that perhaps here was the missing link between Solomon's Temple and the Byrom drawings. This wonder of Islamic architecture was the result of geometric formulas so subtle in conception and so mystical in effect that they became part of a jealously guarded tradition. Learned and copied by the Templars,[14] did they constitute part of a wider philosophy which the Church could only brand as heresy?

CHAPTER SEVEN

The Search for Meaning

IT MAY SEEM unusual for a woman to write about Freemasonry, which from its inception has been a persistently male preserve,[1] although there is now a similar organisation for women. My purpose is not to promote or denigrate the movement or to engage in any of the discussions on whether Freemasonry is incompatible with membership of any particular profession or church. Freemasonry is an historical fact and I seek only explanations to gain an understanding of the nature of the collection.

By the time I had received the drawings I knew John Byrom well as a club man, regular in his attendance at various different groups. Besides being a member of the Royal Society, he was, I discovered, a freemason. He belonged to the French Lodge which met at the Swan Inn in 1730, although its meetings were earlier held at the Golden Lion in Dean Street. He is listed in masonic records in the archives of the United Grand Lodge of England. From a study of Byrom's Journals I also discovered that he recorded visiting both the Swan and the Golden Lion frequently. In keeping with his general habit of secrecy he does not state openly his masonic involvement, but it was appropriate that he should join the French lodge: it was to France that he had retreated when he could not take the Oath of Abjuration in favour of the Hannoverian succession. There he met the exiled Stuart Pretender, and later received a secret letter from France in his own shorthand giving him a full and detailed account of the fate of the defeated Prince Charles Edward Stuart when he was driven from the French court. Byrom's own status as a mason helps to explain the masonic element in the collection and his wish to preserve it carefully.

The starting point of the trail was the two engravings Gerard Thibault commissioned from Michel Le Blon for his treatise on fencing. Both are connected with drawings in the collection. On the allegorical drawing (figure 1) with St Michael at the top there is a geometrical shape right at the centre, a lozenge, in which there are female versions of the Vitruvian man. The entire engraving is heavily female in its personifications. In the Byrom Collection there is a small drawing exactly the same size intended to fit over and represent this part of the engraving – in the same way as the remarkable polygonal design at the centre of the 'Zeus' engraving. It is obvious that the inner geometry of both engravings was a feature sufficiently important for it to be extracted and studied separately. Both engravings, together with additional geometric drawings, found their way into a scrapbook of papers belonging to Sir Hans Sloane. At one time no doubt they had all been part of the same collection, but became separated most probably at the time when Sloane was a member of Byrom's Caba-la Club. Certainly drawings in Byrom's possession matched the two engravings in Sloane's possession and the geometric drawings belonging to Sloane were part of a sequence in Byrom's keeping. One of the most illuminating exercises during my investigations was a discussion of the allegorical engraving with Neville Barker Cryer. He was able to confirm what I had long suspected – that the engraving had symbolic connections with Freemasonry. In addition, as a senior mason, he was able to explain the relevance for masons of so many figures in this engraving.

My first impression was in fact that it was a masonic engraving. It is only on closer examination that one discovers features which almost certainly relate to a wider field than we have so far been able to relate to speculative Masonry from 1690 onwards. Therefore it would be incorrect to say that this is not concerned with Masonry simply because it contains a number of features which are not at the moment directly attributed to what we are familiar with in late seventeenth- and early eighteenth-century Freemasonry.

There are immediately on the engraving at least fifteen items which show how much it is connected with what we know of early eighteenth-century symbolism, and some of the dialogue or catechism we have retained from the 1690s onwards. For example, the two pillars on the left and right of the picture are very prominent still in Freemasonry, but were particularly so at the beginning of specula-tive Freemasonry. They refer to the two pillars built by Lamech, the relative of Noah, who erected a brass and marble pillar in order to retain secrets of ancient knowledge. It is for this reason they have been referred to as the receptacles of the archives of Masonry. On the pillars you have the engraving of what were obviously indications

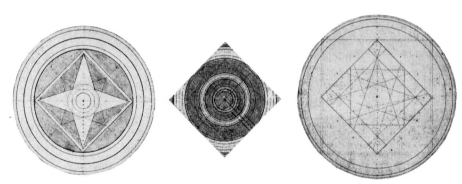

Figure 1: Allegorical engraving by Michel Le Blon, 1615. The Geometry.
Complementary pieces.

of ancient knowledge. On the left pillar are the names of the seven
approved subjects of mediaeval scholasticism: the trivium or group of
three liberal arts of grammar, rhetoric and logic, and the quadrivium
or four branches of mathematics: arithmetic, geometry, astronomy
and music. These were to be studied in the second degree of Masonry.
On top of the pillars you have two figures who represent harbingers
of news or messengers of the deity. Both of these have similarities to
what today we call the deacons in the masonic lodge, carrying news
about the lodge.

At the very top of the picture you have a feature which is now retained in all the oldest lodges but is not used any more, although it was very prominent in the late seventeenth, early eighteenth centuries and indeed throughout the eighteenth century: the flaming sword. This represented the action of God in defending the Garden of Eden from those who had violated the right to remain any longer in that paradise now that they had forbidden knowledge. Thus the flaming sword becomes the judgement of God defending that which is only for those entitled to know. The porcupine on top of the left portico is another ancient masonic symbol. It represents simplicity defending itself. Like the beehive it is no longer used, but it was a recurring symbol in earlier days.

The two figures sitting next to the opening between the two porticos represent two kinds of rulers. One wears a crown of fire, the other a helmet: both bend their sceptres towards the signs of the craft to show how they are subject to the greater control of its mysteries. These are displayed by a regal looking woman holding a globe in one hand and dividers in the other. This is an earlier version of related symbolism in William Blake when he painted the Creator of the world holding a pair of great dividers. Le Blon's symbol is more specifically masonic. Between the dividers we can see the sceptre as the central symbol crossed by the pen or plume of the scribe and the baton of the master of ceremonies, a marshall in fact, as in the days of the Templars. In the top left corner here is the gridiron of St Lawrence, undoubtedly one of the very earliest masonic symbols, which is still used. The dividers are an old form of the compasses. Anderson has a saying: 'Monarchs themselves have not considered it beneath their dignity to exchange the sceptre for the trowel.' And an orb lies discarded by the side of the king on the left. There are other features in the remaining quarters within the dividers, which, if magnified, would undoubtedly reveal themselves as symbols of Rosicrucian or masonic importance. This whole feature, namely the dividers and the symbols inside, is repeated further down at the base of the pedestal on the right. This is an echo of the maxim 'That which is above is like unto that which is below', or a symbol of the earthly practice of a heavenly injunction.

Below, the dividers are held by a woman who in her other hand holds a sword entwined with a serpent. This is another eighteenth-century symbol of justice surrounded by wisdom. Behind her, inside the right portico, is another figure with scales representing justice. Her being in the portico on a pedestal may indicate heavenly as opposed to earthly justice. Similarly on the left, inside the portico, is a figure whose robe is covered with ears. This was a very significant sign to early masons. It meant that you heard everything, saw everything, but said nothing. The woman sitting to the right of her has one hand to her ear while with the other she writes. She represents Wisdom hearing truth and writing it down. Behind her are the open pages of a book or the tablets, another masonic symbol from the eighteenth century. Next to her, on the far left, is a decorously naked female with an hour glass in one hand and a knife in the other. She is in fact Fortune, ready to cut short man's existence with her knife. Her feet can just be glimpsed behind the chariot resting on the wheel of fortune. Masons were taught to 'bear in mind the wheel of fortune means there are masons of affluence and poverty'. Balancing her position on the extreme right of the engraving is another female figure with an aureole above her head. This recalls the sign of the sun which was always displayed over the seat of the Master of the lodge and remained one of the most significant features of a lodge.

At the bottom of the engraving on the left hand side is the figure of Heracles seated in a chariot. In one hand he holds the golden apples of the Hesperides, in the other his club. He represents Strength. Opposite him is the God of War, Mars. Dominating the top of the engraving in the centre is St Michael, his flaming sword aloft, standing over a figure with the tail of a serpent and holding a mirror. St Michael the archangel is slaying the evil one, who learns the truth about himself by looking in the mirror. This recalls the early masonic teaching 'know thyself', a precept which goes back to ancient Greece. It was said to be written up in the temple of Delphi. However, while the central figure is undoubtedly Michael, he himself is not a masonic figure. His presence in the engraving means that it contains christo-hermetic implications which were not taken up directly by the speculative masons later. The attempt was made relatively early to remove any specific saints other than the two saints John from being represented in masonic symbolism. St Michael is shown emerging from the 'shekinah' or glory, the rays on each side of him which resemble the seven rays that symbolise the stars surrounding the moon and sun. This is an emblem often found in early illustrations of the Bible after the Reformation.

So here at the top is a symbol of the Presence, Power, Glory and Majesty of the Divine. I am a little puzzled by the elephant on the top of the left portico, but it is a sign for the oldest Belgian lodge, founded in 1723. The bared leg of the figures standing inside each portico recalls parts of masonic ritual of ancient use. The two medallions which flank the central lozenge, and which have been left deliberately blank, are also symbolic; one is in darkness, the other in light.

The late seventeenth and early eighteenth century is the earliest period to which we can assign with certainty masonic ritual and symbolism, because of our recorded evidence. But before that it is clear there were speculative masons, although we have no evidence of what they actually did, or taught in their assemblies. I would describe this engraving as a neo-classical attempt to represent ancient mysteries in early seventeenth-century guise by learned people who almost certainly had Rosicrucian or hermetic knowledge to hand.

It is obvious from this analysis that the symbolism extended far beyond the immediately overt occasion of a treatise on fencing. It was intended to convey much to the initiated. St Michael, as we shall see, became the patron saint of the swordsman, so his presence is understandable. In the lower foreground there is Hercules confronting Mars, strength with guile opposed to war. So the main body of the engraving is enclosed within a framework of combat. Yet that main emblematic group, even on the evidence gleaned so far, extends back to philosophical and mystical concepts about the nature of knowledge, justice and power. These are concepts which have in part been absorbed into speculative Freemasonry, but existed outside that and even before the formation of the first formal masonic lodges. They are part of the hidden stream of knowledge which obsessed so many seekers after truth. It is present in other aspects of the Byrom Collection, in the formulas for building churches or theatres and in the more abstract investigation into geometry.

It was difficult to know which way to turn to press forward from this point. I reviewed the facts again. Michel Le Blon had engraved this plate in 1615. It is full of seminal emblems of the masonic movement. Michel's descendant, Jacques Christophe Le Blon, came to England where his treatise on colour printing was translated by James Anderson. It was published in French and English in 1725. In April 1731 the secretary of the Royal Society presented a very thorough report on this invention to the Society and requested Le Blon and Anderson to attend the meeting. The following month, on 6 May, the Royal Society received a present from Le Blon of a painting which he had produced by his colour process. Obviously Le Blon enjoyed a very cordial working relationship with Anderson, who was a freemason. In September 1721 Anderson had approached Grand Lodge with the suggestion that he should write an account of Freemasonry. This led ultimately not only to a history but to a revision of the 'Regulations' of the freemasons which, after their approval by the Grand Master, were published in 1723. They have been known ever since as Anderson's Constitutions.

When I considered all the symbols in the Michel Le Blon engraving which Neville Barker Cryer had been able to attribute to the earliest days of Grand Lodge, it seemed reasonable and logical to conclude that, through Jacques Christophe, Anderson had become acquainted with the engraving and all its rich tradition of allegory. In particular Anderson's maxim 'Monarchs themselves have not considered it beneath their dignity to exchange the sceptre for the trowel' could be linked directly to the image of the king with the discarded orb and the signs of the craft. Much of what Anderson learned from Le Blon, I believe, he incorporated into his history and the Constitutions.

One of those thought to have helped Anderson in the preparation of this book is John Theophilus Desaguliers. He became the third Grand Master of Grand Lodge, but he was also a brilliant scientist, the Professor of Experimental Philosophy at Oxford, and a disciple of Newton, whose own work foreshadowed present day theories on the atom, and even the splitting of the atom. He was a friend and great admirer of Byrom. It is quite possible that Byrom was another of the 'learned bretheren' who assisted Anderson in the preparation of his book. This possibility looks even more likely when we learn that Anderson, in tracing the history of Freemasonry, is in effect writing the history of geometry through its connection with building techniques, and that he believed all civilised architecture to have originated in Solomon's Temple, through Greece to Rome.[2] It seemed to me that Anderson was, in a sense, following Byrom's footsteps, or certainly in the footsteps of the custodians of the drawings. The topics in common were too many to be simply coincidental. It is for this reason that we can regard the engraving as a new and important source for the beginnings of Freemasonry, and a summation of much that flows in the underground stream.

There are many other drawings in the collection which clearly indicate a masonic element. They show that some of the masonic emblems included pre-date the foundation of Grand Lodge and thus provide links between the movement and other esoteric groups who, in one way or another, were its antecedents. A good example of this is the swastika (figure 3), not the repugnant insignia of Nazi ideology – the swastika reversed – but the original and true swastika whose meaning was quite the opposite. It is in fact one of the most ancient and widespread of all symbols, appearing in early civilisations not only in Europe but also in India, Japan and both North and South America. Assyrians, Peruvians, ancient Britons and Greeks have all used the swastika in symbolic and decorative ways. This is remarkable in itself. One can readily understand the widespread use of a circle or a square, for these are by comparison much easier to hit upon by chance or experiment. The straight line, the cross, even the triangle, have been discovered and rediscovered in separate cultures in different parts of the world. In the first instance they arose no doubt from sheer necessity and were simply functional, although symbolic asso-

 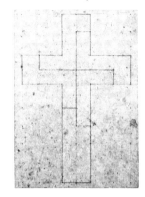 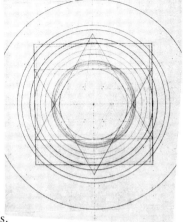

Figures 2,3,4: Masonic symbols.

ciations would rapidly grow around them. The swastika, however, is such a consciously contrived shape that it can hardly ever have been used for anything but symbolic or ornamental purposes. No doubt down the ages all over the world its original meaning has been modified, transformed, even lost, but it has always in its lowest manifestations been associated everywhere with good fortune and luck.

For our purposes we need not look for meanings beyond the sources of European culture, a wide enough field in itself! Evidence points to it being a religious symbol of great antiquity. The four arms closely resemble four cabalistic stages of emanation.[3] They also suggest the four letters of the Tetragrammaton. These are the four Hebrew letters to denote YaHWeH or JeHoVaH. The four Hebrew letters do appear in another drawing. Certainly the shape of the swastika and its context in figure 3 suggest some sort of progression, for the symbol has been placed inside a cross. It has evidently been Christianised, and would imply a continuation from the God of the Old Testament to the God of the New, or even the indwelling of the one within the other. The sign occurs repeatedly on the walls of the catacombs in Rome. The Hebrews moreover expressed the idea of the unity of the divine creation by writing the name of God, base to base, so that above the line it represented good and below the line evil.[4] It is easy to understand why a symbol so rich in resonances and accretions should hold a fascination for the freemason and still be a subject of study.

Another device which links the drawings with the masons is the figure of the interlacing triangles which form an hexalpha or six-pointed star. It occurs in three forms in the collection: as a plain two-line figure (figure 2); sometimes as a combination of a single-line and two-line figure (figures 5 and 7); or as a two-line figure symbolically coloured (figure 6). In this last form it is easy to see the way in which the sides of the two triangles are interwoven. As a result we can see that some of the coloured

165

ones are a variant of the basic symbol. The hexalpha has been associated with Jewish culture since the twelfth century and is known as the Seal of Solomon or the Star of David. According to Jewish folklore, Solomon is supposed to have sealed a spirit up in a bottle with a stopper marked with this device. It is also the name of a plant, Solomon's Seal, so called because of the hexagonal shape of its flower. Today it appears on the national flag of Israel. As a talisman it has a long tradition outside the Hebraic context. The symmetry of its geometry and numbers elicits at one level a purely aesthetic response to a pleasing shape, but at another goes far deeper to induce something more akin to reverence. The interlacing of the triangles results in a six-pointed star and also in an internal hexagon. When the figure is drawn with double lines the six points of the star each contain a further triangle. So there is a constant interplay of sixes and threes in the pattern. Figure 7 has an almost hypnotic intensity about its investigation of a receding series of single and double triangles. It is little wonder that over the centuries its attributes have proliferated and that today it remains still an important symbol in Freemasonry. As a Christian symbol it represents the Trinity, for Hindus it represents fire and water and, by extension, the human soul. It is a masonic sign for the universe.

There are in the collection several drawings which feature a square subdivided into smaller squares. Often these smaller squares total sixty-four, just like a chessboard, and are related to the chequered centre of a lodge floor as anciently shown in a freemasons' meeting place. In a lodge may be found a mosaic of black and white tiles which represent the dark and light alternations in human fortune. It is claimed that the mosaic is derived from the pavement in Solomon's Temple. We have pictures of just such chequered floors in early sixteenth century Bibles (figure 8), and since the Temple was built by Phoenicians and decorated with Egyptian motifs, there may be some basis for the claim. The pavements in Egyptian temples have been found to be marked out in this way for the priests to take measurements of the sun's course as it casts its shadow from pillars or obelisks. It was a favourite pattern for Greek pottery and the floors of

Figures 5,6,7: Variations on the Hexalpha.

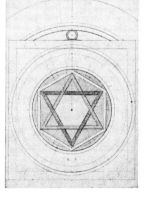

Roman villas. Figure 9 is an example. It has the sixty-four subdivisions, although here they are not shaded. Sometimes they were used to accommodate number sequences and so left blank, or they could be used in association with a swastika imposed on top of the square. The sixty-four divisions could then be used to represent the fifty-two weeks of the calendar year, which was thought to consist of thirty-six solar cycles added to twenty-eight lunar cycles.[5] Certainly for the masons the squares have a long history. With the beginning of the speculative lodges in the early years of the eighteenth century it was the custom to mark out the form of the lodge on the floor of the meeting place. Afterwards it was rubbed out to maintain secrecy.[6] This was felt by some to be a waste of time, and the practice was replaced around 1730 by a floor cloth already marked out, which could easily be laid down and taken up again afterwards. It was at this time that Byrom was attending his French lodge. Meetings were held in inns and so furnishings had to be temporary. The permanent masonic hall is a later development. The whole idea derives ultimately from the days when the original operative master mason would draw up his plans or designs for a building on drawing board or slate. Some mediaeval guilds in Germany opened their meetings by drawing a circle on the floor. Some of the 64 square divisions in the drawings are drawn within a surrounding circle.

One of the drawings has a most unusual watermark in the shape of a pentalpha. This is formed by interlacing two triangles in such a way as to produce a five-pointed star. It is another symbol the collection has in common with Freemasonry. Its presence as a watermark must mean that the paper-maker was either a freemason or a Rosicrucian. For, like so many of the other symbols, it is associated with a number of esoteric groups apart from Freemasonry. It is frequently to be found in works on the Cabala, alchemy and astrology. With the point uppermost the pentalpha is a positive symbol for good and, like other pagan symbols, it became partly Christianised as a symbol of the five wounds of Christ. The watermark appears in figure 10, which is a diagram of the inner geometry of the Zeus engraving by Michel Le Blon, commissioned by Gerard Thibault. The allegorical and mythical figures have been removed in order that the symbolism of the geometry can be revealed and studied.

In addition to the pentalpha in the watermark there is a second one in the body of the drawing itself. It is in the bottom right-hand corner, where it fills the circle occupied in the engraving by the figure representing Earth. The same network of lines can be seen in the background to the figure, but on the purely geometric abstraction the two central triangles forming an upright pentalpha are distinctly highlighted in contrast to the rest of the lines. This is obviously deliberate. Michel Le Blon and Thibault were both conversant with the hermetic tradition, as we have

Figure 8: Luther's Bible, printed LÜBECKE 1533. Chequered floor as in Solomon's Temple.

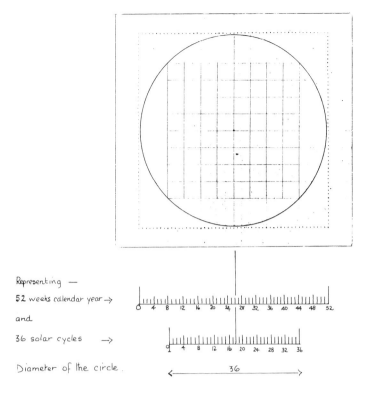

Representing —

52 weeks calendar year →

and

36 solar cycles →

Diameter of the circle.

36

Figure 9: The sides of the large square are measured in 52 units which symbolise the weeks of the calendar year. The inner square consists of 64 smaller ones and represents 36 solar cycles added to 28 lunar cycles.

already noted. The presence of the pentalpha in the schema is evidence of this hermetic element and is another link between the freemasons and earlier groups.[7]

There appear to be other indications of Freemasonry in the use of three dots shaped like a triangle after a person's initials (figure 11). This is known to be an ancient masonic sign. Three dots are also placed strategically on other particular drawings. There are also a number of drawings which explore the properties of the Tau Cross (figure 12). As figure 9, p. 146, showed, it was used in the drawings of the Temple Church as a symbol of the true Christian cross, but it was also studied for its own sake. The Tau cross still has a prominent place in masonic symbolism, and its universal currency as a religious symbol testifies again to the eclectic tradition of Freemasonry.

One of the most intriguing of all the drawings in the collection is figure 13. The basic lines of the design are two forms of the cross – the cross of Lorraine and the cross of St Andrew, a Scottish and a French sign combined. This is made doubly puzzling by the two letters Z and G inscribed each side of the upright of the cross of Lorraine. Two

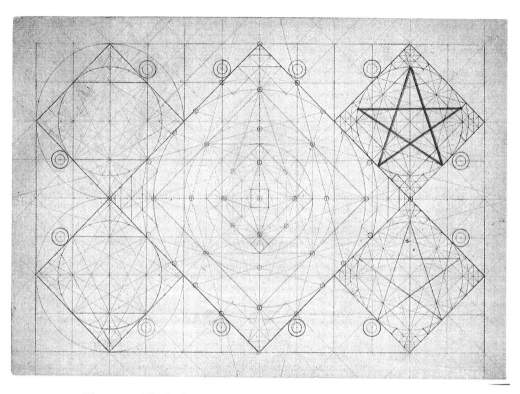

Figure 10: The inner geometry of the Zeus engraving by Michel Le Bon.
The watermark has been highlighted top right.

circles overlap in the background but these are fainter than the two crosses, which are clearly intended to be dominant and of equal importance. Often in England the letter 'G' can be found in the centre of the ceiling of a lodge, and it had been used as a symbolic letter since the beginning of the eighteenth century, possibly earlier. Although there has been some debate among masons themselves as to its exact meaning, the most likely explanation would seem to be that it stands for Geometria, the science which underpins the masons' craft. Geometry is so fundamental that it is associated with God, the great architect of the universe. Mediaeval artists depicted him as such, measuring the universe with a pair of dividers. It was this tradition which Milton drew on in *Paradise Lost* when he described God creating the world out of chaos:

> He took the golden compasses, prepar'd
> In God's eternal store, to circumscribe
> This Universe, and all created things:
> One foot he center'd, and the other turn'd
> Round through the vast profounditie obscure,
> And said, thus farr extend, thus farr thy bounds,
> Thus be thy just circumference, O world.[8]

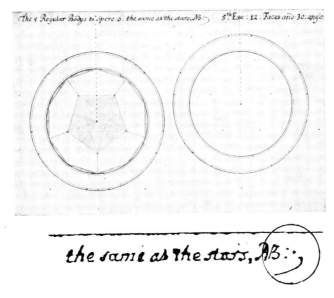

Figure 11: Detail showing three dots (circled), an early Masonic sign.

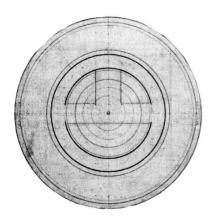

Figure 12: A form of Tau Cross.

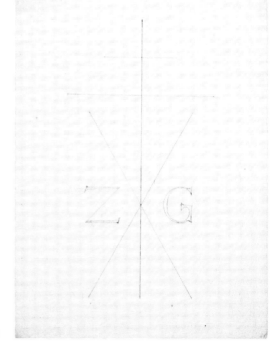

Figure 13

‡ The Cross of Lorraine   Z Zabulon
X The Cross of St Andrew   G Geometria

Masonic archives contain a catechism, dated 1730, in which the postulant is asked:

> Q. Why was you made a Fellow Craft?
> A. For the sake of the letter G.
> Q. What does that G. denote?
> A. Geometry or the Fifth Science.[9]

The letter Z, I am reliably informed by Mr Cryer, probably stands for 'Zabulon', a name for God. It was to remind the mason that God, the Great Architect, is the universal deity to Whom all men of faith aspire, and Who reigns in His Temple.

The St Andrew's Cross had been part of the coat of arms of Michel Le Blon. As already noted he had been responsible for a number of the drawings in the collection; his initials were on the back of some. Was this the reason for the St Andrew's cross on the card? The connection seemed too tenuous. The cross of Lorraine had been used by members of the Lorraine dynasty as a personal emblem, intermittently at least, since René d'Anjou became Duke of Lorraine in 1431.[10] Where was the link between the Scottish and French emblem? The context was obviously masonic. Freemasonry is thought to have reached France with the remnants of the Jacobites after their defeat in 1688, but the first formal French lodge was formed in 1725. The leading personality in its foundation was Charles Radclyffe, the exiled Earl of Derwentwater, whose brother had been executed for his part in the 1715 Jacobite uprising. Charles was also a Jacobite. So too was Byrom, in secret. He also knew Radclyffe and was, as we know, a member of the French lodge of masons in London. In 1725, the year the exiled Scotsman founded the first French lodge, François, Duke of Lorraine, visited London, and was entertained by freemasons during that visit. Later he was himself admitted into Freemasonry by Desaguliers at The Hague in 1731. He must already have evinced sympathy and interest in masonic ideas during that London visit.

All these facts led me to conclude that this particular card in the collection was a commemoration of the Duke's visit and the foundation of the first French lodge by Radclyffe. This would be fully in keeping with Byrom's sympathies. The masonic letters Z and G were placed boldly alongside insignia which recalled territorial loyalties of both Radclyffe and the Duke.

Figure 14 is one of great importance both from the point of view of its content and because of its connection with the Royal Society and Byrom's Cabala Club. In the centre is the six-pointed star, which immediately links it to the masonic movement, but that hexalpha is superimposed on an elaborate presentation of the inner geometry of a church, whose measurements correspond to those of the Temple Church in London. On the back of the card is a third clue, the date 1727. The predominant colour used in the drawing is green. An ancient use of the colour was to symbolise rebirth after death, and it was so used by Templars,[11] freemasons and other hermetic groups. All these features are clues to a cluster of events which took place around the spring and summer of 1727. In the *Freemasons' Guide and Compendium* Bernard Jones states that green, 'always regarded as the symbol of gladness and abundance, has been directly associated with ideas of resurrection and immortality, even of victory. In the ancient mysteries green stood for moral birth or rebirth of the Initiate. The acacia (the Masonic evergreen) has been suggested as a symbol of a moral life or rebirth, and also of immortality'.

I pondered on the most likely candidate to have occasioned the design of this card. Everything seemed to point to one person: Sir Isaac

Figure 14: '∴ 1727 5 by 5 or : 10: by : 10' (written on the back of the design).

Newton. Seriously regarded by contemporaries as the greatest genius who had ever lived, Newton is believed to have dedicated himself to a life of unimpeachable purity. He had many non-scientific interests which overlapped with those of Byrom and his fellow-hermeticists. Although we have no proof that Newton was ever a mason, he was certainly a member of the Gentlemen's Society of Spalding which was a forerunner of a masonic lodge. In addition he spent years on his esoteric studies. In his *Chronology of Ancient Kingdoms Amended* he devoted a whole chapter to the Temple of Solomon, the symbolic significance of its dimensions and its rituals. Some of these he thought contained an alchemical element. Newton owned a hundred books on alchemy and devoted considerable energy to investigating its mysteries. Some of these investigations were in line with a wholly rational approach, others were not. He undoubtedly believed in a secret tradition of learning which he considered could be traced to Pythagoras and to the Chaldean philosophers. He even thought that these ancient savants had discovered the inverse square law of gravitation. Newtonian scholars still argue with some embarrassment about the place of the hermetic tradition in Newton's work, but it was decidedly important to him as he grew older. It was during his last years that Byrom would have known him through the Royal Society where Newton was President from 1703 to 1727.

Newton died on 20 March 1727 and, after lying in state in the Jerusalem Chamber, was buried in Westminster Abbey. His pall was carried by the Lord Chancellor, two dukes and three earls, all members of the Royal Society. One of these was the contemporary Earl of Pembroke. When ill health had made Newton's attendance at meetings of the Royal Society precarious, he had Martin Folkes appointed as his deputy or vice-president. Folkes was a leading freemason and one of Byrom's closest friends. Many other members of the recently constituted Grand Lodge were also members of the Royal Society. Certain of these also belonged to Byrom's Cabala Club, including Sir Hans Sloane. Shortly after Newton died, on 27 April, the President-elect of the Royal Society revived a proposal that had been brought before that august body some years earlier.

> The President Acquainted the Society that there had been a Design and Resolution taken about 8 to 10 years ago to Endeavour to Obtain the favour of his Majesty to Dignify the Society as some of his Royal Predecessors had done with the Grant of his Name under the Title of Patron.[12]

A serious disagreement broke out about the form of wording in which the King, George I, was to be addressed. Byrom, still a secret

Jacobite, was at the centre of this dispute. Tempers became so heated that the affair seriously affected Byrom's relationship with Sloane. Before the embarrassing dispute could be solved, the King conveniently died on his way to Hannover. It so happened that the Temple Church lay outside the jurisdiction of its local bishop and came directly under the King. He, as head of the Church of England, appointed the Master of the Temple, as the chaplain was called. Thus this particular drawing in the Byrom Collection is a record of critical changes taking place at the centres of power, both in the Royal Society and with the monarchy. The motivating spirit which imbued Byrom's inner group led them to commemorate what they saw as significant events affecting their interests. For the initiated the drawing would be both a source of instruction and a means of contemplation.

John Colet

The collection also includes drawings concerned with the work of men whose beliefs have either directly or indirectly foreshadowed the development of Freemasonry. One example is figure 15, which bears the name John Colet. I have chosen to include this card because Colet has a significant place in the tradition represented by the collection and is a figure of interest still to freemasons. He is remembered today chiefly as the founder of one of London's great schools, St Paul's. He belongs to the tradition of English humanist scholars, was a friend of Sir Thomas More and Erasmus and one of the voices calling for ecclesiastical reform. Seven years of study at Oxford had made him a formidable mathematician but he was also widely read in classical literature. He rounded off his education by a tour through France and Italy in 1493 when he was twenty-six, staying and studying at universities on his way. This brought him into contact with the neo-platonist school founded by Marsilio Ficino and Pico della Mirandola at Florence. Another influential contemporary was Johannes Reuchlin, a leading figure in the German Renaissance. His book *De Arte Cabalistica*, which Colet admired, was the first detailed treatise on the Cabala by a gentile. Its emphasis on the importance of number and the value of mystical mathematics in a Christian context appealed to him.

It is not surprising that Colet became a great friend of Erasmus whom he later supported with a pension, for he was a true figure of enlightenment and at Oxford the centre of a group of distinguished scholars. His role in the pre-Reformation church should be mentioned in order that we have a balanced picture of the man. Colet was not simply a student of esoteric schools of thought. In 1504 Henry VII appointed him Dean of St Paul's; he had been left considerable wealth by his father and decided to found a school in St Paul's Churchyard for 153 boys. In his lectures at Oxford

Figure 15: The three Worlds, Collett [sic] – Elemental, Celestial and Intellectual.

and his sermons in London Colet demanded a straightforward exposition of Biblical texts rather than the arid scholasticism of traditional theologians. He showed a similar attitude in the policy of his school. He drew up simple rules for the teachers and staff to follow, translated the Creed and several prayers into English and wanted the active governors to be 'married citizens' rather than celibate clergy. His was not a 'fugitive or cloistered virtue' for he had the courage to denounce Henry VIII's campaign against France. In return the King invited the Dean to Greenwich to discuss how a war might be justified.

For Colet all the new learning of the Renaissance was a means of vitalising his religion both in thought and deed. He was undoubtedly in the forefront of those scholars who were anxious to see a return to proper Biblical criticism and the translation of the scriptures for the masses. Neville Barker Cryer related the drawing in the collection to Colet's Trinitarian beliefs and pointed out that the Church of England as it emerged after the Reformation was the one reformed church to restore the festival of the Trinity after having emphasised Pentecost as the principal feast. For him the drawing asserts that behind the universe there is a fundamental three-fold principle which is God Creator, Saviour and Sustainer.

Colet was also interested in the work of another, highly controversial figure in the hermetic movement, Henry Cornelius Agrippa. He, like Dee, has been much misunderstood and attacked because of his attempt to discover and harness the sources of 'white' magic.[13] Colet acted as host to Agrippa when he visited London in 1510 and together they studied the Epistles of St Paul. Agrippa also adopted some of the ideas of the Christian cabalists in formulating his own theories. In his most famous book, published in 1533, *De Occulta Philosophia*, Agrippa divides the universe into three worlds: the elemental, the celestial and the intellectual. They overlap and are interrelated. I believe that this is also symbolised in the diagram bearing Colet's name. God, according to Agrippa, is present in all three worlds by process of descent from the angels in the intellectual world, to the stars in the celestial world and to the baser elements in the terrestrial or elemental world. Agrippa tries to show, by means of a highly complicated process involving white or pure magic as well as a cabalistic use of mathematics, that man can ascend from the terrestrial world through the celestial and intellectual worlds to the presence of the Creator.

Although the book was not published until long after his visit with Colet, Agrippa had written the manuscript much before that date and could well have discussed aspects of the philosophy he was formulating as early as 1510 with Colet. The ideas are important because they link Agrippa with other groups who pursued the same spiritual and intellectual objectives by different routes. The group which formed round Colet at Oxford, like the scholars drawn to Dee at Mortlake, were forerunners of those speculative scholars who later led to the foundation of the Royal Society and the formalisation of Freemasonry in Grand Lodge. That such groups existed is clear. In 1691 John Aubrey noted on the reverse of one of the folios of a manuscript the following:

> Mdm, this day (May the 18th. being Monday after the Rogation Sunday) is a great convention at St. Paul's church of the Fraternity of the Accepted Masons: where Sr. Christopher Wren is to be adopted a Brother . . . There have been kings, that have been of this Sodalitie.

Other writers, too, talk of meetings held in great secrecy near the newly erected cathedral around this period. In a bizarre footnote to Colet's own career, his coffin was discovered in 1680 under the walls of the old cathedral destroyed by the Great Fire. Members of the Royal Society had it opened for examination but learned little from it. No doubt the Dean, a champion of the search for the plain truth, would have approved.

Robert Fludd (1574–1637)

The next drawing I have included bears the name of another Englishman, Robert Fludd. He comes a little later than Colet, but his work has affinities with some of Colet's ideas. I have deliberately included him for this reason, and because many of Fludd's books were published by the de Bry family. Johann Theodore himself published the first part of Fludd's magnum opus

The History of the Macrocosm and Microcosm (1617–1619); later volumes were engraved by Matthaeus Merian. Accordingly I was not altogether surprised to find Fludd's name included on drawings. This showed to what extent the Byrom Collection is connected with the hermetic tradition preceding the freemasons and other esoteric groups.

In order to see this particular drawing (figure 16) in the context of the collection and of Fludd's own work, it is necessary to look briefly at the career of this extraordinary man. He comes at the end of the Elizabethan age and rises to predominance during the reigns of James I and Charles I. His father had made a fortune as Treasurer of Elizabeth's forces in the Netherlands and was thus able to indulge his son with a long and expensive education. Fludd first went to Oxford where he studied at St John's College, and after taking both his B.A. and M.A. he spent six years travelling through France, Italy, Germany and Spain, supported by his father and working as a tutor to some leading aristocratic families. In 1602 he joined the family of the Duc de Guise where he taught Charles, who became the fourth Duke, and his brother François. For Charles he prepared a lengthy treatise on arithmetic and for François a volume on geometry and military science. He appears to have kept in touch with Charles as late as 1620, long after his return to England. The Dukes of Guise seem to have shared an interest in esoteric learning with their collateral branch, the Dukes of Lorraine, for, as we have seen, François, Duke of Lorraine, became a Freemason in 1731.

It was during his years on the continent that Fludd first decided to become a physician. On his return he went back to Oxford to prepare for his exams, but at first the College of Physicians refused to pass him.[14] He had become a disciple of the Paracelsian school of medicine, which was opposed by traditional doctors, who still believed that treatment for ailments was to be based on balancing the four humours which were thought to regulate the body. Paracelsus had developed what might be broadly described as an 'alternative' school of medicine, one which treated

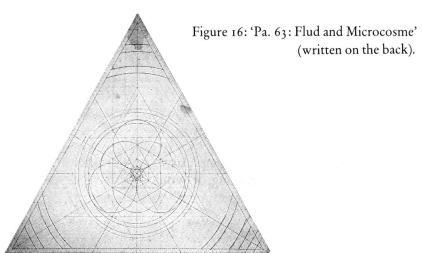

Figure 16: 'Pa. 63: Flud and Microcosme' (written on the back).

the whole person and not just the illness, even to the extent of using astrology, but he made a genuine contribution to the treatment of disease by the application of chemistry to medicine. He believed that health depended on a particular combination of chemical substances in the body and illness occurred when these were out of balance. With all its imperfections this was a great step forward. Fludd's advocacy of Paracelsus led to a three-year controversy with his medical superiors. Eventually he settled down to practise in London, and must have displayed some genuine medical skills for he succeeded in winning the friendship and respect of William Harvey, who discovered the circulation system of the blood.

Fludd's great ambition was to write a work in which all the known facts of the universe, the created world, and man's own creative skills could be presented together within one coherent philosophical framework. He was a true polymath and his writings display an encyclopaedic knowledge of all the arts and sciences as well as a thorough familiarity with the hermetic tradition. The drawing I have selected is related to the section on the Microcosm. Fludd's theories are often very complex but he was able to reduce them to relatively simple diagrams. Figure 16 is of the Threefold Manifestation. The reader will be able to recognise at once its similarity to Colet's triangle with the interlacing circles. For Fludd the triangle represents God. Within this there are three circles which, as with Colet, represent three worlds: the angelic, the stellar and the elemental. In the centre is the inner triangle which represents the Tetragrammaton, the symbol of the name of God that is never spoken. The drawing in the collection is evidently an exploration by a student of Fludd's philosophy of the mysteries encapsulated within this diagram. There is on this occasion even a helpful page reference to page 63 'Flud & Microcosme'.

St Michael

While I was working on that part of the collection concerned with Freemasonry and the hermetic tradition I found myself at times stumbling in the dark. I had entered a world which I had never before imagined, one whose horizons seemed limitless and where the tracks crossed, re-crossed, bent back upon themselves and even suddenly disappeared altogether. Sometimes there were signposts along the way and occasionally the rare encounter with someone who could tell me that I was travelling in the right direction. Along one particular stretch I seemed to be walking in a gloom lit by occasional flashes of lightning in which the name of Michael, saint and archangel, appeared before me. No, I was not hallucinating, but, given the complexity and mystification of some of the texts I found myself reading, it would not have been surprising if I had done just that, for I found myself in the company of people who had been denounced as heretics, witches and magicians. However, certain epiphanies did occur which could not be ignored. The figure of Michael kept reappearing sufficiently to fall into the category of facts that should be faced.

I had come across him first in the Le Blon engraving, the archangel in combat with the dragon. This is the picture we have of him in the Book of Revelation. The traditional Christian view is that he is the protector of individual Christians against the devil, especially at the hour of death when he conducts the soul to God. The Old Testament presents him in the book of Daniel as the helper of Israel.

It is not only in the Le Blon engraving that St Michael appears. He is to be found in the engraving at the front of the Thibault fencing manual, again with sword in hand combating the dragon. In both contexts the Christian saint appears with a classical goddess on either side of him, Minerva and Bellona, the Roman goddesses of wisdom and war. This combination, together with repeated symbols of the masonic dividers and the figure of Hermes, places the figure of the archangel in the wider and parallel context of the hermetic tradition. It is also clear from these engravings, the circle of friends he gathered round him and his own writings, that Thibault was interested in the same tradition. His exposition of the 'mystic circle' for the fencer recalls the mediaeval practice mentioned earlier of starting a guild meeting by drawing a circle on the ground. It is also related to the popular tradition of the circle within which the magus works his skills. It was, moreover, common in eighteenth-century English and French Freemasonry for a circle of swords to be directed towards a candidate during one of the ceremonies. Before Thibault died he made his nephew Hendrick, the Lord of Aagtekerke and Burgomaster of Middelburg, his heir. He, I discovered, was made a knight of St Michael by Louis XIII.

Here was St Michael again. The Order of St Michael was founded by Louis IX in 1469. St Michael was said to have appeared on a rocky island off the north coast of France. This place became dedicated to him and the site of the Benedictine monastery, Mont St Michel. Probably the most famous of all the shrines devoted to St Michael, its reputation as a centre of learning, especially in the sciences, grew far and wide. Later the abbey became part of an impregnable fortress, and from this St Michael came to be regarded as the defender and patron saint of France. The Order of St Michael was the highest order of French chivalry. Membership was limited to thirty-six knights who were chosen from the ranks of men of the noblest blood and highest courage. It was the equivalent of the Order of the Garter and foreign sovereigns were often honoured with the award. Robert Dudley, too, had been made a knight of the order in 1564.[15]

My next encounter with St Michael was still within the ostensible context of fencing. A Confraternity of St Michael was founded in Ghent in 1613 as a guild for fencing masters. Thibault had not yet published his manual on fencing, but he had been brought up in Ghent and his own academy was not too far away in Antwerp. There were undoubtedly other guilds and associations for fencers before 1613, but this was the date when the Ghent guild was formalised with statutes and the approval of local magistrates. While the overt purpose of the guild was to ensure that fencing was held in proper esteem, they could hardly have done so without studying the principles which Thibault was already proclaiming as the fundamental necessity for acquiring a good technique.

So we can see that St Michael became associated with fencing and was almost looked upon as a patron saint of swordsmen, but there was more to the cult than that: in addition to his role as a Christian saint there is an equally long tradition of the archangel in the context of hermetic philosophies. Michael, for instance, plays an important part in the work of Robert Fludd and some of that work is related to drawings in the Byrom Collection.

I have shown that Fludd believed the universe to consist of three worlds, and that there are geometric drawings of this idea. It is necessary to examine this belief a little more. These are difficult waters but I will try to avoid the whirlpool of mediaeval obscurities. Fludd described the act of creation as a ray of light sent out from God into the darkness of the void. This light is obviously pure spirit, but the further it travels from God the weaker it becomes. The first stage of its journey is through the empyrean or Heaven where there is more light than darkness, then comes the ethereal world where the light and darkness are held in balance. The final stage is our own world, the elemental, where the darkness is greater than the light and, as the name suggests, this darkness produces the four elements which were then considered to be basic components of this world.[16] Each of these three worlds was inhabited. In the empyrean were the angels, in the ethereal were the stars, planets and demons, and in the elemental lived man, together with all animal, mineral and vegetable nature. All philosophies which believe in God have to accommodate the problem of evil, Fludd's is no exception: God as the creator of all is also the creator of good and evil, but they are ultimately reconciled in His oneness. The angels are the ministers of light and the demons are the ministers of darkness. They are in perpetual conflict, but in the end good always wins. The demons were driven out of the empyrean by the archangel Michael and his host of angels. Michael, according to Fludd, then took up his residence in the sun.

On the title page of one of his works Fludd has a drawing of St Michael standing in triumph over the defeated dragon. His head has been replaced by the sun in splendour, with three more suns arranged above that. This idea will undoubtedly seem bizarre to many twentieth-century minds, which can just about cope with the idea of angels as decorations for a Christmas tree, but to Fludd they were real, and we can perhaps best understand them as representing forces for good as opposed to forces for evil. With all his embarrassing oddities Fludd, like other hermeticists, was making a serious attempt to explain the nature of the universe and to provide a spiritual ladder by which we might morally, intellectually and spiritually ascend.

Fludd was not the only writer to associate Michael with the sun. It is an idea common to other hermetic philosophers. In fact Fludd's publishers and engravers, the de Bry family, published a book entitled *The Magical Calendar*. No one knows for certain who the author was, but it grew out of a long tradition of belief in number magic, related to the numbers one to twelve. In this book Michael is associated with the number seven. It is at this point that we must return to the relatively safer waters of the Byrom Collection.

There is among the drawings one of a seven-pointed star (figure 17). This is a far harder figure to draw than the six-pointed star because it requires the artist to divide the circumference of a circle at seven equidistant points. Even so this particular example is executed with typical precision. The front of the card consists of a drawing of a seven-pointed star rising out of, or lying on top of, two other concentric seven-pointed stars. The drawing is part of a series prepared with different degrees of complexity and related to what were believed to be attributes of the number seven. Both Fludd and the writer of *The Magical Calendar* (figure 18) drew on the teachings of the Jewish Cabala which lays great significance on number. There are echoes of the Cabala all through the collection. Here behind the geometric sophistication of the figure of a seven-pointed star lie traces of that tradition and its association of the number seven with Michael and the sun (see figure 18). Such traces can be discerned many years later in a number of manifestations. Byrom was a member of a discussion group which called itself The Sun Club. It met regularly and several of its members were freemasons. It was at a meeting of this very club that Byrom announced he was going to form a Cabala Club. One of the members of the Sun Club was Byrom's friend Martin Folkes, a freemason, a distinguished mathematician and successively Vice-President and President of the Royal Society. It would not be by accident that the group was called The Sun Club, nor that it met under the rooms where one of the first masonic lodges held their meetings. We know that now the sun in splendour is seen above the Master's chair in every lodge. St Michael may no longer be a part of the masonic pantheon but undoubtedly the solar associations which grew up around him have in a modified way been taken into masonic ritual.

Figure 17: Seven-petal rose (front and back).

Figure 18: *The Magical Calendar* published by Johann Theodore de Bry. (Adam McLean's translation of the Latin text.)

The Sun, the greatest shining planet, rules the fourth heaven. He completes his course in the fourth sphere in 365 days.

He commands:

Sundays	Sharp
Michael	Sulphur
Grammar	Golden Colour
Justice	Heart
Ruby	Right Eye
Gold	
Lion	
Swan	
The Sea Cow	
Heliotrope	
Fire	
Pure Blood	

Gisors and Templar London

It took thirty years of argument and litigation and two Acts of Parliament for the Hospitallers of St John to gain possession of the Templar lands decreed to them by the Pope when the Templars were suppressed. Indeed, many of the estates changed hands so often that the amount of land the Hospitallers finally took over in England did not represent what the Templars had owned. There seems to be evidence now that some Templar properties passed out of Templar hands in name only. Some of the Templar lands became part of the sites in Southwark where Elizabethan playhouses were built. Paris Garden, where the Swan theatre stood, had been part of the Temple manor. It is very likely that the site of the Rose theatre, which had been owned by Ralph Symonds, had been part of the same manor.

Symonds' widow had left the site to St Mildred's, Bread Street, rather than the neighbouring parish of St Mary Overy. This struck me as an oddity and made me wonder why a parish on the other side of the Thames should benefit from the site rather than the church close by. It was while in search of the background to these two churches that I turned to Stow's *Survey of London*. While reading his account of Vintry Ward I came across a name with distinct Templar resonances. It was the family name of Gisors.

In Vintry Ward there lived at one time a Sir John Gisors who had done sufficiently well in the wine trade to be knighted, become Mayor of London and Constable of the Tower.[17] He was mayor in 1311, just after the suppression of the Templars. His family mansion, Gisors Hall,[18] was in the parish of St Mildred and he evidently established, or belonged to, a prosperous dynasty, for we find another knight living a hundred years later and other Gisors prominent in the city as late as 1486.[19] Two earlier Gisors had rented the Cutlers Hall and other property in the parish of St Michael Paternoster. For this they had to pay rent to the prior and convent of St Mary Overy in Southwark. From this we can see that the church in Southwark had some claim of ownership of property in the parish of St Michael Paternoster, and by some strange quirk, or deliberate design, St Mary Overy (now Southwark Cathedral) contains a window designed in the form of a seven-petalled rose. Rose windows are not an uncommon feature of churches but the division into seven is unusual and the number, as we have seen, was associated in hermetic circles with St Michael.

The Gisors were the English branch of an old Norman family who had an equally long and intriguing history of their own. They took their name from a fortress in Normandy which had become a traditional meeting place between the Kings of England and France. Jean Gisors (1133–1220) owned land in Sussex and Hampshire. There is evidence that the French Gisors were Templars.[20] The family estates at Gisors had been put in trust with the Templars and Jean's grandson, Guillaume, is listed as a knight in France.[21] In 1188 Jean was involved in a famous dispute which took place at Gisors between the King of France and Henry II. It was in Henry's reign that the Temple Church was dedicated in London. Given the closeness of the English Gisors to Henry II and their kinship with the Norman branch, the facts point towards the English Gisors being Templars as well. It may well be that the English Gisors in later years after the suppression of the order made repeated efforts to acquire land once owned by the Templars.

In 1650 another fact can be observed which has implications worth considering. In that year Charles Radclyffe moved into a house in Rose Alley. By then the theatre would have gone, but Charles was a scion of the Radclyffe family whom we have already met. His grandfather had been a soldier whose bravery in battle was celebrated in an ode by Ben Jonson. Later the Radclyffes proved themselves to be staunch Jacobites. This Charles is related to the Earls of Derwentwater, one of whom, as we know, founded the first French lodge of Freemasonry and whose family show signs of being guardians of an esoteric heritage. One is left to wonder what it was that made a member of the family take up residence in Rose Alley. Could Templar loyalties be the reason?

The Gentlemen of Spalding

In 1710 a young lawyer from the Lincolnshire town of Spalding called Maurice Johnson founded the Spalding Gentlemen's Club. It was one of the early antiquarian societies that grew up at the beginning of the eighteenth century and both reflected and contributed to the intellectual climate of England. The formation of the Royal Society had led to an increasing emphasis among the professional and leisured classes on an attitude of enquiry into all natural phenomena. The Spalding society was one of the most successful of such groups and at its height could count as members some of the most distinguished men in the country. These included Sir Isaac Newton, Sir Hans Sloane, Martin Folkes and John Desaguliers. All were members of the Royal Society, and three of them were freemasons.

The topics of discussion at the weekly meetings in Spalding were not confined to local antiquities. The minute books of the society reveal the wide-ranging nature of their enquiries – the latest developments in medicine, Biblical scholarship, the scientific observation of weather, the history of architecture, mechanics. These I have extracted at random and each was an area of concern to Robert Fludd. It is not surprising that the Gentlemen of Spalding should cover topics which reflect some of the interests of Freemasonry. The Society was at its height around 1729. In 1732 Sir Richard Manningham, a leading physician, presented the society with a portrait woven by Le Blon's tapestry-weaving factory in Chelsea (figure 19). It is of the head of Christ, taken from one of the Raphael cartoons which Le Blon was at that time hoping to produce just before the whole enterprise collapsed and Le Blon had to flee. In fact Sir Hans Sloane, no less, proposed that Le Blon should be invited to become a member of the society. There is no record of his acceptance.

Figure 19: Head of Christ by Jacques C. Le Blon.

One can understand the curiosity aroused by Le Blon's new techniques. Colour was a topic which Newton had addressed in his *Optics* and Le Blon was certainly familiar with the great man's ideas. However, Le Blon's value to the members of the Spalding Society was not simply as the artist who had invented a new colour process. He had already shown himself as a valuable source of hermetic knowledge, and his proposer, Sloane, knew that. Byrom did not show any interest in the Spalding Society, although a number of his friends were members. He had direct access to Le Blon's knowledge of the de Bry family tradition in his own Cabala Club. Accordingly, he could afford to remain outside and pursue his own esoteric interests in a group which he controlled rather than belong to another run by someone else. Such an arrangement was more suitable to his own character and interests.

In this chapter I have endeavoured to show how a number of the drawings can be linked with Freemasonry as it developed formally at the beginning of the eighteenth century. At the same time I hope it is clear that many of the ideas expressed in those drawings belong to a wider and even older tradition. The drawings concerned with Colet, the ideas that derive from the cult of St Michael, the drawings connected with the wide-ranging ideas of Robert Fludd, provide a framework within which we can place historically some of the ideas which contributed to the masonic movement. That framework also provides a context for the drawings in their relation to other disciplines to which I shall now turn.

CHAPTER EIGHT

Measures of Time and Space

APART FROM THOSE drawings which are demonstrations of platonic solids, there are few signs of pure geometry. It is in most cases applied. I have dealt with its application in architecture and how it was used symbolically. Later I shall look at the relevance of geometry to the expression of philosophical ideas. Here I would like to concentrate on more finite areas – the application of geometry to technical instruments and in scientific experimentation.

It was clear that several of the drawings were concerned with a variety of mathematical instruments, the most obvious being a design for a compass. This group also contained a number of drawings bearing the names of the engravers or designers. These could be checked and studied in their historical context, mostly that of the seventeenth century. More important still, several of these named drawings had been printed. They were reproductions of engraved plates. There are in the collection other prints, but curiously enough they have no writing on them, nor do they appear to be either technical or scientific. All the same, it was evident that the mathematical prints belonged to a more orthodox tradition and I was able to check basic biographical facts with relative ease. The question of interpretation and evaluation was another matter, that I needed to discuss with experts.

At the Science Museum in South Kensington Stephen Johnston recognised the nature of some designs immediately. They were concerned with navigation and land surveying. One drawing in particular caught his attention (figure 1), bearing the name of Henry Sutton and the date 1661. Another member of staff immediately identified the subject of

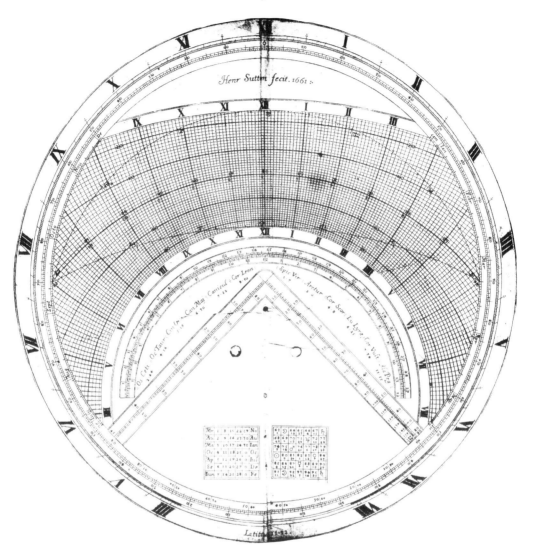

Figure 1: Double Horizontal Dial, 1661.

Sutton's drawing. She explained that it was a sophisticated sundial with a projection of the celestial sphere and constellations from the zodiac. The Museum possessed a model of it in brass, and she was delighted that a paper version had survived in such good condition. Having seen the diversity of the material, she added a word of caution. She could see me going round in a circle, spiralling from one authority to the next and returning repeatedly as each contributed a little more to the growing store of information. How right she proved to be!

188

Sundials

Henry Sutton's printed illustration was in fact a sundial in its own right, would have been sold as such in 1661 and could be so used today. Its correct name is 'Double Horizontal Dial' and it had first been developed in this country by William Oughtred in the early seventeenth century.[1]

The double horizontal dial is an adaptation of an earlier device of Oughtred's, the horizontal instrument. It had been known on the continent earlier, but Oughtred appears to be the first Englishman to develop it independently. He devised the double horizontal dial as a garden sundial and published his work on it in 1636. Various makers produced versions of it through the century. The horizon is projected as a full circle and provides the limb or border of the plate or paper. Around this limb are marked the hours in Roman numerals and within that border is a degree scale and then another border for the months of the year. A fixed pointer or gnomon would be supplied with the projection with two edges which would cast a double shadow as the day progressed. One shadow would fall upon the hours and thus tell the time, the other on the projected horizontal diagrams of the heavens. It is this part which differentiates the double horizontal dial from the normal sundial. It provides all sorts of additional information such as the position of the meridian and the time of sunrise and sunset for a particular day of the year. There are calendars and rules included at the bottom of the diagram for this purpose. These did away with the need for complicated calculations at a time when the mathematical skills of most people were relatively limited.

Oughtred was born about 1574/5 and died in 1660, the year before this particular print appeared. He was educated at Eton and King's College, Cambridge, and had a fine reputation as a teacher of mathematics, especially for his knowledge of algebra. Among his pupils was the young Christopher Wren. Henry Sutton, who prepared this version of the double horizontal dial, was known to be working as an instrument-maker in London in 1637 and died in 1665. He was the son of an instrument-maker, Baptist Sutton, and worked with a kinsman, William Sutton; at least they advertised their skills together: 'All manner of Mathematical Instruments either for sea or land are exactly made in Brass and Wood by Henry Sutton or by William Sutton.' 'Exactly made' was no idle boast: Henry's work was much valued for its precision, and he was also called on to illustrate technical manuals. His shop was situated behind the Royal Exchange in the City; William was closer to the seafarers down the Thames below Wapping. According to a checklist by A.J. Turner, only two of Sutton's version of the double horizontal dial are known to have survived, one in brass, the other in paper. The example once in Byrom's possession is a valuable addition to them.

However, as I studied the checklist, the first name to catch my eye was that of Sir Robert Dudley, who had apparently invented a horizontal instrument like Oughtred's at least as early as 1598! While Oughtred was experimenting with dials at Cambridge, Dudley had designed what he called an 'azimuth dial'. Sir Robert Dudley was the son of the Earl of Leicester and Lady Douglas Sheffield. In 1571 Dudley appears to have contracted himself to Douglas Sheffield, widow of John, 2nd Baron Sheffield. In May 1573 he secretly married her at Esher. Two days later a son, Robert, was born 'of whose legitimacy there can be little doubt' (Dictionary of National Biography). Other sources give different accounts, and the marriage itself remains debatable. Leicester is said to have offered Lady Sheffield £700 a year to ignore their relationship, but she refused the bribe. None the less he did not allow her to stand in the way of his courtship of the widowed Countess of Essex, Lettice Knollys, whom he married at Kenilworth in September 1578. The Queen learned of this marriage from the French Ambassador and ordered Leicester to confine himself to the Castle at Greenwich and threatened him with the Tower, but eventually allowed him to return to Court. Leicester's attitude to his son was characteristically ambivalent, denying his legitimacy yet sending him to Christ Church, Oxford, and naming him among his heirs. Leicester, as we know, had been tutored in mathematics by John Dee and had also studied the sciences. The young Robert evidently inherited much of his father's interests and skills. He was a fine horseman, a highly accomplished mathematician and an engineer of note. When he tried to claim his father's titles, Dudley naturally incurred the wrath of Leicester's widow and her friends, since he could not prove his rights without claiming that her marriage to his father was invalid. He was eventually driven into exile and settled in Italy at the court of Cosimo I, Duke of Tuscany. Cosimo's wife was the sister of the Holy Roman Emperor Ferdinand II, the patron of Thibault's epic work on fencing. Dudley had demonstrated his engineering prowess by draining the marshes between Pisa and the sea. The grateful Emperor created Dudley Earl of Warwick and Duke of Northumberland in the Holy Roman Empire, family titles denied him in England. The gesture was symbolic.

Leicester's scientific interests had been unusual for a man of breeding. Roger Ascham, Queen Elizabeth's tutor, had regretted that Leicester had preferred mathematics to the classics, but Leicester's patronage played an important part in the growth of science and technical knowledge in Elizabeth's reign. In his magnificent riverside palace he collected models of ships, fortifications, compasses, astronomical instruments. All these interests are reflected in this part of the Byrom Collection. In England

James I rejected Robert Dudley's offer to design ships. In Italy he was valued as Leicester's son. Although Leicester had died when the boy was only fourteen, he had ensured that he should be encouraged in the skills he himself valued. Denied the opportunity to use his knowledge in the service of his own king, Robert Dudley found it readily seized upon by Ferdinand II. The genuine achievements of this talented exile are another indication of Leicester's part in the transmission of knowledge represented in the Byrom Collection.

Compass Cards

The discovery of the loadstone was essential for the development of the compass. Loadstone is a natural mineral which was first found in the West at least six hundred years before Christ in the mountains of Asia Minor. The extraordinary powers of this mineral to attract pieces of iron gave rise to many legends about the phenomenon. The same iron ore was later found in other parts of Europe, and the Roman poet Lucretius (*c.* 58 BC) describes how the loadstone could draw iron to it, how it could be used to make bits of iron magnetic and how such magnets could repulse others. Eventually it was discovered that a piece of magnetised metal would, if suspended freely, point towards the north. From this moment the compass became a real possibility. It is first mentioned in the West by an English scholar, Alexander Neckham, in 1187. There are earlier references to it in China, but the Chinese compass was probably an independent invention.

At first the compass needle was suspended in water with the help of straw or cork, then it became possible to support it from a single pivot rather than float it.[2] When this stage was reached the bowl of water gave way to the attachment of a compass card on which the directions were marked. These points were originally wind directions. A rough approximation of the winds of the north, east, south and west provided the four cardinal points, which were gradually refined with half cardinal points, then to sixteen and finally the thirty-two points we use today.

Before the first true compass cards were produced wind directions were indicated by wind roses included on navigational charts. In the 1400s the four cardinal points were painted blue and the four half cardinals red to make it easier for navigators to distinguish between the different directions. Later the east was picked out with a cross. Then, to make it easier still, initial letters of the winds' names were added. Finally the fleur-de-lys came to be used from about 1500 to indicate north. The earliest known compass cards, as distinct from wind roses, employing similar devices date from 1551.

Among the drawings in the Byrom Collection there are at least ten compass cards engraved by different instrument-makers. Those which can be identified include four bearing the name John Henshaw. He was known to be working between 1696 and 1707 from his shop at the Hermitage, Wapping, in London's East End.[3] One of this set of four also bears the initials W.H., who was probably Walter Henshaw, his father (figure 2). It would appear that John used one of his father's blocks to produce reprints. This was not an uncommon practice. The card illustrates a number of the features we have mentioned. North is indicated by a very emphatic fleur-de-lys, the cross for east has become an ornamental flourish of two dolphins, and the three cardinal points other than north have been outlined more heavily to distinguish them from the half cardinals. There are also other, more unusual, features. In the late seventeenth century, there was a fashion for replacing the seven parts (apart from north) with triangular frames enclosing miniature scenes or engravings.[4] Here the three cardinal points have the full blown cheeks of wind cherubs. The four half cardinals are indicated by triangles which contain emblematic creatures representing the four elements: a cow for earth, dolphins for water, a salamander for fire, and birds for air. In the centre of the rose stands Justice blindfolded, the scales in one hand and a sword in the other. At the top of the fleur-de-lys are the initials J.L., prominent and enigmatic. These symbols recall the iconography employed by Michel Le Blon in his two engravings for Thibault.

Even more intriguing is the manner of highlighting a further sixteen by-points around the card. These were evidently inked in after the card was printed. The additions are not uniform, nor are they done with the precision which characterises the later pieces of hand-drawn work in the Byrom Collection. Finally and most revealing of all, the card has been deliberately and carefully cut from the centre across the N.E. triangle. From the same central point another line has been heavily drawn across the S.E. triangle to the limb of the card to provide a folding edge. This enables the flat piece of paper to be folded into a cone. The number of degrees removed from the total circle of 360 in this operation is 106, not a figure which leaps naturally to the layman's mind! On the back of the card various calculations show that this was the figure calculated by whoever cut the card. There are other sets of figures accompanied by comments such as 'this is Broken numbers and hard to doe' or 'again another wai better and very regular'. Evidently the compass card had been used to work out problems connected with circles and cones. This meant that at least one, if not more, of the cards had been used for purposes which were not simply navigational. Since Byrom was a schoolboy of fifteen when Henshaw gave up making his cards, it is likely that these mathematical investigations had been conducted by a previous owner and the card with its calculations carefully preserved.

The dates of the compass cards cover an extended period. One of Henshaw's cards contains at the centre the coat of arms of Queen Elizabeth (figure 3), another that of James I. It may be that one at least of these was another reprint from an earlier block. On that bearing the arms of Elizabeth there are just enough differences in the lettering to make one wonder if there were not an earlier John Henshaw working as an instrument-maker in Elizabeth's reign. This would be in keeping with the existence of another compass card in the collection which has written in hand on the back the name of Mr Gwinne. Another of the Henshaw set, figure 4, is a copy of an elaborate design by John Sellars, who worked for James II around 1671. This card displays the seven academic disciplines and another eight intermediate points represented by four queens and four seamen.

Among the rest is one by Jonathon Sisson who was a contemporary of Byrom. In his journal Byrom records visiting Sisson's shop. 'Thence we went into the Strand, called at Sisson's to see the parallelogram to write by, but it had been sent to my Lord Isla.'[5] This was the beginning of March 1726, and Byrom called again the following week. It was at the time Byrom was meeting with his Cabala Club and regular in attendance at the Royal Society. Sisson had a very high reputation for precise workmanship in the division of scales and his instruments were much prized. Even without an exhaustive study of all the cards it is clear they range from Elizabeth I to George I, and are part of the English contribution to the collection. They

Figure 2: Compass card.   Figure 3: Compass card with Elizabeth I Coat of Arms.

Figure 4: Compass card by John Henshaw (seventeenth century). The figures represent seven academic disciplines.

were owned by several people before Byrom and used in a mathematical as well as maritime context.

In the early days of the wet compass it was still necessary to re-magnetise iron ore needles because iron ore loses its magnetic properties unless specially treated. A loadstone was therefore an essential piece of a ship's equipment and its importance cannot be over-emphasised. With the growth of voyages of exploration, the skills of mathematical instrument-makers were increasingly called upon to provide better instruments. The work of men like Oughtred, Henshaw, Sutton and Sisson shows how the English rapidly caught up with continental craftsmen.

It was another Englishman, Sir William Gilbert (1540–1603), who discovered in 1600 that the Earth itself was a magnet, with one pole in the region of the Arctic and another in the Antarctic. Gilbert had already forged one career for himself as a successful physician, while he gained another for his knowledge of the sciences. His book *De Magnete* brought him international fame with praise from men of the calibre of

Galileo. It has been described as probably the first important work on physical science to be published in England.[6] His own house became a centre for men of like-minded interests who met regularly to discuss scientific matters. Gilbert's book was reprinted in Latin in 1628 and 1633 and this shows the continued importance of and interest in his work. Dryden declared that 'Gilbert shall live till loadstones cease to draw', and certainly the properties of magnetism continued to fascinate serious minds for centuries. James Hamilton, Lord Paisley, later seventh Earl of Abercorn, was one of the many scientists, amateur and professional, who turned their attention to the phenomenon. Paisley conducted a series of experiments into loadstones and published his findings in 1729 in a treatise, 'Calculations and Tables of the Attractive Power of Loadstones'. He presented a loadstone to the Royal Society. Byrom knew him well from these meetings. He records one such for 7 January 1731:

> Saw at the Society and spoke to Mr Sloane, Graham, Hawksbee, Graham Junior, Nesbitt; a long lecture about Chinese chronology, that no European could be told what the characters signified; I had much talk with Lord Paisley about their characters, he said it was not for words but ideas.[7]

Paisley like Byrom was a Freemason. He belonged to the same lodge as Desaguliers and James Anderson. The drawings bearing Lord Paisley's name and illustrating various weights are evidently connected with his experiments (figure 5). Paisley is a possible source for some of those drawings in the collection which have a scientific and purely mathematical bent. Another is a man whose name frequently occurs in the journals, and who was also a fellow of the Royal Society: Francis Hawksbee was present at the meeting just quoted and, like Byrom, regularly attended the Sun Club. He was another successful instrument-maker.

Byrom recorded many of the topics discussed at the Sun Club. He mentions one meeting in February 1726, a month prior to his visit to Sisson's shop, where he talks of 'the experiment with the needle which they tried there, but it would not doe'.[8] Among those mentioned in the entry for September 1731 is the name 'Graham' – a member of the Royal Society, a constant attender at the Sun Club, a man of great creative talent. George Graham was one of the finest craftsmen-inventors of the century, whose contributions to horology and astronomy were fundamental and long-lasting. He invented the mercury pendulum which is still used today and made improvements to astronomical instruments unsurpassed for nearly two hundred years. The elder Hawksbee invented an air pump which set the standard for over a century, and conducted some of the first experiments into electric light. His nephew gave the first lectures in

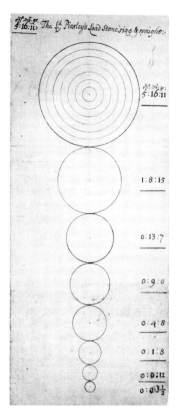

Figure 5: 'The Ld Piesley's Load Stone'.

London which were illustrated with experiments. Graham, in addition to his own achievements, played a part in helping to solve one of the last remaining problems of navigation – the perfecting of a clock that would keep time in the worst conditions at sea. This was the invention of John Harrison who, in 1728, invented a chronometer which would compensate for variations in temperature and the rolling motion of the ship. Graham not only gave freely of his advice but lent Harrison the money to enable him to make his first chronometer. Such, then, was the calibre of men in whose circle Byrom moved during the time he was pursuing his own interests in compass cards, magnetism and the mathematical implications of the instrument-maker's work.

To understand many of the mathematical drawings in the Byrom Collection demanded specialised knowledge. I invited Laurence Goddard, former Professor of Mathematics at Salford University, to look at the collection. Australian by birth, Professor Goddard had worked in British universities for most of his life and I found him delightfully unstuffy, with a warmth and intellectual energy which responded to the mystery of the drawings. Like everyone else I consulted, he had not seen anything resembling them. His first reaction was to associate some with architecture, probably ecclesiastical architecture. The hermetic material and its tradition meant nothing to him, although he could appreciate the notion that geometry could be used as evidence of a great architect of the universe, since the physical world contained so many examples of lines and circles, and its order at times recalled the symmetry of geometry. However, he had not come across such terms as 'the cube of space'. The drawings, he felt, were not really mathematical material as such but applied for the most part to buildings. He suggested a number of people and institutions which I might care to consult, including the Royal Society, the R.I.B.A. and the President of the British Society for the History of Mathematics, Dr Gratton Guinness.

Our discussions taught me several useful things. They also provided one of the most profound experiences of the investigation. In addition I became aware for the first time of just how unfashionable geometry now is in academic circles. Professor Goddard belonged to an older generation, counted himself lucky to have received a university grounding in the subject and lamented its passing from syllabuses today. He pointed out that while a number of universities now had courses in the history of mathematics, mathematicians had regrettably not always kept records of the *processes* they had employed in their work, but simply the *results* of their reasonings. Hence work in progress, which might have been of interest but was abandoned, became lost. Certainly the drawings in the collection showed a great deal of knowledge about straight lines, circles and points of intersection. They revealed a body of sophisticated theory necessary to produce work of this quality. The more he studied them, the more he became convinced that the people making these drawings were not just learning mathematical theory: they were using compass and ruler to work out points of intersection.

He responded superbly to the challenge of assimilating such a vast amount of material in our last meetings between March and September 1987. One of my great pleasures and lasting memories was his genuine amazement and delight at the workmanship. 'How did they do it!' was the exclamation that readily came to his lips. 'With only a compass and a straight edge to work with!' His delight and admiration in discovering something new was a tribute to his own intellectual humility. I was heartened by such a response. I felt that my own respect for the collection, however enigmatic the drawings were and despite the frustration they caused me, was not totally misplaced. I later took up his suggestion and wrote to Dr Gratton Guinness about specific examples. His immediate response was my first experience of a mathematical joke. '(Good Heavens!)² or (. . .)³ even!'

To him they did not seem to have any evident mathematical purpose, but he promised to discuss them further with colleagues. This he did at a meeting of the editorial board of the *Annals of Science*. Dr Guinness's colleagues also felt that the examples were primarily hermetic or occult, and not done with any theorems in mind. Perhaps the sample had been too narrow.

Platonic Solids

One of the groups of drawings is concerned with purely geometrical concepts and they illustrate the five platonic solids (figure 6). They are so named because they are discussed by Plato in his dialogue *Timaeus*, though three of them were originally discovered by the Egyptians, and the others by the Pythagoreans.

Geometry began with the Egyptians. Every year the Nile overflowed its banks and the flood water washed away the boundaries of the land holdings of the peasants. These had to be marked out afresh when the waters receded so that a land tax could be gathered. From this basic act of necessity grew a whole store of geometric skills based on the needs of the moment and tested by practical application. Although their skills culminated in such architectural miracles as pyramids, the Egyptians did not show any interest in geometry as an intellectual discipline. It was left to the Greeks to search for reasons, to theorise and deduce. It was the astonishing series of Greek philosophers and mathematicians who developed geometry into a system of rigorous intellectual training.

One of the most influential of these was Pythagoras. He was born in Samos in 580 BC, but settled in southern Italy where he founded his own school of mathematicians. He and his followers formed something like a brotherhood and appeared at first to work in secret. Since they shared their discoveries with each other, it is not always possible to attribute particular discoveries to an individual, but certainly Plato was greatly influenced by their work. The Pythagoreans introduced ethical and moral concepts into their teachings, and developed a highly complex theory of number symbolism. Although some of these ideas today seem bizarre, the geometrical skills of the Pythagoreans were of the highest

Figure 6: Platonic solids.

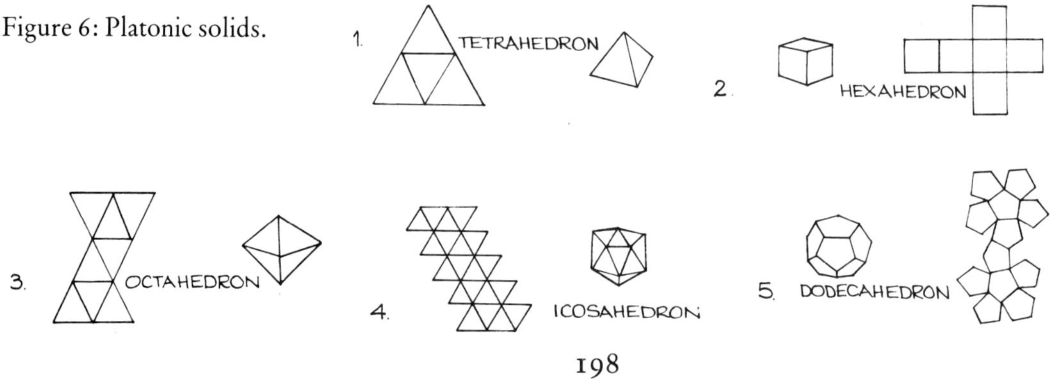

order. They were the first to prove that the earth is a sphere. They also discovered the two additional regular solids – the dodecahedron, which has twelve equal faces each shaped like a pentagon, and the icosahedron, a figure enclosed by twenty equal and equilateral triangles (figure 7).

The other three solids are the cube, the tetrahedron or pyramid, which is a solid enclosed by four equal and equilateral triangles, and the octahedron, which is enclosed by eight equal and equilateral triangles. The regular solids are the expression in space of the square, triangle and pentagon. In the Byrom Collection the flat drawings show the 'net' from which these solids can be constructed by simply folding them together. Some of these 'nets' have already been cut to shape.

One of the important characteristics of the Pythagorean school was to see mathematics in terms of geometry. They envisaged numbers as figures. 1 is a point and 2 a line between two points. However a dot and a line can hardly be viewed as tangible objects. Three was different. Three was seen as a triangle constructed from three points: $\triangle$. It represented the first plane figure and consequently was the first 'real' number.[9] This led Plato to conclude that the triangle must be the basis of all objects because it is perceptible to sense, in other words all surfaces were composed of triangles. It is interesting to note in this context that on the 'net' for the dodecahedron (figure 8) the pentagonal faces have drawn on them their constituent triangles.

The five regular solids have been a source of fascination to mathematicians since their discovery, both for their geometrical properties and their innate beauty. In addition Plato related the first four solids (tetrahedron, octahedron, icosahedron, and the cube or hexahedron) to the four elements and attempted to accommodate the fifth (dodecahedron) in his theory. In so doing he set in train a stream of philosophical commentary, which was revived with the Renaissance. As was shown in Chapter Three, Pacioli devoted part of his treatise *On Divine Proportion* to a discussion of the solids, and Leonardo drew the illustrations. They have continued to engage the attention of philosophers and scientists down the ages. It is not surprising to find examples of them in the Byrom Collection.

A Question of Measures

One of the most interesting aspects of the drawings is the nature of the measures used in making them. Among the papers are two sheets which contain examples of measures (figure 9), one of which is an illustration from a book. The edges of the page have become worn with much use, but the number is clearly visible. Because of the unusual width of the page (46.5 cm) it has been folded down the middle, but that fold is unlikely to correspond with the spine of the book. The page looks

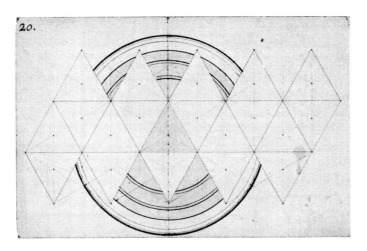

Figure 7: Icosahedron.

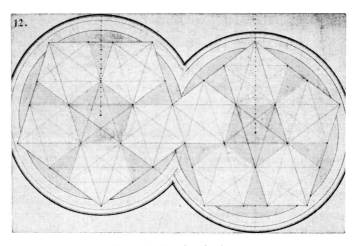

Figure 8: Dodecahedron.

as if it were intended to be folded and pulled out. This particular sheet was probably a printer's copy. Explanations of the scales are indicated in the margins together with numbers and degrees in recognisable progressions. Enough information is presented for the reader to be able to employ the measures. They are concerned with plotting positions of stars and planets, basic procedures in astronomy and navigation. The name of the illustrator, Henry Sutton, is included, so we can attribute a date and context.

Looking at the second measure (figure 10), however, we are faced with an enigma, for there is no writing or number to indicate what kind of measures we are dealing with. Yet here unmistakably is a ruler. The absence of such essential information must be deliberate. Either it was not thought necessary or its absence was to keep it secret.

The ruler contains four different scales of linear measurement. I have labelled the illustration for convenience.

200

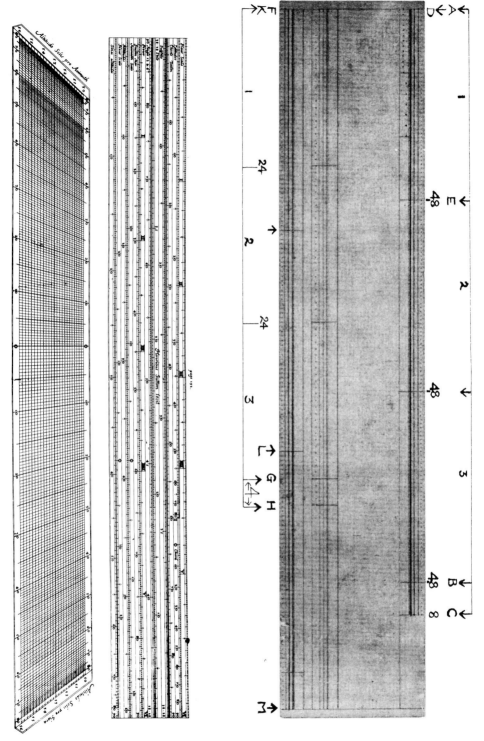

Figure 9: 'Henry Sutton fecit' measure for plotting positions of stars and planets, in navigation.

Figure 10: A measure.

1 A to B is divided into 3 equal sections, each divided into 48 units. At the end there is an additional measure B to C made up of 8 similar units.

2 D to E is equivalent to one of the three sections in A to B. It is itself divided into three equal parts: the first is marked out in 12 units, the second in 6 and the third is blank.

3 F to G is divided into 3 equal sections each subdivided into 24 units. G to H is an extra measure of 4 similar units.

4 K to L is divided into two sections of 48 units, but these are not the same as the 48 units in A to B. The last section L to M is damaged along the edge and an accurate count of the units is not possible.

Some of these measurements are commensurable with each other, most are not. None appears to correspond to our present metric or former standard measures. The mathematical instruments of Byrom's day were precisely designed and, as we know, readily available in London. This ruler bears little resemblance to those advertised by Sutton and his contemporaries. It is a private measure, happy to convey its information by the age-old method of dots. It appears to be employing either base 8 or base 12, and it is evidently necessary for the creation and interpretation of some of the drawings. Sutton's illustration demonstrates the more orthodox aspect of the collection, the ruler typifies the hidden element.

Defence and Self Defence

Among the 'mathematical' cards are a number which have the same format and appear to belong to a special series. They are all printed cards measuring approximately 7 cm by 10 cm. In the top right-hand corners they display a sign from one of the suits of playing cards. Three in fact: clubs, diamonds and hearts; spades are missing. At the top left on each card is a number in large Roman numerals. Any other numbers on the body of the cards are in Arabic numerals. It is clear that they have been cut from larger sheets, possibly containing duplicates or others from their particular sequence, but since so many are missing it is not possible to reconstruct a set. They could easily be carried in the pocket or even used as playing cards in some sort of game, but they are not idly decorated or symbolic. All have the appearance of being instructional in purpose and of dealing with various geometrical rather than arithmetical problems.

One simply identifies the variety of four-sided plane figures: the square, the oblong, the parallelogram, the rhombus and the trapezium.

Another is concerned with simple mechanics, a third with problems of figures with curved sides. I was surprised by the amount of information contained in such a small space. I was particularly intrigued by figure 11. This is the fourth in the set, and the chief geometrical shape strongly resembled a layout for a fortification system which I had come across in the work of Robert Fludd. Since geometry was the basis of all building, it did not seem totally out of place to find a drawing related to the art of military defence. In his *History of the Macrocosm* Fludd includes military science as one of the arts of man. Earlier still Pacioli had lectured on it. Not surprisingly, Fludd illustrates the geometrical basis of contemporary fortification with examples from Italy and the Netherlands. He also produced an ideal conception of a fortified town, a highly involved pattern of zigzagging walls and triangular extensions around a hexagonal centre.

Such designs were relatively modern. Plato, in *The Republic*, had argued that all cities should follow the example of Sparta,[10] which built its towns without any protective walls. Thus the Spartans were always alert and ready for defence. Man's powerful instinct for survival, however, has persuaded him to put his faith in turn in ramparts, stockades, walls, forts and castles.

In England we tend to associate defence with the Norman castle and Hadrian's wall, both legacies of foreign invaders. Our neighbours on the continent have had to be far more watchful over the centuries. Waging an epic war against the Spaniards for eighty years forced the Dutch to develop a system of fortifications so intense that the great military engineer Sebastian le Prestre de Vauban declared it would be easier to conquer the whole of Asia than take the Netherlands.[11] It was after Charles VIII of France had demonstrated in 1494 how easy it was to destroy Italy's mediaeval forts with his new guns that military engineers realised the need to provide a system of defence on geometrical lines. The old circular towers were replaced by more angular projections. These bastions eliminated the possibility of any dead ground which might give cover to attackers. This method of fortification spread across Europe, culminating in the great work of de Vauban in France in the seventeenth century. He was chief engineer to Louis XIV at the time when some drawings in the collection were printed. The geometrical principles for defending towns and cities are expounded at great length in *Les Travaux de Mars* by Alain Mannesson Mallet, 1673, and the reader should compare figure 11 with Mallet's illustration of the square bastion (figures 12 and 13). In 1711 Byrom's colleague Desaguliers published *A Treatise on Fortification*. Such ideas were then so current as to make their presence in a collection of geometrical drawings perfectly comprehensible.

Moreover, the Byrom Collection has links not only with corporate defence but individual self defence through Le Blon's engravings for

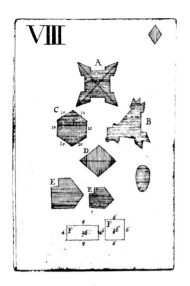
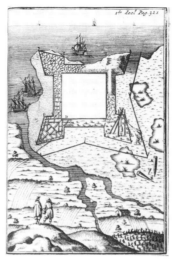
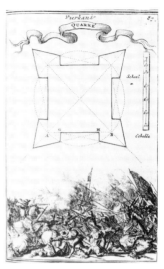

Figure 11: Concerned with fortification.

Figures 12 and 13: Fortifications. (Illustrations from *Les Travaux de Mars*, 1673, by Mallet.)

Thibault's treatise *L'Académie de L'Espée*. Judging by the plates in his book, Thibault's system was highly complicated but his demonstrations were equally successful. There is a touching simplicity in the way Thibault sets out to explain the philosophical basis of the book in his opening discourse. Writing in French, he begins by declaring the supreme perfection of the human body:

> Man is the most perfect and most excellent of all creatures in the world. In him one sees, amongst other signs of divine wisdom, such an exquisite representation of the complete universe in his entirety and in his principal parts that he has rightly been called by the ancient philosophers 'Microcosm', that is to say 'the little world'. For apart from the dignity of his soul, which is so very superior to all that is perishable, his body contains an epitome, not only of all that one sees here on earth, but even all that is in Heaven itself, representing everything with a harmony so gentle, beautiful and complete, and with such an exact correspondence in Number, Measure and Weights, that it relates miraculously to the virtues of the Four elements and the influence of the Planets, so that there is nothing like it to be found anywhere else.[12]

As he develops his argument Thibault summons Pythagoras, Plato and

Vitruvius as his classical authorities. Man's body is so well proportioned in its construction that:

> Architects both ancient and modern have not been able to find anything else in the world which could serve better as a measure according to which they should design the arrangement of their works than this model, man.[13]

Thus the Temple of Solomon was built to conform with the proportions of man. Noah was commanded by God to build the Ark according to the same formula. Pythagoras had called man 'the measure of all things'. Vitruvius, the great Roman architect, was the authority for all the new architecture of the Renaissance and the inspiration behind the great Gothic cathedrals and churches of Europe.

So Thibault starts from the basic premise of man as the microcosm, unifying classical philosophy with Christian precept. Le Blon's Zeus engraving sets the god in a geometric network of squares, circles and triangles and expresses many of the beliefs outlined in the beginning of the manual. Since he uses Pythagoras as one of the authorities it is not surprising that Thibault's geometry is endowed with some mystic qualities. To begin, the swordsman must draw on the ground a mystic circle with diameters and chords, enclosed in a square. To do this he uses his rapier as a pair of compasses. The rapier itself has to be perfectly in proportion to the stature of the combatants. After the points of intersection in the circle have been numbered, the contestants take up their position at the opposite ends of the diameter and then proceed to move to new positions precisely laid down. An incorrect move or a 'false move' exposes the fencer to a wounding lunge.[14]

The Twenty-four-hour Clock

Among the hand-drawn figures in the collection is one (figure 16) which bears no writing, no dates, but is devoted on both sides to drawings of a circle with many bisections. The front shows a number of concentric circles, the outermost of which is pricked out all along the circumference with dots, totalling 360 in all. The circle is bisected twenty-four times. The lines are scored not drawn. They cannot be compass points or wind directions since the number twenty-four does not tally. It is much more likely that the lines represent hours and the fifteen degrees between each hour line represents the time the sun would take on average to travel between one hour and the next. In other words the drawing is a basic representation of the face of a twenty-four-hour clock. Such clocks have a long pedigree. There is a particularly fine example in Wells Cathedral,

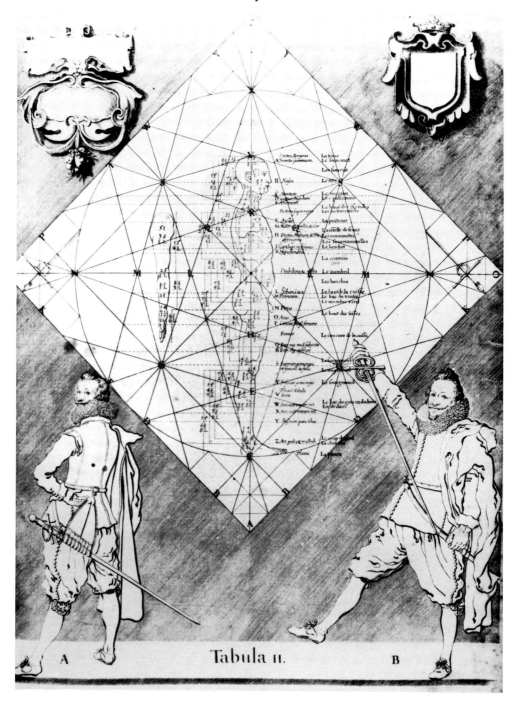

Figure 14: Gerard Thibault's treatise on the art of fencing, based on the proportions of man, 1628.

206

Figure 15: 'Fencing by Arithmetic':
Romeo and Juliet, Act III Scene I.

with its splendid astronomical clock dating from the fourteenth century (figure 17).

Oughtred's sophisticated garden sundial was an alternative way of telling the time. The clock, however, is more accurate, because it always runs at the same speed, whereas the sun's motion across the sky varies slightly in the course of a year, and the position of the sun varies with the place from which it is observed. Sundial time is noticeably different between different places, even in England. Bristol, for example, is about ten minutes behind London. It has long been realised that the orientation of the Elizabethan theatres was taken into account in their construction. In the past it was thought that, since the plays were performed in broad daylight, the stage would have to be so positioned as to take full advantage of the sun. Only relatively recently has it been proved that the theatres were built so that the stage received *indirect* sunlight.[15] Figure 16 has no watermark but it may well be that it is one of the early drawings made to calculate the sun's position during the day. This could then be included in later, more detailed drawings to help with the orientation of the theatres.

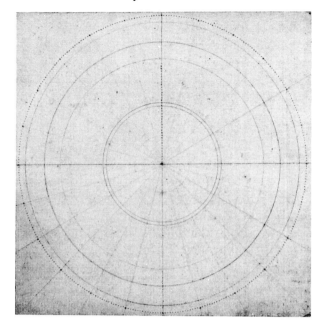

Figure 16: Twenty-four-hour clock.

Figure 17: Wells Cathedral, fourteenth century.

Among the sequences of drawings is one devoted to circles which enclose a wide variety of stars. They grow in complexity, starting with four-pointed stars and ending with nine-pointed ones. Each time the 360 degrees of the circle is divided with assured skill. Many stars are coloured to highlight certain features in the patterns they create. They can be appreciated as much for their beauty as for the geometrical truths they demonstrate. They appear to have been drawn at different times by different people, for there are at least three distinct tints of yellow and the variation in colour cannot be attributed to fading. Moreover, the quality of the card on which they are drawn varies. There is none of the traditional 'working out' which one might expect in theoretical calculation. They present the appearance of the finished article, and some look like models from which later drawings were to be made. Numbers in the top left corner indicate the shape of the stars on the card. Thus figure 18 is marked 6:12 and the drawing reproduces a six-pointed star within a twelve-pointed one. Each star is contained in a related polygon: the six-pointed star in a hexagram, the twelve-pointed one in a twelve-sided polygon. The regularity of such a relationship is repeated like a unifying principle which demonstrates an inherent order.

Figure 18: Six-pointed star with elaborations.

Figure 19: '9 pointed star'. The most difficult to construct.

There are a number of smaller cards concerned with the details of the patterns at the centre of the larger circles. Again the stars vary in shape. Those with nine points caused Professor Goddard the greatest astonishment. He did not know of any mathematical procedure which would demonstrate how these drawings had been produced. Such a reaction from a man with his knowledge left me in awe.

Images of Science?

When I was assessing the scientific element among the drawings I returned to figure 20. This drawing is based on a figure from Robert Fludd's *Microcosm* which describes his conception of the universe (figures 21A and 21B). God the Trinity is represented by a triangle which encloses three circles. These are the three worlds which he has created and which were looked at briefly earlier. They are shown to overlap, and at the centre God is found once again. This is a visual way of saying that God has no beginning and no end. The point is emphasised by writing His name so that it can be read continuously around the inner triangle: Iod, He, Vau. All the symmetry, carefully contrived, represents the mathematical organisation of creation. The inclusion of names of musical intervals shows that the world is held together by divine harmony. The illustration is a highly compressed image of ideas which Fludd took from Greek, Hebrew and Christian tradition and wove together into his own philosophy.

For example, the triangle which is so important in this illustration harks back to Pythagoras and the association of number with shape. Plato, building on this idea, concluded that, below the surface of everyday normal perceptions, objects are made up of these theoretical shapes.

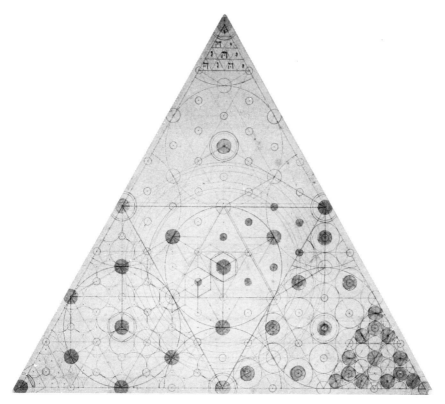

Figure 20: Microcosm.[16] Geometry in the service of Science.

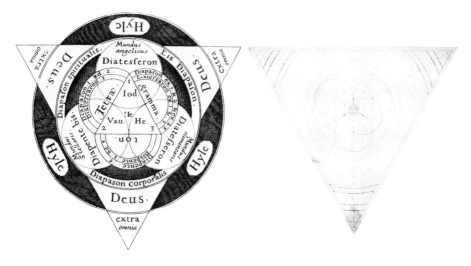

Figure 21A: Robert Fludd.[17]

Figure 21B: The threefold nature of God.[18]

This now strikes us as very odd, but is it more odd than our acceptance today that the chair we are sitting on is, in reality, made up of a mass of atoms or molecules? We can immediately justify the atomic theory by citing scientific evidence, but in so doing we must not discount entirely what Plato or other philosophers have written in the past. Many used mathematics and geometry to push forward the frontiers of knowledge to the stage where we think we are right to see the world around us, whether a desk or a diamond, as molecular in structure. It was Pythagoras or one of his followers who discovered that harmonic progressions are basically mathematical by relating the length of a string to the pitch of its vibrating note. It confirmed their belief that numbers were the elements of all things. Few would go so far today, but that differences in kind in what we perceive by our senses may be dependent on mathematics is an idea of fundamental importance to scientists. How else do we explain the difference between ice and water?

I felt, as I moved through the collection, that I was watching the development of scientific thought from the pseudo-scientific ideas of mediaeval scholars to the first genuine discoveries of modern science. This is understandable since the collection covers the period where one mode of perception begins to give way gradually to another. It can be seen in the careers of men like Newton and Boyle, living in an age of profound religious belief while laying the foundations for a mechanistic view of the universe. None of us can escape entirely the shackles of contemporary belief. William Gilbert when he wrote his great work on magnetism also made the first genuine distinctions between magnetism and electricity, but he expressed what he knew in the language of contemporary thought, in terms of 'effluvium' and the four humours. Translated into modern terminology Gilbert's ideas are still close to present-day notions.

Although many drawings lack explanation, the ideas they represent can be seen to develop. Figure 20 is an example: it is, I believe, a development of Fludd's theories, by an extension of his basic geometrical pattern with circles and triangles repeated in a sequence which draws the eye to the centre. The drawing should be compared with figure 22, a large equilateral triangle filled with a pattern of smaller triangles, starting with one at the apex and increasing with arithmetical regularity to thirty at the base. Each of the angles of the main triangle is bisected to produce lines which help in the construction of the central hexagon. In effect the card can be seen as an enlargement of the central pattern on figure 21B, a close-up of its 'heart' as it were. It is a classic demonstration of the Platonic idea of surface being made up of triangles.[19] Figure 22 is a print. There are two of these prints in the collection. Written in pencil close to the apex is the very early masonic sign of the three dots.

The same geometrical relationships are dealt with in innumerable

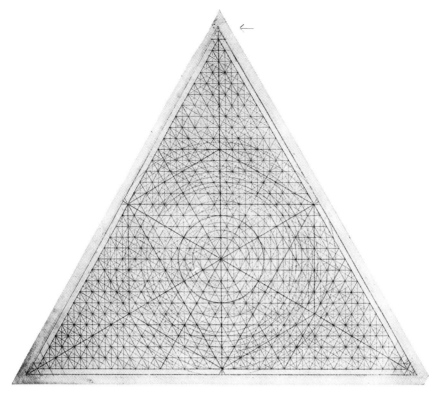

Figure 22: A study in a surface composed of triangles (Plato).

cards in the collection. Each of them differs to emphasise in turn some special feature such as the triangular element or the hexagon. Figure 23 is of particular interest. Here the card is shaped as a hexagon but the surface is again made up of innumerable triangles. Moreover the intersecting points have become changed to small circles. All the triangles and circles have been drawn by hand in red pen. In addition, certain of the circles have been coloured to produce a pattern within the pattern: the Tree of Life. The card has the appearance of belonging to those of the seventeenth century; it is again marked with the three dots of the early masons, linking it and figure 22 with some type of masonic movement.[20] However, the pattern of linked circles recalled to me representations of modern theories of molecular structures, such as the nitrate ion with its triangular structure and the phosphate ion with a tetrahedric structure. The different spatial arrangements displayed in models of simple molecules put a new gloss on ancient Pythagorean ideas about numbers and solids.

It was yet another Greek philosopher, Democritus, who around 400 BC propounded the theory that all substances are built from particles that cannot be subdivided. In 1666 Robert Boyle, in his *Origins of Formes and Qualities*, returns to this hypothesis and postulates one uniform kind of

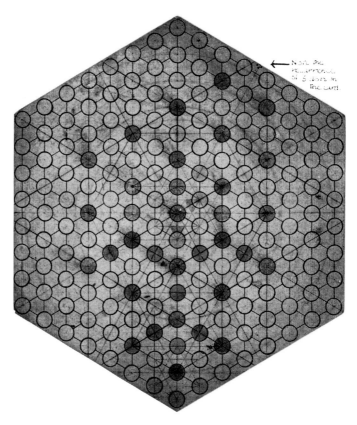

Figure 23: Hexagon – this figure demonstrates a variety of structures (see below).

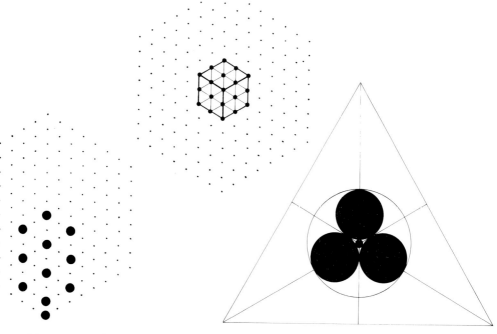

Figure 24: Hidden patterns: Tree of Life, atomic structure, and (right) a triangular structure of atoms.[21]

matter. He sees the visible world in terms of moving atoms and accounts for the diversity of substance by the variety of ways in which the atoms are grouped. This is in keeping with much of modern physics. Could the hexagon in figure 23 be an attempt to illustrate such a concept? If so, how was one to account for the Tree of Life inscribed into the pattern? The fusion of ideas from the Christian Cabala and new scientific speculation seemed to point to a date around the time of Boyle's work. Boyle was a devoted Protestant. While in scientific matters he proceeded by strict reasoning, he was also very much aware of the limitations of reason. Did someone who knew and sympathised with Boyle's work seek in this diagram to represent and combine the processes of a *mystical* search for truth about creation with new *scientific* theories about the structure of the created world?

This syncretic approach would be typical of the Royal Society in its early days.

CHAPTER NINE

In Pursuit of Truth

BOTH THE ARTISTS who were responsible for the drawings and the philosophers who inspired them were engaged in the pursuit of the truth about the nature of the universe, man's place in it and his ultimate destiny. The collection preserves this continuity of ideas in a unique form. Already in unravelling the mystery of the drawings the teachings of the great Greek philosophers have been examined. This survey has been limited to essentials, for the content of those beliefs is extensive and the subject of continuous and detailed study. Along the road of my investigations I have met a procession of figures, to each of whom I have been able to allot a part of the collection. Although their contributions are different, they have much in common. To understand the drawings better it is necessary now to look at two sets of ideas which coloured the beliefs of many Renaissance scholars and thinkers, particularly those belonging to the esoteric tradition: the Corpus Hermeticum and the Cabala.

Corpus Hermeticum

Cosimo de' Medici (1389–1464) used the enormous wealth created by his father, Giovanni, and his own business interests to gain control of Florence, which he then set about turning into the greatest centre of learning and art in Europe. He encouraged painting and sculpture, spent lavishly building churches and palaces, financed the first public library and set up an academy for the study of Plato and the Greek philosophers. In 1463 he ordered the translation of a group of Greek texts known as the Corpus Hermeticum. These were supposed to have been written by an Egyptian philosopher, Hermes Trismegistus, a shadowy figure who derived ultimately from the Egyptian god of learning and medicine. It was believed that Hermes had written his works before Plato, and that Plato acquired many of his ideas from studying the texts during his stay in Egypt. Hermes was thought to have been a contemporary of Moses; therefore the ideas expressed in the Corpus were regarded with the same veneration as Mosaic law.

Marsilio Ficino, head of the academy, completed the translation of fourteen tracts before Cosimo died in 1464.[1] They were accepted as genuine for over a hundred years. Then, in 1614, a Swiss philologist, Isaac Casaubon, who settled in England, proved that the texts were written at different times between AD 100 and 300 by a variety of writers and contained a mixture of Greek and Jewish thought. This undermined the authority of the Corpus Hermeticum but ideas they contained continued to influence many writers. According to Peter French the writings fall broadly into two categories: the first and earlier group is concerned with astrology, alchemy and magic; the later is more philosophical and religious in intent. The central idea is that man should study the world around him to regain awareness of his own divine nature. The texts state that a loving God created man in his own likeness, but separated Himself from man because of some lapse or offence. (The parallel with the Garden of Eden is obvious.) However, by using his intellect, in a spirit of humility, man could rediscover the spark of divinity with which he was endowed. The pursuit of knowledge accompanied by faith is the means to self-fulfilment. This is set in the context of a world governed by the seven known planets which exercise real power. Superimposed on to this cosmology were the angels and archangels of Judaic tradition. These could be reached by contemplation and, through them, the 'first cause' of the philosopher, the 'great architect' of the masons, or the 'God' of orthodox Christianity. In many ways the texts differ radically, however, from those of Christian belief, especially in the emphasis on white magic and man's own potential divinity. This emphasis was obviously open to misunderstanding and could lead to disaster.

The Cabala on the other hand is a mystical tradition within Judaism, claiming to have originated with Moses. Central to it is the Tree of Life, which is an image of the attributes of God. There are a number of drawings in the Byrom Collection bearing this Tree (see figures 1 and 2). The divine attributes are ten in number; they are called the Sefirot and are all held in a state of perfect balance. This is expressed in the three columns of the Tree. The central pillar represents the principle of Equilibrium, the one to the right represents the active principle, the idea of Expansion, and the one to the left is the passive principle, the idea of Constraint. The starting point of the tree is at the top in the centre. From here the Divine Will manifests

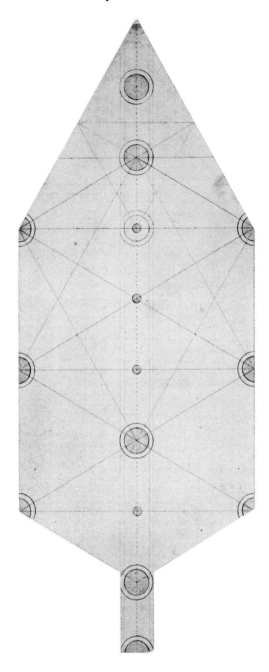

Figure 1: The Tree of Life.

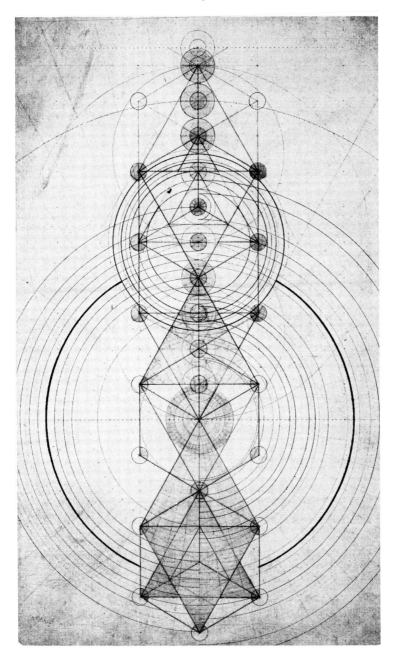

Figure 2: Trees of Life.

itself in a zigzagging progress first to the right then back across to the left and so on. If we follow this path we encounter each of the divine attributes in turn. These are named the Crown, Wisdom, Understanding, Mercy, Judgment, Beauty, Eternity, Reverberation, Foundation and the Kingdom. 'Science' is the on-Sefirah (Pas Sefirot) of Daat – see Chapter 6, p.134. The names should be taken as approximations for the original Jewish words, which have many layers of meaning. For example, the Kingdom (Malkhut) represents the presence of God in matter.[2]

The Cabala was an oral tradition which therefore developed into a number of different schools, and the ten attributes, while constant, can be reinterpreted in other ways. They can be replaced by the Ten Commandments, and the pattern is a guide to personal obedience to the Almighty. They can be employed to illustrate the celestial hierarchy of angels and archangels. Around the basic pattern there grew a set of doctrines rooted in the twenty-two letters of the Hebrew alphabet. Cabalists delighted in producing highly elaborate meanings from different combinations of letters, and they used this system to wrest equally involved interpretations from the books of the Old Testament. Over the centuries the system was developed to present the most subtle and profound perceptions about the nature of God, the universe and man's place in the divine plan. It is still much in use today.

The Cabala presupposes correspondences or parallels between all levels of existence, spiritual, intellectual and physical. For example a tree can be divided into four parts: the root, the trunk, the branch and the fruit. This fourfold nature was thought to be repeated in man, whose body contained the four elements: fire, air, water and earth. There was a further correspondence with the four letters of the Tetragrammaton, the most holy name of God, YHVH, or Jehovah. Another correspondence was made with the four levels at which man was said to exist in relation to God. These are the level of the Will (Fire), which is the nearest to God, then came the Intellect (Air), the third level was Emotion (Water) and finally Action (Earth). Each of these levels or worlds contained the qualities inherent in the one before it. (The reader will recognise the similarity here with the ideas of Robert Fludd; his worlds owe much to Christian Cabalism.) Diagrammatically these four worlds can be represented on the Tree of Life by overlapping circles. There is in fact much geometry based on circles, triangles and the square in the Tree. It indicates important relationships, paths of interaction and patterns of order (see figure 3).

Christian Cabalism

The first Christian philosopher to attempt to take advantage of the insights of the Cabala was the Catholic Ramón Lull (1233–c. 1316) in Spain. He

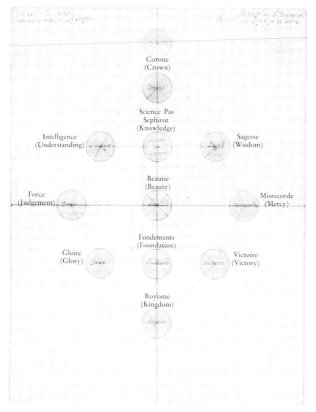

Figure 3: French names of the Sephirot of the Tree of Life.

hoped to blend aspects of the three great religions which were then to be found in Spain into one philosophic system which might help to unite the three communities: the native Catholics, the large influx of Jews and the Moorish invaders. But Lull wrote in Latin and did not concern himself with the linguistic elaborations based on the Hebrew alphabet. Christian Cabala can be said to begin properly with the Italian philosopher Pico della Mirandola (1463–1494), one of the brightest stars in the constellation of scholars and artists which shone at the court of the Medici in Florence. He studied the Cabala with Jewish adepts and produced a version similar to the Jewish system but one which still employed linguistic acrobatics. For example, he was somehow able to demonstrate to his satisfaction and that of many others that the name of Jesus was equivalent to the Tetragrammaton with the addition of a symbolic 'S' in the middle.[3] In so doing he presented the Cabala as predicting Jesus as the true Messiah. The details of his argument are complex but it was sufficiently understood to convert many Jews. Pico was also steeped in hermetic lore and thus there is a union of Hebraic and hermetic elements in Christian Cabala. Pico became convinced that it was possible through study of the Cabala to achieve a mystical communication with angels and through them with God. Christian Cabala is a typical Renaissance combination of philosophy, theology and cosmology and even some form of white or positive magic. Since the Cabala proved that the longed-for Messiah was Jesus, the use of magic through angelic powers was permissible.

John Dee

The work of John Dee was heavily influenced by Christian Cabala. He published the *Monas Hieroglyphica* in Antwerp in 1564 and dedicated it to the Emperor Maximilian II. It is thought that he travelled to Vienna to present the book to the Emperor in person. When he returned to England, Dee was summoned to Greenwich in June, where he instructed Queen Elizabeth in some of the mysteries of the book.

The title refers to a sacred symbol or hieroglyph which represents the idea of the ultimate, irreducible unit of being, the Monad (figure 5). On the physical plane that unit is material, on the spiritual it is God. The symbol is an epitome of Dee's beliefs after seven years of hard study. As the symbol is unfolded with ever increasing complexity the student would be instructed about the nature of the universe, and this knowledge would free him from the limitations of his physical existence and help him to achieve a union with the creator. At the same time the treatise contains half-veiled references to alchemical formulae. These were to be used in experiments to demonstrate on the material plane the validity of Dee's spiritual views of the universe. The real theme of the book is concerned

Figure 4: John Dee (1527-1608).

Figure 5: Frontispiece from *Monas Hieroglyphica*.

with the transformation of the human soul from its corrupt state to perfection.

Reading through the *Monas* and commentaries on it, I recalled Dr Ryan's warning at the outset of my investigations on the dangers of the journey ahead. Certainly the treatise is difficult and obscure. Dee made it deliberately so in parts to protect his 'secrets' from being misapplied. I shall confine myself to explaining as simply as I can the relevance of the hieroglyph to the Byrom Collection. There are two drawings (figures 6 and 7) which are obviously related to the monad. They include all the external features of his symbol except one, which I shall account for later. Both cards have drawings on each side, making four versions of the symbol. They display the skilful execution, symbolic colouring and geometrical development characteristic of the collection. The drawings on the card should be compared with the complete monad which adorns the title page of Dee's treatise.

The symbol begins with a dot or point. On the most basic level of geometry the dot is the starting point for any line or circle. The point

223

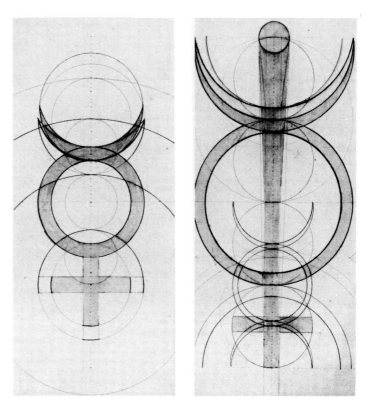

Figure 6: The monad.

Figure 7: The monad, with elaborations.

is also the centre of the circle from which the compass leg moves round to describe the circumference. Dee uses this as an analogy of the universe as interpreted by Ptolemy. The point is the earth, the circle around the point is the sun and also its path and that of the other known planets. At the top of the circle we see it is intersected by a crescent. This is the moon. The intersection of crescent and circle represents the proximity of the moon to the sun. Dee points out that although the moon is shown above the sun, the sun is superior in majesty to the moon and all other planets.[4]

The sun and moon rest on a cross, as one might expect. It is endowed with a multiplicity of symbolic associations. Dee then proceeds to dismantle the cross into different components to wrest various numbers from it. Where an untutored eye might simply see two crossed lines, Dee sees two straight lines and a point, thus obtaining the number 3. He then splits the cross into four right angles and obtains the number 4. With similar geometrical dexterity he produces the number 7 and even 8. These numbers are all important in the tradition of number symbolism which hermetic scholars inherited and developed from the Pythagoreans and the Cabala. With great delight Dee proclaims these hidden properties as proof of the comprehensiveness and power of his monad.

On Dee's title page we can see that the bottom of the cross joins two half circles. This is the sign for Aries and also the sign of the element fire. Dee also uses the four lines of the cross as symbols of the four elements and their respective compounds (dryness, cold, moisture and heat). Finally, the hieroglyph is contained within an oval shape, which we are told represents the alchemist's egg. At this point in the exposition the treatise becomes more obscure and the uninitiated is soon lost. Dee is evidently hinting at a formula which he wishes to protect from imposters. On a very simple level the oval shape represents the universe. Dee later describes how the disciple can construct the monad in its correct proportions. Dee's belief was that the monad brought an understanding of creation, and with that understanding came power over the created world.

The book was highly popular with hermetic scholars of the time. Among the writers influenced by it were Dee's successor Robert Fludd, the German mystic Jacob Boehme, and the alchemical physician Count Michael Maier. It is significant that there are drawings connected with all three men in the collection.

The modern reader may well tire of the obscurity of Dee's text, but that obscurity belonged to the hermetic tradition of secrecy. The Cabala also encouraged secrecy because of its claim to be part of a tradition that could be traced back to God's revelation to Moses. The early Pythagoreans had guarded their discoveries too. Mathematics had a long tradition of secrecy. In a papyrus dating from 1700 BC Egyptian priests collected a number of problems in geometry and arithmetic which they entitled 'directions for knowing *all dark things*'.[5] To the unlettered in England, mathematics in its simplest forms still smacked of magic. It is not surprising therefore to find Dee writing in evasive ambiguities. He genuinely believed that his monad was a key to knowledge which could be dangerous in the wrong hands. Even today we delude ourselves if we believe all knowledge can be openly available to everyone.

An interesting feature of the four drawings in the collection is that they omit the sign for Aries. If, as Dee explains, Aries is the sign for fire as well, the omission of fire from the drawings may reveal their purpose. No experimentation is possible without fire to heat the alchemical process, so perhaps the drawings were used for their purely spiritual and contemplative value. Without the sign for Aries the symbol becomes the sign for Mercury, the supreme hermetic sign.

Across the title page of the treatise Dee had written:

> Let him who does not understand
> either keep quiet or learn!

Apparently Elizabeth I, a woman of formidable intellect, told Dee she was prepared to learn and to practise, 'whereupon', he says:

> her Majestie had a little perusin of the same with me, and then in
> most heroicall and princely wise did comfort me and encourage me
> in my studies philosophicall and mathematicall etc . . .[6]

Perhaps there was something not a little heroical about Elizabeth's attempt to master the mysteries of the monad. Was she, I wondered, relieved to turn from its complexities to the encouragement of her learned doctor?

Dee's importance is not that of an original thinker, but of a great disseminator of knowledge. He did not make any new advances in mathematics but he saw its value both philosophically and practically. We are in his debt for encouraging so many technical skills in this country and he is now accepted as the single most important influence in the development of navigation in the Elizabethan age. He advised many leading seamen, including Sir Humphrey Gilbert and Martin Frobisher, and was on close terms with four of the backers of Drake's voyage around the world (1577–1580). One of those four was the Earl of Leicester.

As the leading hermetic exponent in England, Dee taught Philip Sidney chemistry. This was another of the interests Philip shared with his sister. According to John Aubrey, Mary, Countess of Pembroke, 'was a great chymist and spent yearly a great deal in that study'. At Wilton, the Pembroke country house, Mary employed her own private chemist, Adrian Gilbert, half-brother to the seaman Sir Humphrey Gilbert. Adrian Gilbert used to visit Dee at his home at Mortlake.

Around Sidney grew a circle of literary friends calling themselves 'the Areopagus', after the supreme court of justice in ancient Athens. The group included the poets Gabriel Harvey and Edmund Spenser and met informally to discuss literary topics, in particular the development of a carefully contrived form of verse, and the relationship of verse to music. In a letter to Spenser, Harvey refers to Dee's 'mysticall and supermetaphysicall philosophy',[7] so the two men were undoubtedly aware of Dee's hermetic ideas. It is possible then, as French suggests, that Sidney's ideas on poetry were influenced by Dee's ideas on music expressed in the *Preface*. In the *Apology for Poetry*, Sidney states his belief in the 'divine force' of poetry which arises from a combination of the 'exquisite observing of number and measure in words' and the poet's imagination. Both Dee in the *Preface* and Sidney in the *Apology* drew attention to the magical power of music as illustrated in such classical legends as Orpheus taming the wild beasts with his lute. The Pythagoreans emphasised the mystical value of music because of the mathematical relationship of harmonic intervals. Dee believed music enabled man to attain harmony with the worlds around him. Sidney made similar claims for poetry. He adds Poetry to a list of sciences and arts – including Music, Astronomy and Mathematics – all of which enable man to 'know, and by knowledge to lift up the mind from the dungeon of the body to the enjoying of his own divine essence'. This is the quintessential hermetic attitude. Sidney differs only in arguing that poetry is better able to achieve this than any other discipline.

Another great hermeticist known to Sidney was the Italian friar Giordano Bruno who visited England in 1583 and stayed for two years as guest of the French Ambassador. During that time he wrote three Italian Dialogues. In one, *Ash Wednesday Supper* (published 1584), he describes how he was visited by John Florio and Matthew Gwinne who took him to dine with Sidney's great friend Fulke Greville.[8] In the dialogue Bruno pays a handsome compliment to an unnamed Knight who was present, probably Philip Sidney. The following year Bruno dedicated a sequence of poems to Sidney. Sidney took the trouble to travel to Oxford to hear Bruno preach his hermetic philosophy and on his return visited Dee. Bruno, however, took his enthusiasm for the hermetic texts much further than Dee, and openly proclaimed the value of magic. (The Florentine scholars had rediscovered ancient texts on magic as well as classical philosophy and adapted them for their use.) Bruno had developed a philosophy which was a blend of hermetic and cabalistic doctrines which he hoped would lead to a reform in Christianity. His extreme views led to his arrest in 1600, when he was tried and burned for heresy in Rome.

What was the relevance of these philosophical ideas to the collection? Many of the names connected with the drawings were involved in various attempts to combine science and mysticism into theosophical systems which might have a wide appeal beyond the confines of orthodox Christianity. The Platonists of Renaissance Italy, John Dee and Robert Fludd in England, the Rosicrucians in Germany, each saw the divisions of Christianity as discordant with the natural harmony of the world. Each sought to resolve the dissonances. The philosophical content of the drawings seemed to be concerned with mystical experimentation arising from geometrical studies. For example, figure 8 should be looked at as consisting of two congruent squares. The bottom represents the material world of the earth, the top is the spiritual world to which man aspires. The similarity of the two reflects the hermetic maxim 'As above so below'. An extended Tree of Life leads from the bottom square to the top indicating that the two are connected. The top is crossed at intervals by a sequence of arcs which represent the wider cosmic order beyond the earth. The intervals between the arcs carry their own significance spiritually and harmonically. I believe the drawing is a commemoration

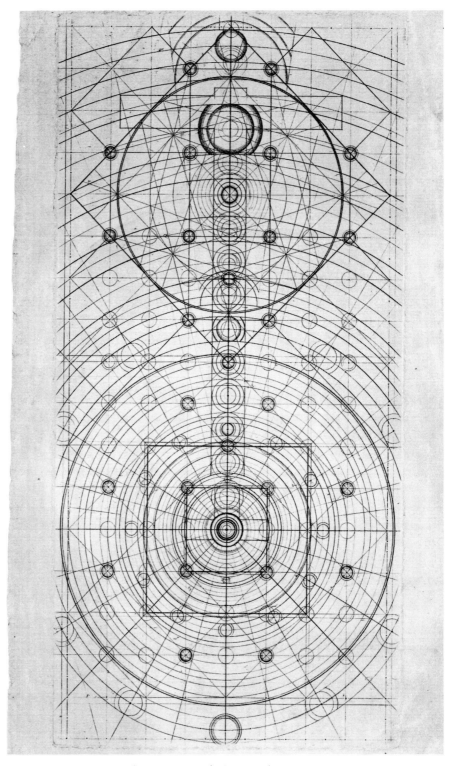

Figure 8: A study in sacred geometry.

of the Fortune Theatre. The frame of each square, measured by the 72 rule, conforms to the dimensions of the Fortune's frame, and the square enclosing the smaller circle in the top half corresponds to the Starrs mall at the Fortune. Built at the beginning of a new century, 1600,[9] it was the only square theatre to exist at the time and appears to have had a special significance, which Byrom, according to his own shorthand note (Chapter 4, p.91), was anxious to suppress. This drawing embodies the philosophical and architectural ideas behind its construction.

Robert Boyle

The geometry of the drawings required consummate skill. Were special instruments employed to make them? In March 1724/5 Byrom was enquiring among his friends at the Sun Club if they knew of a device called an arithmetical wheel. Perhaps that was the instrument used. None of Byrom's friends had heard of it. Those he asked included George Graham, Martin Folkes, Dr Jurin, the Secretary of the Royal Society, and Hawksbee junior. Given such an array of technical knowledge Byrom was surprised by their blank response. The wheel sounded like a device for drawing or making calculations. It had to be identified. The Science Museum referred me to the work of a Scotsman, George Brown, who in 1700 published a device called the 'rotula arithmetica'.[10] This was an early form of calculating machine which undertook the basic arithmetical procedures of addition, subtraction, multiplication and division. Brown was granted a licence to make and sell it in Scotland but not in England, and that could account for the ignorance of Byrom's friends. Later, Sir Robert Sibbald, a leading patron of science in Scotland, wrote to Sir Hans Sloane in an effort to get the patent extended to England. Sloane could well have been the person who mentioned it to Byrom. The device had nothing to do with the drawings, nevertheless it led me to a most unexpected find.

While I was tracing the wheel I received a letter from the Science Museum which mentioned a manuscript of geometric drawings in their care. It belonged 'to a collection, chiefly of geometric solids, which is thought to have been owned by Robert Boyle. This "Boyle Collection" is now part of a larger collection associated with George III'. The references to geometric solids recalled the drawings of regular solids in the Byrom Collection. Perhaps the two sets of drawings should be compared. In September 1990 I visited the Science Museum Library where I was handed MS 471. This is a small vellum bound book, rather like a pocket notebook. I had seen similar books used by Byrom for his own shorthand notes.

The manuscript book was made up of blank pages to some of which drawings had been stuck in the manner of the Schweighardt scrapbook.

Figure 9: Robert Boyle (1627-1692).

With one exception these accounted for the first twenty-five pages. There were one hundred and fifty blank sheets followed by another series of geometrical drawings. One page had two drawings on it but the rest had only one drawing to a page. Many were black and white, but a few were coloured in the same symbolic manner as Byrom's. The similarities were uncanny. This was partly explained by the fact that the drawings in the Boyle manuscript and companions in the Byrom Collection were prints with various additions made by hand to both.

The manuscript was a major discovery which I can only liken to finding the Schweighardt scrapbook in the British Museum Library, but the manner of the discovery was as surprising as the find itself. Two independent investigations converged so fittingly that John Dee would have believed it to be astrologically ordained, Jung would cite it as an example of synchronicity. Both books contained material which complemented some of Byrom's drawings. Whereas the Schweighardt text had been owned by Byrom's contemporary, Sir Hans Sloane, this new book appeared to be older. Robert Boyle (1627–1692) had died the year Byrom was born. The implications of this were considerable. It meant that the material in the Byrom Collection which was the same as Boyle's was now incontestably older than Byrom. I knew Byrom's work on such material crystallised around 1725 in the formation of the Cabala Club, but his interest obviously started earlier. Even so there was a gap of some thirty years between Boyle's death and Byrom's club. What had happened to Boyle's drawings in the meantime? Had they remained with his papers or had someone else been working on them? Moreover, when had Sloane's interest begun? Sir Hans Sloane was born in 1660 and died in 1753. He was thus thirty-two when Boyle died. Had his interest started with Boyle and continued with Byrom? There were noticeably fewer drawings in the Schweighardt scrapbook than in the Boyle manuscript. What was the common link between these three men? Given the perishable nature of paper I had been surprised that Byrom's drawings had survived so long. Paradoxically, the deliberate but caring neglect by his descendants had been their salvation. Sloane and Boyle had taken the trouble to put their drawings into books, no doubt because they considered them *worth keeping*. When I considered this fact, the common link appeared to be the Royal Society. All three were members. Boyle had been a founder member and was even offered the Presidency in 1680 but declined to serve. Sloane was President from 1727 to 1742.

Earlier in the investigations the librarian at the Royal Society had pointed out there were gaps in its records. Like so many institutions in their infancy, the Royal Society had lacked the administrative services to record, preserve and locate information about all its activities. There were the minute books and the Philosophical Transactions, the famous series of papers written by the Fellows. However, in the eighteenth century there was room for the knowledgeable amateur, in the best sense of the word, in the ranks of the Society. Certainly it took time to evolve into the exclusively scientific academy of today. Indeed today Byrom and others would not even be proposed for consideration as members. In addition to the problems of a society still in its youth, there were others caused by changes of premises. It was conceivable, therefore, that material brought to the meetings, discussed, perhaps informally, among members, even possibly left there for a while, could have been distributed for investigation. Alternatively it could have been lodged with a secret group within the Royal Society. Beyond question the drawings common to Boyle, Byrom and Sloane were one aspect of the collection which had engaged the attention of distinguished men of previous generations. I had come to this conclusion already about other material in the collection; the discovery of the Boyle manuscript confirmed it. Despite the problem of dating caused by the absence of watermarks on so many drawings, the 'Boyle group' also emphasised the continuity of ideas in the collection.

When I returned to Manchester I was able to make a detailed comparison between the Byrom drawings and photocopies of the Boyle book. A number of interesting facts emerged. Byrom had more drawings in the Boyle category than Boyle himself. Byrom also possessed more than one copy of a drawing. The Byrom Collection contained either a simpler or more complex version of drawings in the Boyle book, and together these showed a sequence. Byrom also had several drawings which were much larger versions of similar geometrical designs owned by Boyle. Byrom had two drawings attached to pages torn from a pocket book similar to the Boyle manuscript. Byrom had separate, narrow, oblong drawings which looked as though they were intended to lie alongside a larger drawing in the manner of one on page 4 in the Boyle book. Some of Byrom's drawings had been trimmed. Some were simply identical. It was at this stage that I noticed the same flaw in two of the drawings, figure 11 from the Byrom Collection and figure 10, which is page 4 in the Boyle book. They had been printed from the same plate.

It was essential to confirm with the Science Museum the provenance of the Boyle manuscript. Why were they so sure that it had belonged to him? In due course I was sent a copy of a handwritten inventory. It is entitled:

A List of Some Curious Mathematical Bodys, Figures Etc., from the Collection of the *Great* Mr Boyle . . . Supposed to be made two centurys Agoe, as described in a German book of that Date which was sent (with this collection) to be placed in His Majesty's Observatory at Richmond 13 March 1770.

The inventory included brass models of five regular solids, a load-stone, and brass plates of 'astronomical, astrological and mathematical delineations'. The German book, I later learned, was *Perspectiva Corporum Regularium*, written by Wenzel Jamnitzer and published in 1568. Jamnitzer was a distinguished German goldsmith and a master of his guild in Nuremberg. As such he, like de Bry, would be privy to the 'secrets' of German masons. He dedicated the *Perspectiva* to Maximilian II four years after Dee had presented the Emperor with his *Monas Hieroglyphica* which employs geometry to express his secret philosophy.

The tenor of the list attached to the inventory was mathematical and scientific. This was perfectly in keeping with the public career of Boyle, and reflected that part of the Byrom Collection described in Chapter Eight. I was not surprised, therefore, to see mention of the regular solids once more or reference to astronomical plates, but the most important feature of the Boyle drawings for me was that they were not concerned solely with geometry (which may account in part for the presence of Jamnitzer's book). Some of Boyle's drawings contained the pattern of the Tree of Life, which also occurs in the Byrom Collection. The most striking of Boyle's cabalistic designs had, superimposed on the Tree, the figure of Christ suspended as if from a cross. Solemn and mysterious,

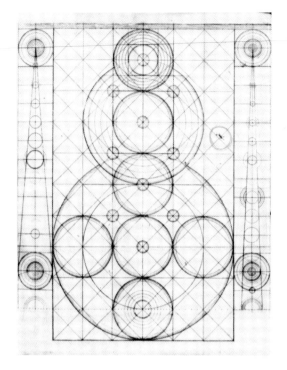

Figure 10: 'Manuscript 471' (Boyle) – the same flaw occurs in figure 11.

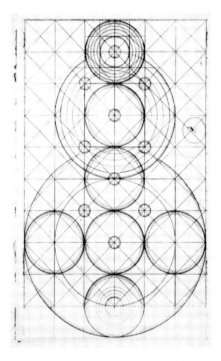

Figure 11: Byrom's companion piece, printed from the same plate.

this was the clearest example I had yet seen of the Christian element in the Cabala.

At the Science Museum I had been given one name connecting the manuscript book of Boyle to Byrom, that was Demainbray. This man had written to Byrom in 1750, but there is no mention of Demainbray in either Byrom's journals or letters. By 1750 Byrom had retired to Manchester. What had prompted Demainbray to write to him? Stephen Charles Triboudet Demainbray (1710–1782), as his name proclaims, was of French extraction. His family had sought asylum in England with other Huguenot refugees. He was eighteen years younger than Byrom and, after being left an orphan, was boarded with Desaguliers. He could have been the initial link with Byrom. At seventeen Demainbray went to Leyden University and then spent much of his university career at Edinburgh, Dublin, Bordeaux and Montpellier. While in Edinburgh he experimented with the effect of electricity in promoting the growth of shrubs. In 1750, the year he wrote to Byrom, he was appointed to give a series of lectures on mathematics and science to the Prince of Wales, the future George III. This appointment may have been the cause of his letter to Byrom. Perhaps Byrom's reputation among members of the Royal Society or some other group had inspired it.

I returned to Robert Boyle. The presence of a man of his stature in the collection demanded attention. One of the pioneers of modern science, he is universally known for Boyle's law, the discovery that the volume of air varies inversely with the pressure. This resulted from a series of brilliant experiments which also proved that air was necessary for life and that sound was impossible in a vacuum. Yet the drawings show that he was connected with the esoteric tradition which was part of the philosophies of Dee and Fludd. Where was the relevance of sacred geometry and the Cabala to Boyle's career?

After four years at Eton he was sent at the age of twelve to a private tutor in Geneva and at fifteen was in Florence, about the time of Galileo's death, busy reading Galileo's *Dialogue on the Two Chief World Systems*. His precocious genius was already showing an interest in cosmology. It has been claimed that Boyle pursued esoteric studies on the continent. Certainly Florence was an ideal centre to do so. When he returned to England in 1644 the country was divided by the Civil War, his father had died and the family's wealth was depleted. His sister, Katherine, Viscountess Ranelagh, took him under her wing and remained his great support all her life. After a short while he settled at a family house in Dorset, where he began to assemble a private laboratory; for this he made several trips to the continent to purchase what he describes as 'hermetic equipment'.

Like Byrom, Boyle had a gift for language and, apart from the tradi-

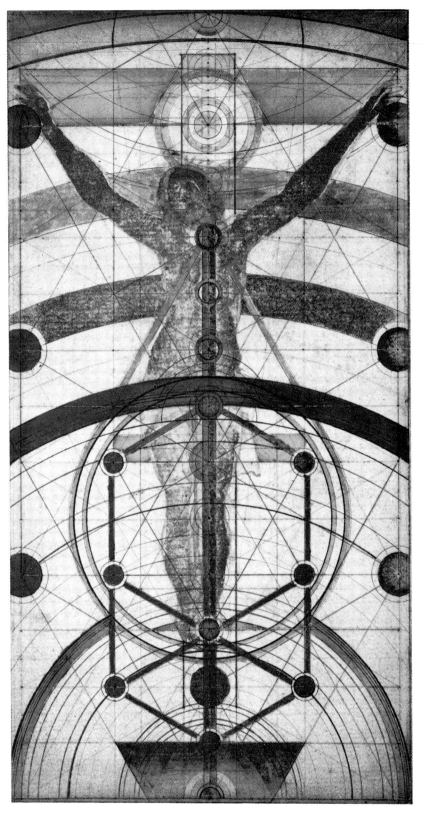

Figure 12: Christian Cabala, from Manuscript 471.

tional Greek and Latin, he also mastered Hebrew, Syriac and Chaldee at an early age. These last three would have enabled him to study hermetic source material, particularly the Cabala. There were family links with cabalism. Edmund Spenser had married a member of the Boyle family during his service in Ireland, and John Milton (1608–1674), whose poetry also contains cabalistic influences, was a close friend of Boyle's sister. The benefit of historical perspective gives a new importance to both these relationships with Boyle. The closer I looked the more natural Boyle's association with the drawings seemed. Throughout his life he was a devout Christian and his naturally religious disposition would attract him to Christian cabalism. This in no way conflicts with his status as the most revered and influential scientist of his day, on a par with Newton. The 1770 inventory was right to call him the 'Great Mr Boyle'.

Apart from his achievements as a chemist and physicist, Boyle wrote extensively on philosophy and religion, subjects which few scientists would attempt to cover today. He wrote much on natural theology, that area where religion and science met. He comes towards the end of a tradition which sought to explain Creation in terms of an all powerful and loving God, and at the start of a new age which chose to describe the universe in terms of scientific laws. As a scientist he insisted on thorough method and proper experimental procedures, and he applied the same criteria to the Christian religion. Whatever had been revealed in the scriptures had to be believed, but with the help of reason and experience.

Like Fludd, Robert Boyle believed the universe consisted of three worlds, but Boyle's worlds are easier to understand.[11] For him there was a spiritual world inhabited by angels and other intelligent beings, a second world, visible to our unassisted sight, which can be felt by our sensations, and a third world which such relatively recent inventions as the microscope (1590) and telescope (1608) were making visible for the first time.

Boyle is important to the collection for another reason – his association with the Invisible College, the forerunner of the Royal Society. It was Boyle who invented the term 'Invisible College', which was meant to describe a small circle of men meeting regularly in London. He uses it first in a letter to his old tutor in Geneva, Isaac Marcombes (written in October 1646). Boyle tells him how his time is occupied with the study of 'natural philosophy, the mechanicks and husbandry, according to the principles of our new philosophical college, that values no knowledge but as it has a tendency to use'. He goes on to say that Marcombes will be 'extremely welcome to our invisible college' if he should decide to visit England. In February 1646/7 he wrote to a friend at Cambridge describing the members of this group as 'the invisible or (as they term themselves) the philosophical college' who are

> men of so capacious and searching spirits . . . persons that endeavour to put narrow-mindedness out of countenance by the practice of so extensive a charity, that it reaches unto everything called man . . . they take the whole body of mankind for their care.[12]

The clear note of idealism here is strongly reminiscent of the ambitions of Samuel Hartlib, a Lithuanian refugee whom Boyle had met through his sister. Hartlib was a great friend of Milton, who had dedicated to him his essay on education. Before coming to England Hartlib had been a member of a mystical sect in Prussia which had drawn its inspiration from the Rosicrucian manifestos. He was a great admirer of Dee's *Preface to Euclid*, urging its translation into Latin so that it would gain wider international currency. It undoubtedly agreed with his own ideas on education. Hartlib hoped to set up an academy of learning which was utopian in aim and intended to be as much a bulwark to strengthen the Protestant state as to promote the advancement of knowledge and religion. Boyle, a keen Protestant, was very much in sympathy with his aims. Science and Religion were still partners in a marriage which had not yet disintegrated under the advance of rationalism.

Although Hartlib's dream was never realised, Boyle met regularly a small circle of leading men of letters and scholars at his sister's house in London on his visits from Dorset. Katherine was a woman of great intelligence and wide interests who won the respect and friendship of leading intellectuals. Members of her circle were the nucleus of the Invisible College which met each week to discuss 'natural and experimental philosophy'. These meetings started in 1645 and took place sometimes at an inn in Cheapside, at other times at Gresham College. Three of the founder members were appointed to academic posts in Oxford. These included Dr John Wilkins who became Warden of Wadham College. The meetings of this new breed of scientists continued at Oxford, and Wilkins tried to persuade Boyle to join him at Wadham with the promise that the college would provide everything he needed for his experiments. Boyle, however, preferred his independence and instead set up a private laboratory in Oxford. After Wilkins moved to Cambridge the group continued to meet at Boyle's lodgings.

The Alchemical Tradition

Although he was later to attack and demolish the alchemists, the starting point of Boyle's new science was itself alchemy. This has been defined as the attempt to apply the principles of mysticism to the physical world. The basic belief is, as exemplified in Dee's Monad, the essential oneness of the universe. There is also a correspondence between the spiritual realm and the physical world. What happens in one affects the other. The Pythagoreans considered that all things were made from different combinations of earth, air, fire and water, but these in turn were only different manifestations of one basic matter. It was not long before this principle was applied to metals. Since these were found underground alchemists viewed them as living things, seeds growing in the womb of nature. As with other forms of life, metals did not mature equally. Gold was the most highly developed and therefore the purest. The other metals descend in a scale of increasing impurity to the basest of all, lead. By analogy, gold became the symbol of purified man, cleansed of sin: lead became the symbol of all that is corrupt in his nature. We still talk of base metals and indulgently refer to a well behaved child as being 'as good as gold'. These are echoes of our alchemical past.

With time alchemists came to believe that metals were all composed of two elementary principles: sulphur and mercury. These terms were not used as we would use them today. In fact it is not always easy to decide what some alchemists mean by them, but in general sulphur meant that quality which accounted for the colour of a metal and its ability to burn. Mercury meant that property which made a substance malleable, fusible and gave it lustre. Roger Bacon (1220–c. 1292) was one of the famous alchemists who believed in the sulphur-mercury theory. Later it was extended to include a third 'element', salt. This was the quality which was considered to give solidity to a metal and enable it to resist fire. The combination of these three – sulphur, mercury and salt – in different proportions explained the different properties of metals. The vivid colour of copper was due to a predominance of sulphur, whereas the strength of iron was caused by the large amount of salt it contained.

The most important of these principles or elements was mercury, and it was thought that all metals could be reduced to mercury and then be reconstituted into gold or any other metal by adding the requisite quantities. The ideal to aim for was gold because that was the condition to which all metals aspired. It was only some flaw in nature which prevented this.

> All metallic seed is the seed of Gold; for Gold is the intention of nature in regard to all metals.[13]

On the spiritual level the philosophic alchemists argued that all men aspire to fulfilment through purification. So in his laboratory the alchemist sought to discover the process whereby a metal could be changed into gold.

That process was called the Philosopher's Stone.

The difficulty of finding such a formula made the alchemists blame themselves not their theories. Thus they had to lead a life of austere self-denial to be vouchsafed such sacred knowledge. Just as the metals had to be stripped of all impurities, so too had the alchemist. More and more the analogy with the spiritual level held, to the point where on the level of spirit the Philosopher's Stone becomes Christ. In this way the experiments of the alchemists can be viewed as attempts to seek a mystical truth by discovering the secrets of the physical world.

The pursuit of the Philosopher's Stone to purify metals led to the search for medicine which would cleanse the body of all its impurities and so ensure perpetual health. The Elixir of Life was to be found by mixing the Philosopher's Stone with suitable ingredients in a solution of wine. The most important ingredient inevitably was gold. Frequently the claim is heard down the centuries from doctors, alchemists and charlatans that they have discovered a panacea made from gold in some drinkable form, but those alchemists who claim to have discovered the Philosopher's Stone kept their formulas closely guarded secrets. When they wrote about them, they usually did so, like Dee, in language so obscure that it is difficult to be certain what they are saying. The claims for the transmutation of metal to gold are patently ridiculous, but even today gold injections are still administered by doctors for therapeutic purposes in this country. Moreover, on the spiritual level the analogy of the process, whereby man's corrupt and baser instincts may be raised to perfection, and the finite limits of material life be transcended by an immortality of spirit, is one that has engaged the attention of men of undoubted intelligence, skill and moral probity.

It should not surprise us, therefore, that such a sensitive, intelligent and religious nature as Boyle's should be attracted, at least at first, to the claims of the alchemists. Although his scientific work demolished those claims they still retained their attraction. In 1661 he published *Certain Physiological Essays* in which he first outlined his hypothesis on the nature of matter. He elaborated on this in *Forms and Qualities* in 1666. These essays together with *The Sceptical Chymist* (1661) laid the foundations of the new science of chemistry. Boyle believed that corpuscles were the only thing universally present in all bodies and backed up his hypothesis with prolific experimentation. After Boyle it was no longer possible to accept the four elements of the Greeks or the sulphur, mercury and salt theories of the alchemists.

Even so a mystery remains. Boyle's first biographer was Thomas Birch, Secretary of the Royal Society. According to Birch, Boyle announced his intention to set aside certain days (in his laboratory) for particular experiments –

of a more difficult and elaborate kind than those I have hitherto published and more of a kind to the noblest Hermetic secrets or as Helmont styles them 'arcana majora'.[14]

Concerning these experiments, he confessed that he could not be as open with the public as with his other work 'partly because, in spite of my philanthropy, I was engaged to secrecy'.[15] This is an astonishing assertion from a man who was accustomed to providing exhaustive accounts of his experiments.

The paradox is that Boyle always believed that the transmutation of metals was possible. In 1676 he informed the Royal Society that, as far back as 1652, he had been able to purify mercury to such an extent that, when mixed with gold in the palm of his hand, it generated heat.[16] This he thought was an essential preliminary to transmutation. He had kept the process hidden for over twenty years because, as he admitted, he was unsure about the wisdom of divulging it. He was anxious for the advice of fellow members, and got it from Newton. His advice to Boyle not to publish his findings clearly implied that he thought Boyle to be mistaken. Nevertheless Boyle chose indirectly, through an account supposedly related to him by a third party, to make known a process for changing gold into silver. Even more significant, he obtained in 1689 an amendment to an Act of Parliament against fabricators of gold. This amendment would now permit 'the art of melting and refining metals . . . and extracting gold and silver out of the same'. That Boyle should go to such trouble can mean only that he thought he was on the threshold of discovering the Philosopher's Stone. If that was so, then his work would have been for the highest motives only, to justify the ways of God to man. It is important that we should bear this in mind when considering the nature and purpose of the drawings in the Boyle MS471. They are closely connected with that alchemical interest, which represents in part the mystical side of the chemist and physicist.

Bartholomew Close

Boyle's interest in alchemy brings us once more to Bartholomew Close. In the church of St Bartholomew the Great is an alabaster monument to Dr Francis Anthony (1549–1623). He was a physician and alchemist who invented 'Aurum Potabile', a gold extract which could be dissolved in liquid and was said to be a cure for all kinds of diseases. The preparation made Anthony both famous and wealthy. He was able to buy several houses 'in St Bartholomew's', and when he died he left his potion, practice and property to his son, who continued to live there until at least 1653. John Anthony composed the epitaph for his father's monument:

Religion, virtue and thy skil did raise
A threefold pillar to thy lasting Fame
Though poisonous envye ever sought to blame
Or hyde the fruits of thy intention
Yet shall they all commend that high desygne
Of purest gold to make a medicine
That feel thy helpe by that thy rare invention.[17]

In 1616 Francis Anthony wrote a defence of the claims made for his panacea and dedicated it to Michael Maier (1568–1622). The same year Maier included Anthony among the dedications of his book *Lusus Serius*.

Maier's name appears on drawings in the collection, and so clues may be revealed in his English connections. Maier visited Anthony in Bartholomew's Close and also met Robert Fludd. Like Anthony he was a physician, and at one time he was court physician to Emperor Rudolf II, who was very interested in science and, in Prague, surrounded himself with astrologers, alchemists, artists, engravers and engineers. It was he who ennobled Leicester's son, Robert Dudley, for his services in Italy. Maier he made a count of the Holy Roman Empire. On the death of the Emperor in 1612 he appears to have come to England and spent considerable time here intermittently between 1612 and 1616. Elias Ashmole states that he came to live in England purposely that he might 'so understand our English Tongue, as to translate Norton's *Ordinall* into Latin verse!'[18] Whether that is so or not, he was here in time to congratulate James I on the betrothal of his daughter Elizabeth to the Elector Palatine. In November of the same year he was one of the Elector's household in attendance at the funeral of the young Prince Henry, son of James I. He was still here in 1613, for he gave copies of his book *Arcana Arcanissima* to Sir William Paddy, head of the College of Physicians, Lancelot Andrewes, Bishop of Ely, and Francis Anthony.

Maier's favourite form of writing was either the fable or the allegorical narrative similar to *Pilgrim's Progress*, though much more obscure. Profusely and beautifully illustrated, his books were published by the de Bry family, one of them engraved by Matthaeus Merian. These two names provide further links between Maier and the collection. Maier was also a Rosicrucian. In his *Symbola Aurea* (1617) he claims he first heard of the Brotherhood in England – no doubt from Robert Fludd. Fludd's first publications (1616/17) were tracts defending the Rosicrucian manifestos from attacks by Catholics. (Fludd was an Anglican, Maier a Lutheran.) When Maier sent a Christmas card to James I he chose a design which included a rose and a cross. He was highly regarded for the breadth of his reading and extensive knowledge of mythology, especially Greek and

Egyptian. For many later writers he became a source of material concerning Hermes Trismegistus, and his reputation lasted for much of the seventeenth century. Newton studied his books with care and left behind over eighty pages of annotations.

One of Merian's engravings for Maier's *Atalanta Fugiens* shows a philosopher pointing with dividers to a geometrical figure which consists of two circles, a square, a triangle and, at the heart of the pattern, a man and woman (see figure 13). It is entitled 'Monas or the One', a clear reference to the work of John Dee – yet another link between Maier and the collection. The geometry in Maier's engraving is reproduced in one of the drawings in the collection (figure 14). Maier's English connections, then, do provide a cluster of clues. He is linked with Dee, de Bry, Merian and Anthony. Anthony himself is linked with Dee, as the following entry in Dee's private diary shows. It is dated 30 September 1600 (Manchester).

> After departing of Mr Francis Nicholls, his daughter Mistress Mary and his brother Mr William, Mr Wortley, at my return to Deansgate to the end whereof I brought them on foote, Mr Roger Kooke offered and promised his faithful and diligent care and help, to the best of his skill and powre, in the processes chymicall, and that he will rather do so then to be with any in England which his promise the Lord bless and confirm! He told me that *Mr Anthony considered him very liberally and frendly*, but he told him that he had promised me.[19]

The Mr Cooke who here so touchingly protested his loyalty was an astrologer. He started as Dee's assistant as a boy of fourteen, and undoubtedly had great skills since both Dee and Anthony were anxious for his services. Dee instructed him in many of his secrets, but unfortunately Cooke was morose and had a violent temper. Even so, Dee did not want to lose him; perhaps because he had taught him too well during their alchemical experiments. Eventually, however, they parted company.

In the light of all these facts it is clear that there was an hermetic group in Bartholomew Close based around John Dee's kinsman, David, and Dr Francis Anthony. The original priory of St Bartholomew, an Augustinian house, was founded in 1123 together with a hospital. The priory was suppressed by Henry VIII in 1539 and plundered to replenish the royal coffers. The hospital survives as one of the great teaching hospitals of London. The priory had been large and prosperous, and many of the buildings were destroyed or converted to secular use. Part for a long time served as stables, the Lady Chapel became a printer's workshop and the north transept a blacksmith's forge, but even in decline its setting was colourful and cosmopolitan. The immediate neighbourhood of the priory attracted a number of distinguished residents. Sir Walter Mildmay

Figure 13: Maier's *Atalanta Fugiens*, published by Merian.

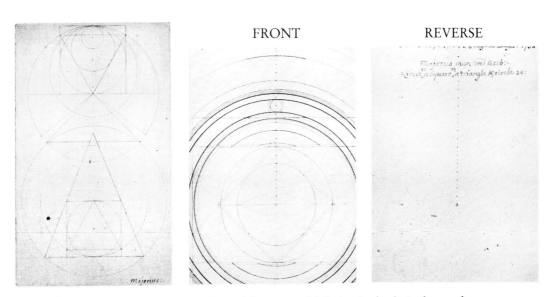

Figure 14: A geometric interpretation of figure 13, Majerius is the latin form of Maier.

Figure 15: Maier's 'man und Weib', 1732 – the latest date on any card in the collection.

(1520–1589), Chancellor of the Exchequer to Elizabeth and founder of Emmanuel College, had his London home there. He was a firm defender of the Puritans when they came under attack from Elizabeth's bishops. Another eminent householder was Sir Edward Cary, Treasurer to James I. In 1630 the French Ambassador was living in the Close with a suite of twenty. This may account for a colony of French citizens which grew up near St Bartholomew's, among them two sculptors, Hubert Le Sueur and Maximilian Colt. The State Papers Domestic record the deliberations of a commission set up to look into the use of some sheds as a workshop for purifying gold and silver. It was important enough to include Inigo Jones. The sheds, which adjoined part of the French ambassador's house, were moved to prevent the stench causing further annoyance to Gallic noses.

The lists of immigrants for Bartholomew Close reveal a large number of Protestants from Germany, Holland and Bohemia who chose to settle there. Mildmay often urged Elizabeth to champion the cause of the Protestants in the Low Countries against Catholic Spain. This may have played a part in making Bartholomew Close a refuge for them. The priory had been famous for centuries for the fair which was held each year around the feast of the patron saint. It brought the church considerable revenue since it was the chief cloth fair in England, growing in importance until it lasted for fourteen days. By Byrom's time it had fallen into decline, but at its height it attracted not only honest tradesmen but half the crooks and riff-raff of the city. In 1614, when Anthony was busy with his panacea, Ben Jonson used the fair as the setting of his comedy of the same name, and gives us a vivid picture of the low life of the area.

As we now know, David Dee had been appointed Rector in 1587 and, although he was removed from office, he was buried at the church. John Dee's grandson, Rowland, came to live in the street named Poultry, while Rowland's own son, another Rowland, lived in nearby Bow Lane. The street directories for 1677 list both men, and Rowland senior appears separately as a goldsmith 'in the Poultry at Bartholomew Close'. By then the family's fortunes had changed. In 1605 David Dee had been deprived of his living after litigation over property in the parish had caused resentment. Although the lawsuit may have provided a convenient excuse, it was nowhere put forward as the official cause of his dismissal. This remains a mystery, particularly since the same year the hostility of the Fellows of Manchester College drove John Dee to relinquish the Wardenship and flee to Mortlake. It looks very much as if David Dee had been a link between John Dee in Manchester and kindred spirits who gathered at Bartholomew Close, as if to a safe meeting place. After Dee left Dr Anthony took over as intermediary until he died. The two Rowlands' choice of livelihood is significant. The disreputable, esoteric pursuits of John Dee were replaced by the not unrelated but respectable profession of goldsmith. Ironically the two Rowlands would be living in Bartholomew Close at the time Boyle revealed to an incredulous Royal Society his own secret experiments with gold.

The influx of Protestants from the continent was not, of course, confined to St Bartholomew's: Huguenots settled elsewhere in and outside London, but some deliberately sought the precincts of the former priory. Among the aliens were 'Bartholomew Gasper and Gasper Gorris. Two ministers borne at Prague in Bohemia who lodged here a year and a half.'[20]

Prague – the name is full of resonances. Rudolf II had moved his court there from Vienna and made it the centre for esoteric studies in Europe. Maier lived there. Dee visited the Emperor. Under Rudolf the city enjoyed a liberal and enlightened rule. The Bohemian church, which had become almost a national church, had risen out of the ashes of the religious reformer Jan Hus, burned at the stake on 6 July 1415. Although a Catholic, Rudolf adopted a very tolerant attitude towards the Hussites, but when he died things changed dramatically. After the brief rule of Rudolf's brother, who was an old man, the throne passed to a fanatical Catholic, Archduke Ferdinand of Styria. He was determined to suppress the Hussite Church, and this led to violent conflict.

In August 1619 the Bohemians decided to offer the crown to Frederick Elector Palatine, now married to Elizabeth Stuart, daughter of James I. The Habsburg supporters confirmed Archduke Ferdinand as Holy Roman Emperor and as such a strong candidate for the throne of Bohemia. Frederick's attempt to reign was doomed. James I refused support even for the sake of his daughter. The other Protestant princes in Germany faltered and Frederick was defeated at the Battle of the White Mountain. He fled to The Hague where he lived for a while on a pension from the English and the Dutch. In Bohemia the Habsburgs took full revenge on the Hussite church. Both clergy and their adherents had to flee. Bartholomew Gasper and Gasper Gorris appear to have been part of that exodus. Despite the behaviour of James I, England was still a Protestant haven and Bartholomew Close, through Dee, Anthony and their continental contacts, a spiritual and intellectual refuge.

Gresham College

The history of Gresham College is significant to the collection for two reasons; first, because the name of Matthew Gwinne is written on the back of one of the drawings; and second, the college has a place in the emergence of the Invisible College. Sir Thomas Gresham (c. 1519–1579) was a successful financial agent who entered the service of Henry VIII as king's merchant. His main duty was to negotiate loans for the crown with merchant bankers in Germany and the Netherlands. In this capacity he also served Edward VI and Elizabeth I. His duties meant that he was based for much of his career in Antwerp and in the process made an enormous fortune for himself. He was more than a little unscrupulous, but undoubtedly a shrewd businessman. For a while he was appointed ambassador to the court of the Regent of the Netherlands and throughout his financial negotiations acted as a spy for Henry, and later, Elizabeth. The death of his only son in 1564 made Gresham reconsider the purpose of his financial ambitions. He decided to devote some of his wealth to the public good and built the Royal Exchange as a centre of business for London merchants in 1568. When he died in 1579 he left his London home and the rents from the Royal Exchange to found a college for the free instruction of the public. Seven 'professors' were appointed to lecture each day in turn on divinity, astronomy, geometry, music, law, medicine and rhetoric.

The lectures were to be given in English first for the benefit of anyone who wished to hear them, and then in Latin for foreign visitors. They were, however, formal lectures with no demonstrations or experiments in those areas which could be called science: geometry, astronomy and medicine. This was in keeping with the practice of the universities. The first lecturer in medicine was Matthew Gwinne, from March 1596 to September 1597. He left because he was irked by the stipulation that the lecturers should not marry. Other professors, not unnaturally, were to do likewise. While Gwinne was compelled to follow the age-old method of formal lecture, it is as well to remember that he was a friend of Sidney and met Giordano Bruno at the house of Sidney's close associate Fulke Greville. They discussed at length new Copernican theories of the sun-centred universe and evidently Gwinne was a supporter of the new learning, which, at the time, was received with contempt at Oxford. Copernicus had published his theories forty years earlier in 1543. Members of the Invisible College were still championing these theories a century later against disbelievers.

This does not make Gresham College the forerunner of the Royal Society, but it is clear that even when appointments were made from the two universities they were not all as opposed to the new learning as some scholars thought. Later, when enlightened members of the Invisible College were being appointed to professorships at Gresham, it provided them with a platform for the new learning, and incidentally a home for the Royal Society.

The Invisible College and the Royal Society

Francis Bacon (1561–1626), Lord Chancellor under James I, owes his place in the history of science to his foresight in arguing in his *Novum*

Organum (1620) the need for a more 'scientific' approach to the study of natural philosophy. At that time the method of enquiry common to all universities in Europe was based on mediaeval conformity to Aristotelian logic. Scholars and teachers followed a deductive method divorced from careful observation and analysis of facts, and with little or no experimentation to confirm such observations as they cared to make. Facts were gathered only to confirm preconceived theories. Few dared to challenge the correctness of the original premises. When they did – like Bruno – they were disbelieved.

It was not only hermetic thinkers who were ignored. The end of the sixteenth and beginning of the seventeenth centuries saw some remarkable advances in science. The discoveries of Galileo (1564–1642) helped to confirm the Copernican theory of a sun-centred universe, but they led to his imprisonment in Italy. William Gilbert produced his great work on magnetism in 1600 and laid the foundations of modern physics. Johann Kepler (1571–1630) made further advances in astronomy when he established that planets moved round the sun in ellipses, not circles. His three laws paved the way for Newton to discover the law of gravitation. For a long time Oxford and Cambridge ignored all these achievements and their implications.

It was in reaction to this outmoded attitude that the group of men whom Boyle christened the 'Invisible College' gathered together to reform the teaching of science in this country. They were meeting during the difficult years of Cromwell's Protectorate, before the Restoration of Charles II, and they had to proceed with discretion because of the opposition of the university establishment. Is it possible to establish their connection with the stream of knowledge which is represented in the collection of drawings?

This private group of experimental scientists was led by John Wilkins, Warden of Wadham College at Oxford, who was a compelling personality with tolerance and breadth of vision in a very partisan age. Although he made no scientific discoveries, he drew around him men of undoubted talent and inspired them with his intellectual energy. In 1638 he published *The Discovery of a World in the Moone*, in which he foresaw that man would one day be able to reach the moon. In the book he states:

> Twere a superstitious, a lazie opinion to think Aristotle's works the bounds and limits of all humane invention, beyond which there could be no possibility of reaching. Certainely there are yet many things left to discovery, and it cannot be any inconvenience for us, to maintain a new truth or rectifie an ancient errour.[21]

During the Civil War Wilkins was a Puritan, and in 1656 he married

Cromwell's sister. After the Restoration he became an Anglican and was later made Bishop of Chester. I was intrigued to discover that before his career in England he had been Chaplain to the Elector Palatine, the eldest son of the ill-fated King and Queen of Bohemia, whose court at Heidelberg had been the centre of much Rosicrucian activity. Theodore Haak, a German from the Palatinate, was a friend of Wilkins and a member of his group during an early meeting in London in 1645.

In 1648 Wilkins published *Mathematical Magick*, which, despite its title, has nothing to do with magic but is concerned with mechanical inventions. It is based on Robert Fludd's theories about mechanics in his magnum opus *Utriusque Cosmi Historia*, and Wilkins openly admits his debt to Fludd and to Dee's *Preface to Euclid*. John Evelyn, the diarist, reports that, in his rooms at Wadham, Wilkins had a hollow statue which was able to utter words by means of a long concealed pipe, and that he possessed other similar curiosities. The figure sounds very like the mechanical wonders which were constructed to decorate the castle and gardens of Frederick and Elizabeth in Heidelberg. These included a statue of Memnon which uttered strange sounds when the sun shone upon it. Both book and statue link Wilkins to the hermetic tradition.

Six years later another Puritan divine, John Webster, attacked the Aristotelian attitude to the natural sciences in a pamphlet dedicated to the Major General of Cromwell's army. In it Webster appeals to all who truly love the Advancement of Learning in the universities of Cambridge and Oxford, or elsewhere. He, like Bacon, argues the need for a new philosophy, but unlike Bacon he would include alchemy, astrology and a study of occult doctrines. This is a surprising indication of the survival of hermetic tradition into the Protectorate. Webster also supported the Paracelsian theories about illness and medicine which were championed earlier by Fludd, and praises Dee for his contribution to mathematics in this country.

Webster's proposals were denounced by another member of the Oxford group, the astronomer Seth Ward. He complained that the Dee-Fludd tradition relied on mysticism at the expense of experimental verification, and went on to attack the Rosicrucians. In this he was supported by Wilkins, who wrote a prefatory letter to Ward's book. This marks a change in attitude by Wilkins from his earlier acknowledgment of his debt to Dee and Fludd.[22] It shows the distancing of the Oxford Group as a whole from Dee and the hermetic tradition. In 1614 Isaac Casaubon had exploded the theory of the ancient authenticity of the Corpus Hermeticum. His son, Meric, delivered the *coup de grâce* to Dee's reputation in 1659 by publishing excerpts from his secret diary which recounts Dee's attempts to converse with angels. Scholars are not decided on Meric Casaubon's reasons for doing this. He claimed it was 'to do good and promote religion',[23] but his true motives are entangled in the web of religious divisions of the age. He had been a bitter Anglican opponent to Cromwell's party and lost his living in Canterbury. By 1659, with Cromwell dead and succeeded by his son, the country was weakened by further religious and political dispute. It may be that Casaubon chose this moment to embarrass the government for it was very anxious to suppress the diary but was unable to do so. Years later, in 1677, John Webster denounced Casaubon for his attack on Dee, and claimed that Dee was still 'the greatest and ablest Philosopher, Mathematician and Chymist of his age',[24] but the damage had been done.

In 1658/1659 the Oxford group moved back to London. They were still outside the main stream of academic thought in Oxford and still found it necessary to question the narrow prejudices of the Aristotelians. Laurence Rooke, one of the Oxford group, was elected to the post of Professor of Astronomy at Gresham College in 1652. Five years later he changed to Gresham Professor of Geometry, and Christopher Wren, an old pupil of Wadham College, became Professor of Astronomy until 1662. So, indirectly Gresham College did become a base for spokesmen of the new philosophy and a home for the members of the 'Invisible College'. With the return of Charles II the meetings at Gresham College continued on a regular basis. It was after a lecture given by Christopher Wren on 28 November 1660 that the group, now enlarged, decided to form a Society for promoting Physico-Mathematical Experimental Learning. That was the beginning of the Society which was granted its royal status in 1662.

By this time all that remained of Dee's work was his emphasis on the value of a utilitarian teaching of mathematics. The shift among the new scientists towards experimentation and verification sounded the death-knell of the hermetic tradition. Although as an institution the Royal Society rejected that tradition, individuals within it continued to pursue their own investigations for some time. An example of this can be seen in Boyle's work in alchemy. The mystical elements of that tradition (particularly the Christian Cabala) still exercised the attention of Boyle, and later Sloane and Byrom. Thus the collection is an important record of a continuity of interest from the Elizabethan age to the eighteenth century. Even as the interest in hermeticism and the Cabala declined, one quality was shared with the founding fathers of the Royal Society. Christian Cabalism started with Ramón Lull's attempt to use it to bind the three separate cultures of Spain together. That harmonising principle was a distinguishing mark of later religious hermeticists Dee, Bruno, and the Rosicrucians. The impulse was symbolised in the enlightened court of Rudolf II, whose Catholic faith did not prevent him from welcoming the Protestant Kepler, when he fell foul of the Catholic authorities in Austria.

The same ecumenical spirit is evident in the writings of Francis

Bacon: 'whatever deserves to exist deserves also to be known, for knowledge is the image of existence'.[25]

However, there is an important distinction here too. Knowledge is the image of existence but its acquisition does not make us the equal of God, as the hermetic tradition claimed. Bacon strikes the same note of piety which French notes in the Corpus Hermeticum:

> the entrance into the kingdom of man, founded on the sciences, being not much other than the entrance into the kingdom of heaven, whereinto none may enter except as a little child.[26]

The distinction is repeated: the sciences lead us to the kingdom of man, not the kingdom of heaven. This is one of the earliest signs of the ultimate effect of the new academic rigour, proclaimed by Bacon and the new scientists – the separation of science and religion. Bacon could not have foreseen this, for he was a devout Christian, disturbed like many by the divisions within the faith. Bacon hoped that Protestants and Catholics would join together in the advancement of learning.

By 1660, however, religious beliefs had become more polarised. Nevertheless Bacon's wish for tolerance and harmony was shared by the Royal Society. Its council included a Catholic as well as Anglicans and Non-Conformists. The official historian of the Royal Society, Thomas Sprat, explained that the members:

> freely admitted Men of different Religions, Countries and Professions of Life. This they were obliged to do, or else they would come far short of the largeness of their own Declarations. For they openly profess, not to lay the Foundation of an English, Scotch, Irish, Popish or Protestant Philosophy; but a Philosophy of Mankind.[27]

In 1663 the Society had been granted a Second Charter with a coat of arms and a motto taken from Horace. 'Nullius in verba':

> Ac ne forte roges, quo me duce, quo lare tuter,
> Nullius addictus iurare in verba magistri.[28]

'And do not ask me by chance what leader I follow or what god protects me. I am not bound to revere the word of any one master.' The secularisation of science began.

CHAPTER TEN

$\mathcal{J}$nfluences for Change

ELIZABETHAN ENGLAND WAS a rapidly developing world, building on the consequences of the Reformation and the spread of recently acquired knowledge which opened up new horizons geographically, politically and theologically. The protagonists in two of Marlowe's plays reflect the sense of enormous potential before man and the dangers awaiting its fulfilment: Tamburlaine in his desire to conquer the world, Faustus in his pursuit of complete knowledge. Dee, with his wide range of activities and his acknowledged position as the leading exponent of the hermetic tradition in England, in the end posed a similar threat to those in authority. Yet, at the outset of his career, Elizabeth was receptive to many of his ideas and was ready to make use of his abilities in her own statecraft.

Elizabeth I and John Dee

John Dee became involved in a programme to promote the Queen's claims to territories abroad, once supposedly ruled over by the mythical King Arthur. In 1576 he wrote his *General and Rare Memorials pertayning to the Perfect Arte of Navigation*. Published in 1577, it was intended as the first of four books to celebrate the British monarchy, but the others did not materialise. Part is made up of tables for mariners, but it also contains an argument for a strong permanent fleet for defence and expansion. In conversation with the Queen, Dee encouraged her to believe she was entitled to rights of land in Scandinavia and Greenland. She spoke to him about the matter again in 1580.[1] Dee himself is responsible for the original drawing of the title page for the book (figure 1).

Figure 1: Title page of John Dee's *General and Rare Memorials*, 1576.

It shows a seascape with a Galleon entitled *Europa* in which Elizabeth sits enthroned, her hand upon the tiller. The ship is being blown by winds sent by God: the Tetragrammaton appears in clouds at the top right-hand corner. Elizabeth is beckoned landward by the figure of a woman standing on top of a rock rising behind a fortress. She represents Opportunity. On the coast another figure, representing Britain, kneels, begging Elizabeth to land. There is much hermetic symbolism in the illustration such as the death's head and an ear of wheat turned upside down.

Two features in particular caught my attention. Once again the figure of St Michael appears, this time shown descending from the Heavens, the sun, his own kingdom, behind him. Sword drawn and bearing his shield, he is the vanguard of the ship, protector of the Virgin Queen and a reminder of the chivalric element in the order of things. We must remember that Leicester had been made a Knight of St Michael ten years earlier. Dee has deliberately placed the figure of Opportunity balanced on a geometrical solid. Her foot rests on a tetrahedron or pyramid which in turn rests on the rock below. The tetrahedron announces again the importance of geometry, its centrality in his own work, its use in navigation and thus, indirectly, in Elizabeth's expansionist dreams. Its presence reminds us of Dee's advocacy of applied mathematics and is linked with the tradition of the drawings and their examination of the Platonic solids.

Dee gradually lost favour before the end of Elizabeth's reign, and by the time James I succeeded to the throne several influences combined to destroy or distort his achievements. The witch hunts which had started earlier on the continent began to infiltrate to England. James had already published his treatise condemning witchcraft.[2] In it he denounced those men who believed that they could communicate with spirits by drawing circles and making conjurations. This reads like a condemnation of cabalistic rituals and an oblique but hostile reference to the *Monas Hieroglyphica*. Dee was easy prey for the witch hunters. When a fresh attack on him was launched in 1603, he appealed to James asking for those who accused him to be brought to court, but James ignored him. Dee's persistence with his experiments in 'angel magic' in the face of continued hostility looks more and more like the delusions of a man now desperate at almost any cost to prove the integrity of his life's work.

James I

In the circumstances it is not surprising that Dee's genuine achievements in mathematics and science were not acknowledged by Francis Bacon, who did not himself enjoy the full confidence of James I. Knowing of the King's abhorrence of witchcraft, Bacon may have felt it politic not to draw attention to the worth in Dee. James, despite his own formi-

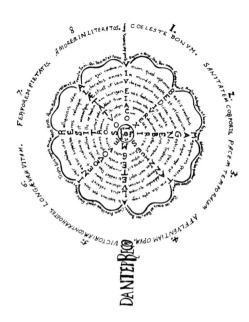

Figure 2: A Christmas Greeting to James I, 1612, from Michael Maier,
copied by Adam McLean.

dable intellect and his penchant for running into print on theological
and philosophical matters, was not interested in science. He never fully
understood the importance of Bacon's argument for a new approach to
scientific enquiry. When James was presented with a copy of Bacon's
Novum Organum in 1620, he sighed cynically that it was like the peace
of God which passeth all understanding.[3] Yet he could not have been
entirely unsympathetic to aspects of the esoteric tradition. How else do
we account for the Rosicrucian Christmas Greeting (figure 2) sent to
him by Michael Maier in 1611/12? James could not have been incensed
to receive it, for it has been carefully preserved and can still be seen in
the Scottish Record Office. Drawn on a parchment measuring three feet
by two,[4] it consists mainly of an eight-petalled rose covered with Latin
inscriptions. Encircling the petals are wishes for the King's health and
prosperity. It is unmistakably a Rosicrucian symbol, and Maier must
have thought it an appropriate compliment to pay James. In fact the
first of the Rosicrucian manifestos had still not been published when
Maier sent the card, although we have evidence that it was circulating in
private. I thought of Maier's own Rosicrucian sympathies, his friendship
with Fludd, the English Rosicrucian champion, and began to suspect
that Maier had tried to influence the King personally in favour of the
Rosicrucian ideals. James's reputation as a scholar was internationally
known. Maier may, mistakenly, have thought that James might support
the movement and be sympathetic to its idealism, its hope for a world
reformation leading to enlightenment and truth.

Another hint that this might have been so came from Robert Fludd, much of whose major work was published in James's reign. He dedicated the first part of his *History of the Macrocosm* to James in 1617, addressing him as 'Ter Maximus', a Latin echo of the name Hermes Trismegistus. To Fludd, Hermes was one of the most important sources of ancient wisdom, and he claimed that James had been 'my just and kingly patron all his life'.[5] How true this is, we cannot be sure. Fludd wrote two further treatises which he dedicated to James, but they were not published. This may be an indication of a change of attitude towards Fludd on the King's part. He may have declined the dedications, thus showing his disapproval. This royal indifference was one of the influences which contributed to a change in direction in applied mathematics, away from science towards mechanical technology in other areas – for instance the theatre.

The masque now became the favourite theatrical entertainment at court. It was the preference of the Queen, and during the reign of James I it reached its highest point of development, mainly through the combined talents of Ben Jonson and Inigo Jones. It became a complex and ornate spectacle, elaborately and expensively presented with music, dancing, poetry and singing displayed from within a proscenium arch in a sequence of breath-taking settings devised by Jones. He developed a striking innovation in perspective. On a slightly raised stage he arranged a series of wings painted with foreshortened views to direct the eye of the spectator up the stage and towards the backcloth which completed the scene and consisted of two sliding partitions. These could be drawn aside to present further vistas. The masques were lavishly dressed and contained lighting effects only possible indoors.

Starting in 1605, Jones worked with Jonson in an uneasy partnership, fraught with professional jealousy on Jonson's part. He felt offended by the assumption of pre-eminence by Jones as the architect-designer. Their differences came to a head in 1631/2 and Jonson was replaced by another poet, Aurelian Townshend, largely because Jones did believe the architect was more important than the poet. As if to make this clear, he decorated the frame of the stage for his new masque with two figures, one each side, representing the Theory and Practice of Geometry. Jones had travelled at least twice on the continent, studied theatres there, and read Sebastiano Serlio's treatise *On Architecture*, as well as Vitruvius. The classical principles enunciated by Vitruvius, and first introduced through Dee in the public playhouses, returned in a new and brilliant way in the inspired stagings of the court masques. The stagings demanded great technical skills, and the ingenuity expended on them involved the application to theatrical needs of the mathematical skills and techniques advocated by Dee.

Frances Yates drew attention to a caricature of Inigo Jones by Ben

Jonson in 1624 in *Neptune's Triumph*, where he likened him to a master cook who knows all the ingredients necessary for art:

> He has Nature in a pot! 'bove all the Chemists,
> Or bare-breeched brethren of the Rosie-Crosse!
> He is an Architect, an Inginer,
> A Souldier, a Physitian, a Philosopher,
> A generall Mathematician.[6]

This description together with an earlier reference to the cook's ability to make citadels 'with fifty-angled custards' can be applied to Robert Fludd and his encyclopaedic works. If that is so, then Jonson made the comparison fit because he felt Fludd had too great an influence on Jones. In other words Jonson sees Fludd as helping to encourage in Jones the importance of architecture's role, and thereby geometry. Thus, despite James's lack of interest in science, the technological skills were preserved and indeed promoted through the demands of the masque.

Elizabeth of Bohemia

James was succeeded by Charles I in 1625 but he is not remembered as either a patron of science or a student of hermeticism. He was not an intellectual like his father but an aesthete, a great collector of works of art for whom Michel Le Blon once worked. It was left to James's daughter and Charles's sister, Elizabeth of Bohemia, to influence briefly the course of the tradition Dee had set in train in England.

Elizabeth was much more open to hermeticism and played a positive part in encouraging certain aspects of it. All her life she was passionately fond of the theatre. British actors travelled to Germany to perform before her and even in exile she retained her own company. It was when she took up residence in Heidelberg with Frederick, however, that their joint interests in hermetic skills began to show. She had taken with her from England the French surveyor Salomon de Caus who had worked originally for her brother, Henry, designing gardens with a variety of wonders. He served Elizabeth and Frederick in the same capacity, transforming the gardens of their castle at Heidelberg, where he levelled part of the steep hillside on which it stood to provide a platform for vast formal gardens laid out geometrically in strict Renaissance tradition. Here he built grottoes to illustrate mythological scenes, musical fountains and mechanical statues. All were designed to give a magical effect to the surroundings, and, like the devices used by Jones in his masques, called for the highest technical skills. Like them they derived from applied mathematics. Both Elizabeth and Frederick had an intelligent interest in hermetic studies, and seem to have attracted like-minded thinkers to them during their brief spell of prosperity at Heidelberg.

For example, some time before 1614, Johann Theodore de Bry moved his publishing firm in Frankfurt to Oppenheim, possibly in anticipation of Frederick's return with his bride. Like others, de Bry may have had high hopes from the union of the Elector with the Protestant princess from England. Curiously, the end of Frederick's reign coincided with de Bry's resumption of publishing at his old base in Frankfurt. In addition, a large part of the works of Fludd and Maier was published either by de Bry in Oppenheim or by his relative, Lucas Jennis, at Strasbourg during the reign of Fredcrick and Elizabeth. This led Frances Yates to conclude:

> These publishers were bent on publishing quickly a large amount of material by these two authors and this must have been a definite policy – to publish material congenial to the Palatinate movement. Considerable sums of money must have been available to subsidise these publications.[7]

Figure 3: King James VI of Scotland, James I of England (1566-1625).

Figure 4: Elizabeth Stuart, Electress Palatine and Queen of Bohemia (1596-1662).

One of the books Elizabeth took with her when she moved to Bohemia was Raleigh's *History of the World*. Raleigh made a number of sympathetic references to the Hermetic tradition in this book, and believed in the power of natural magic. To him it was 'the wisdom of nature'. It was a process which 'bringeth to light the inmost virtues and draweth them out of nature's bosom to human use'. It was intended for the 'help and comfort of mankind'.[8]

Had Elizabeth and Frederick not embarked on the Bohemia adventure, their court at Heidelberg would undoubtedly have become a centre of learning. The city already had a great university and a magnificent library collected over generations by Frederick's family. Similarly, if Elizabeth had remained in England she would have been an influence of enlightened encouragement which could have ensured the continuity of the tradition in this country and perhaps accelerated the reform of scientific education. Bacon's pleas in this matter would certainly have met with more support from her than her father. *The Advancement of Learning* (1605) had appeared when she was still a child. In it Bacon deplored the stagnation of learning in the universities, and argued for an international approach to the study of the natural sciences, a brotherhood of scholars. I was interested to note that, in her exile in The Hague, Elizabeth received Samuel Hartlib, John Dury and Comenius. All three men were idealists, eager to set up new institutions of learning. By 1640 all three were in England campaigning for the reform of education, and each acknowledged his debt to Bacon. Although the outbreak of the Civil War disrupted their dreams, Hartlib stayed in England and became a friend to and influence on Boyle.

Commonwealth

The reign of Charles I was bedevilled by his high-handed dealings with Parliament. After his defeat in the Civil War and execution in 1649, power passed to Oliver Cromwell (1599–1658). Space does not permit a thorough examination of all the impulses moving towards a more technically minded and scientific age, but it is especially instructive to examine the careers of three men close to Boyle and the group which led to the foundation of the Royal Society. Each inherited the Baconian desire for reform in science, and was indirectly indebted to Dee. Their careers show the influences which made them change allegiances in pursuit of their objectives. One, John Wilkins, we have met before; the others are John Wallis and Jonathan Goddard.

John Wallis (1616–1703) was one of the great mathematicians prior to Newton. His interest in mathematics started early and, at fifteen, was for him 'a pleasing diversion at spare hours'. He himself says that at the time mathematics was still not an academic discipline 'but rather mechanical – as the business of traders, merchants, seamen, carpenters, surveyors of lands and the like'.[9] During this period this artisan class tended to be Puritan and they were the inheritors of Dee's exhortations on the value of applied mathematics. Wallis studied a number of subjects at Cambridge – ethics, physics, anatomy and medicine – and then took Orders. In the Civil War, while he was serving as a private chaplain, a letter in cipher arrived at the house concerned with the capture of Chichester. Wallis was able to decipher it within a remarkably short time and became a decipherer on behalf of the Parliamentarians. His future was assured. He first received a living in London and later by parliamentary decree was awarded a fellowship at Queens' College, Cambridge. On his marriage he returned to London, where he met Boyle.

Cromwell had a great respect for Wallis. He made him Savilian Professor of Geometry at Oxford in 1649. Like many others around him, Wallis cannot be wholly acquitted of dissimulation. It is easy, at this distance, to disapprove of men whose loyalties went with their preferments, but for them the ends justified the means. Wallis is said to have deciphered the personal correspondence of Charles I after his capture but not to have revealed everything to the King's enemies. This he made sure was known to Charles II, so he was still secure on the Restoration. However, he had already made his name as a mathematician. He was a genuinely original thinker and his book *Arithemetica Infinitorum* (1655) placed him in the front rank of scientists. Newton read it as a student and was inspired by its brilliance. Wallis later devised a method for teaching speech to patients who were deaf and dumb, which he demonstrated before Charles II, Prince Rupert and members of the Royal Society.

After the Glorious Revolution (1688) he continued to work as a decipherer, now for William III. The rewards appear to have been meagre indeed, for he was compelled to write to the Earl of Nottingham 'for some better recompense than a few words'. In 1697 he justified his ambivalent allegiances by saying:

> It hath been my lot to live in a time wherein have been many and great changes and alterations. It hath been my endeavour all along to act by moderate principles, between the extremities on either hand and in a moderate compliance with the powers in being.[10]

To those who insist that men around them must be 'one of us', this can never be enough, but it is for many an understandable and sensible accommodation.

John Wilkins (1614–1642) certainly changed allegiances to suit his career. From the outset he sought patrons whose influence would realise his ambitions. In this way he mounted to the service of Charles Louis, brother of Prince Rupert, son of Elizabeth of Bohemia, who was living in exile in England. Wilkins's adherence to the Puritan cause brought in due course the wardenship of Wadham College. In 1656 he strengthened his position in the Commonwealth Establishment by marrying Cromwell's widowed sister, Robina, and was allowed to keep his position at Oxford, despite his marriage. On the return of Charles II, however, that alliance proved a handicap and he was removed from office. His great charm and abilities had already won him many royalist friends and he soon received a series of church livings, culminating in the Bishopric of Chester. Charles II had a high regard for Wilkins, partly no doubt because of his high intellectual gifts, though the religious tolerance Wilkins exercised and encouraged would appeal to the King more.

Our third Puritan, Jonathan Goddard (1617–1675), was the most committed. After studying at Cambridge he joined the College of Physicians and caught the attention of Cromwell who appointed him physician in chief to the army. Goddard accompanied the Protector on his Irish campaign in 1649 and to Scotland in 1650/51. Like Wilkins and Wallis he was rewarded with a university post as Warden of Merton College in 1651, and also became a councillor of state. In 1655 he was appointed Professor of Physic at Gresham College. Charles II later removed him from Merton to replace him with a royalist. Goddard was not so pliant as his two colleagues. After that he concentrated on his work at Gresham. His house in London became another meeting place for members of the Invisible College and his laboratory a base for experiments conducted on behalf of the Royal Society. Goddard also produced his own secret remedies for various ailments. One of these was for use in apoplexy and fainting fits. By what one might term a stroke of irony he died in the street of apoplexy on his way home from a meeting.

The Millennium

The careers of these three men typify those of many during the Commonwealth. It was a time of great social, political and religious turmoil. At such times in history another phenomenon has been known to occur and that is the emergence of millenarianism – the tendency to seek hope and reassurance in the expectation of the millennium, the end or beginning of a thousand-year cycle linked with the second coming of Jesus Christ, or, in the case of the Jews, the coming of the Messiah. Many Puritans saw this as the only meaningful explanation of the upheavals they were experiencing. The year 1666, because of the very number, seemed ominously significant, the possible harbinger of a Messianic age. That year a Jew in Smyrna, Shabbethai Zebi,[11] proclaimed himself the Messiah, much to the consternation of Judaism. It was the climax of a growing fervour among orthodox Jewish cabalists. Some Jews apparently had earlier considered the possibility that Cromwell might be the promised Messiah and attempts were made to ascertain whether he could be of Jewish descent.

This coincided with the Jewish attempt to gain readmission into England. A leading figure in this was Manasseh Ben Israel,[12] whom I had first encountered in the career of Michel Le Blon. He was a leading cabalistic Jew, a member of the community in Amsterdam. He had made a great name for himself with a scholarly interpretation of some of the most difficult passages in the Old Testament. He also wrote a number of texts on the Cabala; one, *Nishmat Hayim*, dealt at length with cabalistic magic and had considerable currency among hermetic scholars. As we know, Michel Le Blon tried to sell some of Manasseh Ben Israel's cabalistic drawings to the Queen of Sweden and Manasseh corresponded with the Queen himself. He believed that the restoration of the Jews could not take place until the Jewish race had spread into every corner of the world. In 1644 he became convinced that the North American Indians were the lost tribes of Israel, and corresponded widely on the subject. He sent his son to England to negotiate with Cromwell on the readmission of the Jews, who had been expelled originally by Edward I in 1290. The Protector, a deeply religious man, convinced that he had been called by God into His service, listened with sympathy. There was still some resistance to the suggestion, however, and it was left to Charles II to allow the full return of the Jewish community to England.

Manasseh Ben Israel lived for most of his time in Amsterdam, and his beliefs influenced gentiles such as Abraham von Frankenberg, the disciple of Boehme (see figure 5). Cromwell gave him a pension of £100 and, when his son died in England, made a further grant of £25 to defray the expense of taking the body back to Amsterdam. Cromwell's generosity indicates a sympathy which sprang up between many devout Puritans and Jewish mystics. The Protestant work ethic, the idea of making the world a better place, leads naturally to the idea of improving it in readiness for the coming of the Lord. Such an atmosphere was conducive to the encouragement of the technological revolution. It is part of a complex web of influences leading to the promotion of learning. Education was seen as a necessary part in the salvation of man. That was its purpose. For the first time, in the Commonwealth, the state sees itself as responsible for universal education. Hence the activities of men like Hartlib and Dury and at a different level the Oxford experimental philosophers. The gradual emergence of science from the hermetic tradition is a transmutation as magical as any alchemist could wish for.

Although the Royal Society was granted its charter by Charles II (1630–1685) he cannot be regarded as a great supporter of science at a personal level. It was not his wishes which brought the Society into being but the energies and activities of men such as John Wilkins and John Wallis, and also the encouragement given to the King on their behalf by Sir Robert Moray, Secretary of State for Scotland. Charles was intelligent, tolerant and curious about a wide range of subjects, but most of his interests did not go very deep. He had not been trained to be an intellectual, though he enjoyed most fashionable pursuits, which now included an interest in the world around. Similarly, he may have liked beautiful objects but did not become a great collector. He showed no special interest in either literature or music. His mind was, if anything, drawn towards science, in particular chemistry and mathematics. It was not until the reign of George I that we find a member of a royal family deeply interested once more in those traditions connected with the Byrom Collection.

The Hannoverians

George I, Elector of Hannover, a grandson of Elizabeth of Bohemia, became King George I of England in 1714 at the age of fifty-four. He never took the trouble to learn to speak English, looked on Hannover as his real home and his new throne simply as a means of extracting money for his own pleasures. He surrounded himself with a German-speaking court, left his wife in prison in Germany on a charge of adultery and consoled himself with singularly unprepossessing mistresses. He died in 1727 when he was succeeded by his son George II. Neither of these men could be regarded as intelligent; on the contrary, both were stupid, obstinate and complicated. George II (1683–1760) had a good memory, a detailed knowledge of the pedigrees of European aristocracy and an abiding interest in his regiment of guards. Undeniably a brave little man, he was the last English sovereign to lead troops into battle, at Oudenarde. Apart from his mistresses, who were less ugly than those of his father, his favourite pastimes were gambling and listening to Handel's music. It is due to him that Handel settled in this country, but George II had no real interest in either art or sciences. Coarse-grained and brutish, he was nevertheless devoted to his wife, Caroline of Ansbach (1683–1737). Her character contained a streak of vulgarity, which undoubtedly appealed to her husband, but she was a much stronger personality and highly intelligent. In Germany she had been a friend to Leibniz, the great mathematician and philosopher, and, even after coming to England, corresponded with him regularly on philosophical matters. Caroline was genuinely interested in theological speculation and sympathetic to the mystical side of religion in an age of growing rationalism. She flattered the weaknesses of her husband to gain control over him, and was content to be the power behind the throne, almost working in collusion with Sir Robert Walpole in managing the King. Caroline was equally fond of George despite his infidelities. Separated from his mother at an early age because of his father's suspicions, George had received a cursory education and never managed to speak English fluently.

Since George I had left his wife in Germany, her place at court was taken by Caroline as Princess of Wales. Eventually she set up her own household, but even before then had created her own salon. Her husband lived to a routine of meticulous regularity which almost turned punctuality into a vice. Caroline arranged her own life accordingly. One evening a week was set aside for the discussion of philosophy and the elderly Newton was a frequent visitor to meetings at Leicester house, to which he could be carried in a sedan chair from his home in nearby St Martin's Street. Caroline, already fully aware of the intellectual stature of Leibniz, truly appreciated the measure of Newton's genius. She remarked that it was the greatest glory of the House of Hannover to have subjects such as Newton in one country and Leibniz in another. Some of these meetings centred on a discussion of Newton's greatest work, the *Principia*, and were attended by Dr Samuel Clarke, at that time Rector of St James's and a prominent philosopher, together with Bishop Hoadly. At Caroline's request Clarke conducted a correspondence with Leibniz on the nature of time and space and free will. The letters of the two men were read aloud at her gatherings and led to lively discussions. Yet she was shrewd enough to leave her serious debates to join in the inane festivities of her husband's circle when required.

At other times Caroline discussed the education of her children with Newton. This led him to reveal his unpublished researches into dating the events in ancient history. The Princess was sufficiently interested to ask for a copy of the work, which was still in an unfinished state. Newton organised the papers into a presentable form for her to study. This was the origin of *A Short Chronicle from the First Memory of Things to the Conquest of Persia by Alexander the Great*. Newton later showed it to a Frenchman, Abbé Conti, and allowed him to make a copy on condition that he kept the contents secret, because there might still be errors in it. Conti, however, broke his promise and showed the copy to several people in Paris, where, unknown to Newton, it appeared in print and became a source of prolonged vexation to him and the subject of controversy.

Newton had based all his calculations on the Biblical tradition of the date of Creation being 4,004 BC. The entire history of Western Man had to be accommodated from that starting point. In this he expended much effort and ingenuity, but inevitably the chronology is of little value now. One section of the text, however, is part of the background to those drawings connected with the recreation of Solomon's Temple. At the age

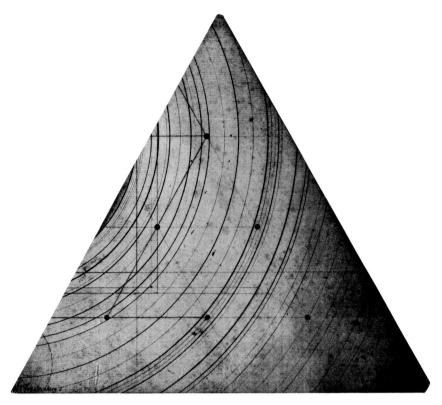

Figure 5: A working drawing bearing the name of Abraham von Frankenburg, disciple of Jacob Boehme.

Figure 6: A companion to the previous figure, illustrating Jacob Boehme's place in the pedigree of the drawings.

of eighty-one and in poor health Newton spent three years preparing an edition for the press but died in 1727 before it was finished. It was left to his nephew, John Conduitt, to oversee its publication with a dedication to Queen Caroline.

Newton and Leibniz independently of each other discovered calculus as a method of extending our ability to make different calculations. But although mathematics was the base from which Newton had made his great discoveries about the laws of the universe, he never completely lost interest in alchemy. Apart from his library of books on the subject, his manuscripts include one of 113 pages listing the usage of alchemical terms in authors he had studied. In 1669 he asked a friend at Trinity to verify some alchemical observations he had collected from the work of Michael Maier. Newton, as well as Boyle, was still sufficiently near to the hermetic tradition to sense the possibility that some alchemical truth might yet be revealed even while his own work in mathematics was beginning to put together a purely mechanistic view of the universe. Stukeley refers to a paper by Newton, which had been accidentally destroyed by fire, in which the great man had been working towards a mathematical explanation of elements as different geometrical groupings of a universal substance. Newton and Boyle both read the works of alchemists carefully while publicly denouncing them. The names of Ripley, Norton and Flamel feature in Newton's manuscripts as they do in the Schweighardt scrapbook owned by Sir Hans Sloane.

When I returned to consider these facts they confirmed for me the continuity of interest from one President of the Royal Society to another. Moreover, Newton took seriously the view held by early philosophical alchemists that the truth was only to be revealed to seekers who were morally above reproach. Fludd, Boyle and Newton all led chaste lives by conscious choice. It should no longer cause us disquiet that one of our greatest scientists clung to some shreds of past traditions. It is perhaps a sign of great minds that they have the greatest capacity to hold knowledge sometimes in a state of suspension in case of its potential value.

Similarly Leibniz could not entirely ignore the hermetic tradition in the evolution of his own mathematical concepts. His work contains many references to the Rosicrucians, and one authority believes he joined a Rosicrucian group in Nuremberg in 1666.[13] Early in his career in the 1670s he sought to devise a system of universal symbols which could represent all the essential concepts of thought.[14] As he considered the best form such a system should take, he dismissed in turn the ambiguities of everyday language, astronomical signs such as Dee's Monad based on the seven planets, and the hieroglyphs of Egypt and China. The one language which might have served was that supposed to have been spoken by Adam when he named the creatures in the Garden of Eden, since it was the first, the nearest to created reality, but that was lost. In the end he concluded that the only notation clearly universal was that of mathematics. This project never came to fruition, but later out of this examination of the unique nature of mathematical notation emerged an extension into infinitesimal calculus, with the invention of signs for operations hitherto impossible without them. The distance travelled in this search by Leibniz from the emblematic engravings of the alchemists to the new notation of calculus is symbolic of the progress from magic to science we have been observing in England.

Before introducing the next card from the collection in this book I pause to catch my breath. I feel I have been running through the centuries, crossing from one country to another. Those two bulky envelopes seem to have led me on a paper-chase in a whirlwind through time. The card is in the shape of a triangle and on it is a series of dates which span nine centuries, a span in keeping with the long pedigree of knowledge that lies behind the finished artefacts left in Byrom's custody. The card is meant to be studied as an entity and the dates conceal some hidden unity. On the reverse side of the card, precisely behind the dates are arrangements of dots in groups of three or four, deliberately added. They are nothing to do with the triangular pattern, but must have been intended to convey some message to the initiated in connection with the dates, events or people commemorated on the other side. One date, 1622, occurs twice – at the centre of the left side and at the apex. Bearing in mind the nature of material in the collection, I searched hard and long to relate the dates to events and people in recorded history. The first to yield up its secret was 1622, the year Michael Maier died. This date being the last on the card signified some sort of break, pause, or end. I felt that pause to be some time before the Commonwealth. We have seen Michael Maier impinge on the collection in a number of ways. His work is directly referred to, in particular his drawings associating alchemy with geometry as illustrated in *Atalanta Fugiens*. In the light of this, and his connections with Robert Fludd, Dr Anthony, James I and his employment in the service of the Holy Roman Emperor Rudolf II, it seems certain that the card is commemorating the year of his death during the Thirty Years War. Maier disappeared in Magdeburg when the city was occupied by foreign troops.[15]

The date of 1414 may have been assigned by whoever drew the card (which is very much in the Fludd tradition) to the death of Jan Hus, who was burned for heresy. The coronation of Frederick and Elizabeth of Bohemia had been celebrated in Prague Cathedral by Hussite clergy. Maier was a Lutheran and the Hussites were one of the most important pre-Reformation groups in Europe. Later Comenius, the campaigner for educational reform, who inspired Hartlib and Dury, was a member of the Bohemian Brethren, a mystical branch of the Hussite movement. The burning of Hus was an important stage in early Protestant history. Maier's death, with the date placed at the apex of the card, may have been seen as of similar importance within the Protestant hermetic tradition.

With 1154 we come nearer to English history, for that was the year King Stephen died and was succeeded by the first Plantagenet, Henry of Anjou, as Henry II. A great ruler, who set about restoring order after the ineffectual reign of Stephen, Henry is unfortunately best remembered for the murder of Thomas à Becket, carried out by men who thought, mistakenly, they were serving their King. Henry had been anxious to keep a measure of control over the Church of Rome in England, as he had done with the nobles, but Becket's death ruined this policy.

William the Conqueror, the first Norman King of England, is associated with 1051. It was in that year he was promised the English throne by Edward the Confessor. Edward was the last but one of the Saxon kings and, although the throne was inherited by the bloodline, it was not automatic that the eldest son should succeed. The death of a Saxon king was followed by a council which elected his successor. When the council chose Harold, William invaded to make good his claim by force.

There is another possible link between the dates 1154 and 1051. Sompting Church was granted to the Templars in 1154, the year Henry II became King. (Much later in his reign, Henry would be present at the consecration of the Templar church in London.) Hewett has calculated that the building of Sompting could be as late as *c.* 1050, which would mean possible completion and consecration in 1051. Time had to elapse before a new church was consecrated. We know there was a persistent belief that the Templars acquired a store of secret knowledge in the Middle East. Certainly they gathered ideas and designs for building their churches. Why were they interested in acquiring Sompting Church, with its extraordinary tower and Saxon arches modelled in Roman style? The two dates may be connected with the church, consecrated in 1051 and acquired in 1154 by the Knights Templar. Perhaps there is some specialised knowledge of geometry involved.

The last of the dates is 713 and this is the most difficult to assign to readily known events. When retreating into the eighth century there is the danger of being confused as much by legend as by lack of information. I had hunted even longer for the relevance of this date and then returned to the *Royal Genealogies* of James Anderson (1732), a lengthy work of great erudition and, in those parts concerned with Biblical pedigrees, of some speculation. Yet from Anderson I learned that in 713 there had been another power struggle, and one leading to a death connected with the Merovingian dynasty of France.

Franks in origin, the Merovingians established a dynasty from which were created several kingdoms. They were by the seventh and eighth centuries rulers with some civilised values, but the centre of power had gradually shifted from the king himself to a chief minister called the 'Major Domus'. This separation between real and symbolic power was dangerous and bound to lead to conflict. In the end the Merovingian dynasty was usurped by the Major Domus Pepin III, who appealed to the Pope for confirmation of his right to rule and was successful. This was in 751, but earlier attempts were made, and in the year 713 the Major Domus, Grimoald, was assassinated by a rival, Theobald, in Liège. Towards the end of the dynasty the Merovingian adherence to Rome was weakening and it may be that the assassination of 713 is in some way connected with moves hostile to Rome's ambitions. A tendency to independence, separation or opposition to Rome does seem to be a common factor in some of the dates on the card. Many of the drawings in the collection are connected with Protestant hermeticists: Dee, Fludd, Maier. Perhaps Fludd, or a member of the de Bry dynasty, brought all the dates together to commemorate the death of Maier who was seen as the latest in a line of martyr-like figures.

Whatever the common link between these dates, the card is closely related to the last drawing to be introduced. Together they provided me with one more surprise and further evidence of the profound richness of the Byrom Collection. Neither drawing has a watermark. Figure 7 is a six-pointed star, composed of two large triangles, and is, I believe, concerned with one of England's most sacred national monuments. Both the front and reverse of the card contain dimensions and details of Westminster Abbey. The front is in effect equivalent to the parametric drawings of Elizabethan playhouses, since from it can be extracted measurements for both the horizontal and vertical planes. Whereas the grid on the setting-out plan of the Globe is composed of small squares, here the grid is made up of small triangles, each of which represents a measure of 16 units from the centre of the base to the apex.

A ground plan of the Abbey to the same scale is shown in figure 11 for comparison. As with the parametric drawings of the theatres, it is the central column of the triangle A. B. C. which contains the key to the interpretations of the measure. The artist was concerned with highlighting significant features in a straight line from the West Door to the end of Henry VII's Chapel. If a tracing of the scaled ground plan is placed on top of figure 7, the geometry of the coloured circles and arcs matches exactly important stages down the building from West to East: the choir screen, the choir, the sanctuary, the Confessor's chapel and, finally, Henry VII's chapel. The precision of this alignment is truly remarkable and cannot be due simply to coincidence. According to Neale's *Westminster Abbey* the internal length from 'the western towers including

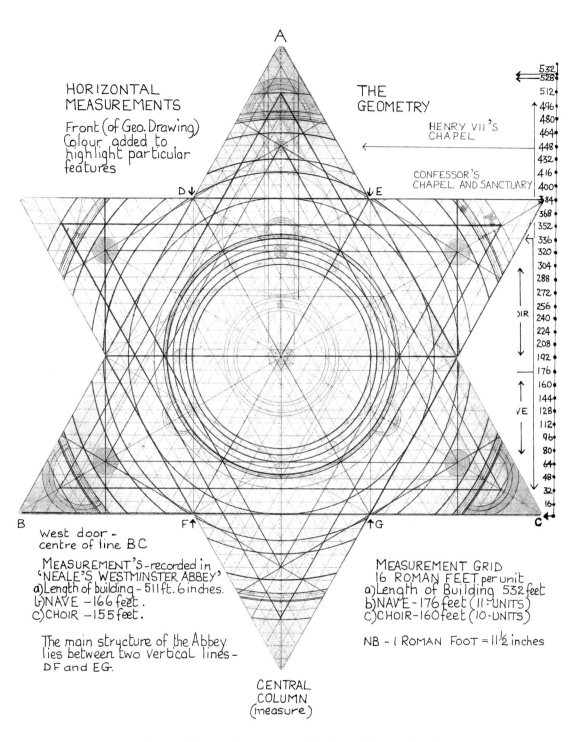

Figure 7: Westminster Abbey in the Byrom Collection, giving units of Roman measure.

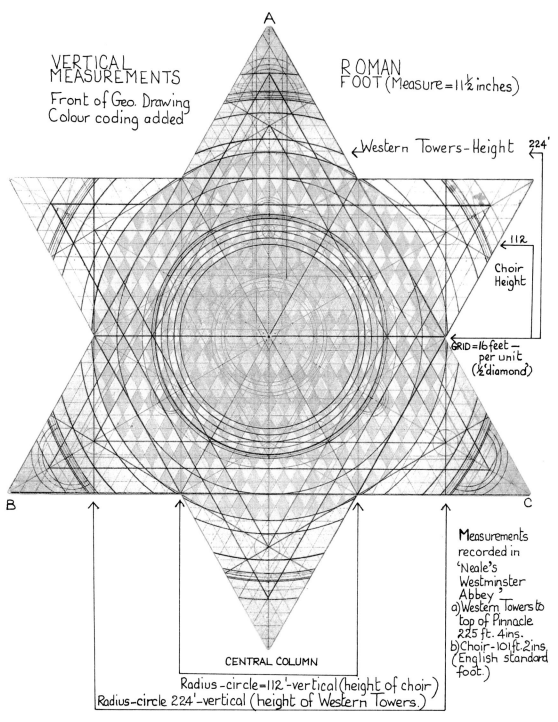

Figure 8: The proportional geometry of Westminster Abbey, giving vertical measurements. The colour coding has been added to the original drawing.

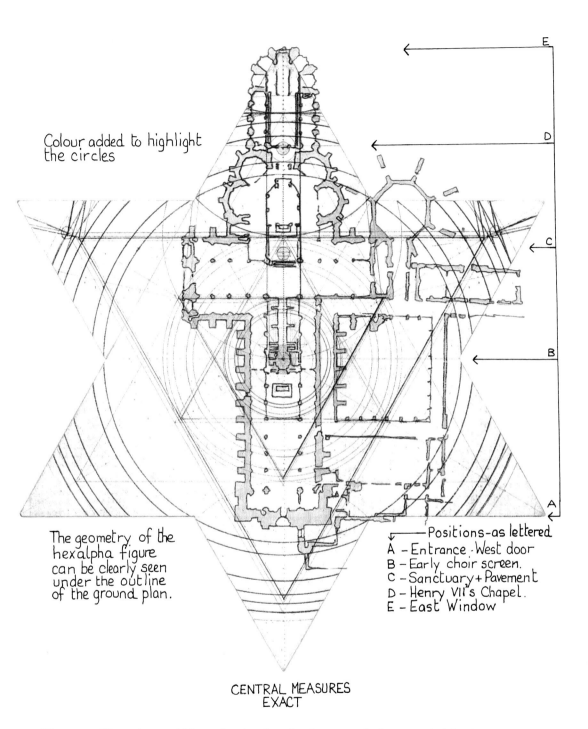

Colour added to highlight the circles

E

D

C

B

A

The geometry of the hexalpha figure can be clearly seen under the outline of the ground plan.

Positions - as lettered
A – Entrance. West door
B – Early choir screen.
C – Sanctuary + Pavement
D – Henry VII's Chapel.
E – East Window

CENTRAL MEASURES
EXACT

Figure 9: Westminster Abbey: focal points in the ground plan revealed in the geometry. (The ground plan is superimposed on the reverse side of the drawing in figure 8.)

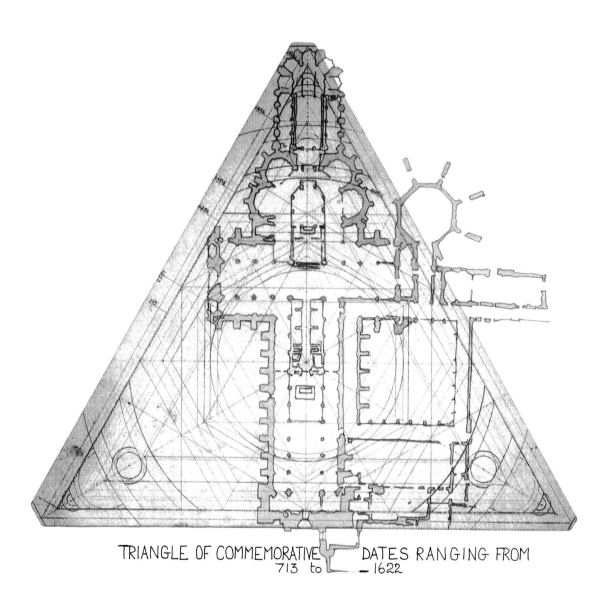

TRIANGLE OF COMMEMORATIVE DATES RANGING FROM
713 to 1622

Figure 10: History expressed in number and geometry, the ground plan of
Westminster Abbey superimposed. The two dates 1051 and 1154 draw the eye
towards the intersection in the Chapel of the Confessor. The other main
intersection at the entrance to the choir leads to the date 1622. Thus number links
with geometry to demonstrate concepts to be found in the Abbey – sanctity,
destiny, harmony and continuity.

Henry the Seventh's chapel' is 511 feet and 6 inches. Using the grid of triangles the distance on the card measures 532 units. This discrepancy can be accounted for when one realises that the unit employed on the drawing was a Roman foot, which is half an inch less than the standard English foot. When 532 Roman feet are converted into English measures, the length of the Abbey as shown on the drawings becomes 509 feet 10 inches.

There are other features in the Abbey, such as doors and towers, indicated by the geometry of figure 7. It should be noted that the artist has employed a system of circles to demonstrate aspects of the Abbey's geometry similar to that in the King's College Chapel drawings (page 136).

In figure 8, which is another version of figure 7, I have used a simple colour-coding to show the Abbey's adherence to the laws of proportion and highlight some of the measurements incorporated within the geometry. In doing so I have not added any lines to the original drawing.

The reverse of the card is shown in figure 9. It is much simpler by comparison since the grid of triangles has been omitted. This enables significant features of the Abbey to be emphasised once more when a tracing of the ground plan is superimposed. Clearly seen are the choir screen (indicated by the blue circle), the sanctuary with the Great Pavement, and the entrance to Henry VII's chapel.

The triangular card with the dates down the side (figure 12) is the same size as the triangle in figure 7 which contains information about Westminster Abbey. The two cards clearly had geometrical features in common. Accordingly I placed the Abbey ground plan on top of the dated card to see the effect. The dates on figure 12 relate to specific lines in the pattern of the drawing, and I had been searching for an explanation of this for so long that I was interested to see whether these lines coincided with any features on the ground plan of the Abbey.

Two dates were conspicuous: 1154 marked the entrance to the Confessor's Chapel and 1051 the place where the Coronation Chair had stood for centuries. As we knew, 1051 was the year Edward the Confessor promised his throne to William the Conqueror. After his death the many miracles attributed to Edward led to his canonisation. In 1163 the royal saint's body was removed to the shrine prepared by Henry II in the Confessor's Chapel in the presence of the King and the Archbishop of Canterbury, Thomas à Becket. It seemed appropriate that 1154, the year of Henry's succession, should indicate the entrance to the chapel where Edward was finally laid to rest and which is regarded as the most sacred part of the Abbey. The effect of this discovery was to confirm the connection between figures 7 and 12 and give a final demonstration of the system of measurement I had discovered in those drawings concerned with

Figure 11: The ground plan of Westminster Abbey.

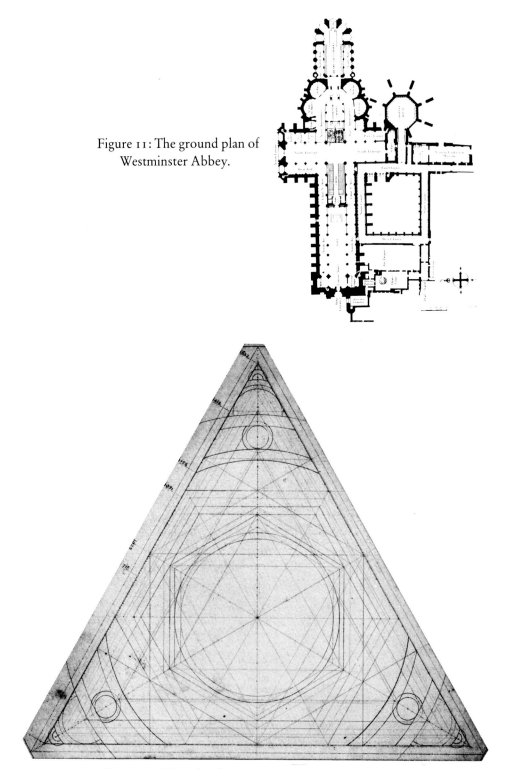

Figure 12: Triangle of commemorative dates, 713-1622.

buildings. The dates combined with geometry to provide new insights for me into the relevance of the cards. Furthermore, 1622, the date of Maier's death, reminds us of his belief that Rosicrucian ideals might be a means of reconciling different religious factions in Europe. Discord resolved by the harmony of music is suggested by the intersection leading from the date to the centre of the early choir screen. 1414 directs the eye to the centre of the Henry VII Chapel. Through his marriage to Elizabeth of York Henry finally ended the Wars of the Roses. Firm but wise, he established the Tudor dynasty and the pre-eminence of law, and facilitated the transition from the Middle Ages to the Renaissance. Thus he can be seen as a consolidator of change, just as Hus was revered as an initiator of change. The points of intersection highlighted on the ground plan of the Abbey emphasised ideas of sanctity, destiny and universal harmony. The two cards also strengthened my long-held view that the drawings are a collection of source material belonging to some group which remained consistent to its ideals across the centuries.

The earliest date connected with any of the cards centres on a happening in Liège in 713. Theodore de Bry, the motivating spirit of a great publishing enterprise, had originated from Liège, a city which stands as a reminder of the war-torn history of Europe. When I read of the assassination of Grimoald at Liège, I felt I had come full circle. Could Theodore de Bry have been influenced not by that date but by events it set in train? Was he not a Huguenot refugee fleeing from intolerance? Perhaps the impulse which led him to establish his printing press was the desire to disseminate ideas asserting the dignity of man's capabilities, the richness of his potential.

The last date on the drawings is 1732; Byrom died in 1763. There were thirty-one years left in which he could have disposed of the drawings, handed them on to some spiritual or intellectual successor to carry on the tradition they represent. Why did he not do so? The answer to that question lies in Byrom's own complex history and the secret Thomas Siddal refused to reveal. The collection has been treated as an entity in itself. The fascinating life of its custodian must be told elsewhere.

Appendix One

This Appendix consists of four parts. Part One is a note on the 'Starrs mall' provided by Leon Crickmore. Part Two shows a diagram of the standing arrangements in the Globe theatre, followed by an extraction from the parametric drawings giving supplementary information which will help the discriminating reader to understand more fully the principles of the design of the theatres. The drawings selected are those concerned with the Globe, and this information was used in making the Globe model by M.E.I. Young. They should be studied with those already included in Chapters 4 and 5. They have been placed here in order not to interrupt the flow of the narrative. Part Three contains a note on the wooden models and drawings of the Globe's staircase and roofing. Part Four consists of independent commentaries from other contributors with appropriate experience and expertise.

Figure 1: 'Starrs mall'.

A Note on the 'Starrs mall'

The name 'Starrs mall' suggests a passage open to the stars, or (more poetically and by association with the game *pall mall*) a playground for the planets. However, since this drawing is on card, cut out, and fits into the eight-sided figure of the Globe, as well as serving as a template for the other Elizabethan theatres (see figure 11, Chapter 4), for its maker it must have carried some special significance. To interpret this, one needs to recall the Ptolemaic cosmology, even though, at the time of the building of the first Globe in 1599, Copernicus had proposed his alternative heliocentric theory some fifty years before, and Kepler had already published the basis of his Laws of Planetary Motion. For Ptolemy, the earth was the unmoving centre of the universe. Around the earth Ptolemy postulated seven concentric spheres to carry the planets or 'wandering stars' (the Moon, Mercury, Venus, Sun, Mars, Jupiter and Saturn), and, ultimately, an eighth sphere to bear the 'fixed stars' as well as the structure of the entire planetary system. It is probably to this that Lorenzo is referring in *The Merchant of Venice* (Act V, Scene 1) when he says: 'Look how the floor of heaven is thick inlaid with patines of bright gold.' It was believed that this eighth sphere revolved from East to West once in every twenty-four hours (as indeed is still our own everyday perception), while the planets also moved, more slowly, from West to East in their respective cycles through the zodiac. The 'Myth of Er' – a tale about the experience of a soldier, revived from the dead – which occurs towards the end of Plato's *Republic* (X, 617b), describes how on each of these rotating rings there stands a Siren, singing a note of a rising scale: a kind of ladder to heaven; the 'music of the spheres'.

On the reverse side of the 'Starrs mall' drawing there is inscribed: 'Underneath is the sets of the brass patterns for the Larger and Lesser Starrs mall' – a reference, presumably, to the sidereal worlds of the sun and moon, the two luminaries so described in the Book of Genesis (1, v.16). The significance of the phrase 'sets of the brass patterns' is unclear: it might imply that circles based on the arcs illustrated were to be used in the design of other theatres or engravings – though etchings were normally made on copper; or that spherical shells derived similarly and cut in brass were intended to serve as part of a cosmic model like that of the solar system included by Kepler in his *Mysterium Cosmographicum* (1596); or even, perhaps, that plaques the size of these circles were to be made in brass to commemorate certain members of some Cabala Club.

Several of the drawings in the Byrom Collection are compatible with the hypothesis that the Globe ('This wide and universal theatre', to borrow a phrase from just before the 'All the world's a stage' speech in *As You Like It*, with which the Globe may have opened) was meant

277

to be understood as a symbol of the cosmos. Compare, for example, the fourteenth-century astronomical clock in Wells Cathedral, with its inscription: 'Sphericus archetypum globus monstrat hic microcosmum' ('This round ball represents the world in microcosm') – see figure 17, Chapter 8. If this be so, other connotations follow. A circle is a symbol of eternity, the 'spiritual world'; in various mystical traditions it represents God or the Self. The square, on the other hand, symbolises the 'material' world. In a number of Renaissance drawings, a male figure is placed within the cosmos represented by a circle or square, to show man as a 'microcosm' within the 'macrocosm', and at the same time a mirror of it. Sometimes it is significant whether the hands and feet of these figures touch the circle or the square, and at what point of the zodiac the contact is made. The human figure is so placed that the centre of the circle or square sometimes coincides with the navel and sometimes with the genitals. In a drawing called *Vitruvian Man* (*c.* 1490), Leonardo da Vinci has constructed a figure whose hands and feet, in two alternative positions, touch either a circle centred on its navel, or a square centred on its genitals, the navel dividing the body in the 'golden proportion'. Such geometry expresses the harmony which was traditionally perceived between human and cosmic proportions. A square containing a circle, a square contained within a circle, a square and a circle of equal perimeters, and attempts to construct a square and a circle of equal areas fascinated the geometers of ancient times and were respected as archetypes of the order in the universe. Variations of these patterns seem to underlie the geometry of utopian plans as various, for example, as those of Plato's ideal cities, St John's vision of the New Jerusalem and actual constructions such as Stonehenge, the astronomical clock in Wells and Shakespeare's Globe.

However, much of this tradition has been lost, and so, lest the reader finds my line of thinking fanciful or irrelevant, I cite a passage from Frances Yates's book *Theatre of the World* (p. 134):

> A theatre with a name such as the Globe, and which was recognised as representing the world ('See the world's ruins' exclaimed Ben Jonson when surveying the charred remains of the first Globe after the fire) *must*, in my opinion, have been based on the classical theatre plan of the equilateral triangles within the circle of the zodiac. A theatre which was one of those which sprang up in London in the atmosphere of popular Vitruvianism generated by Dee is almost certain to have aimed at expressing in terms of symbolic geometry attitudes to man, to the cosmos, to God, which lay behind Renaissance architecture. Thinking along these lines one is more likely to arrive at a possible plan of the Globe than by spinning out imaginary technical details from insufficient evidence.

To return to Lorenzo's speech:

> There's not the smallest orb which thou behold'st
> But in his motion like an angel sings,
> Still quiring to the young-eyed cherubins:
> Such harmony is in immortal souls;
> But whilst this muddy vesture of decay
> Doth grossly close it in, we cannot hear it.

As Frances Yates goes on to hint, the plan of Shakespeare's Globe was probably in some profound sense 'musical': for only a theatre, embodying within its structure some of the mathematical proportions which generate the 'music of the spheres', could serve as a fitting vehicle for the richness of his 'vast Renaissance imagination'.

LEON CRICKMORE

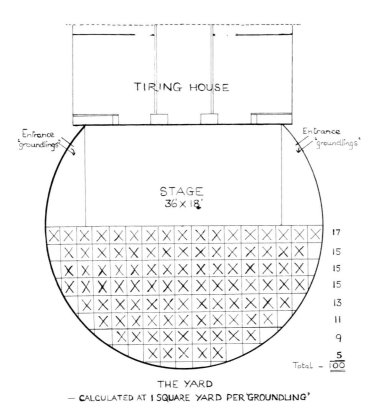

Figure 2: The 'Groundings' area of the Globe theatre – diameter 51 feet.

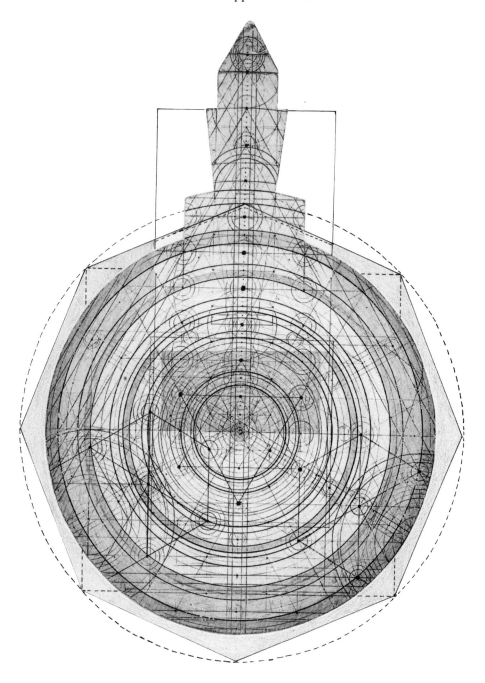

Figure 3: The geometry of the separate components of the Globe combine to product the overall harmony of the structure.

To ensure firm foundations piles were driven into the ground. "A quavery or maris and unstable 'foundacion must be holpe with great pylys of alder rammed down, and with a frame of tymbre called a crossaundre"*(Wm. Hormon) * "Cross andrews" occur at Westminster Abbey ᶜ1475. (Yulgaria. 1519).

St. Andrew's cross. * " Presumably they were balks notched to-gether crossing diagonally like a St. Andrew's cross." "Such a method was known in very early times and was used for instance, by the Romans when building the walls of Anderida (now Pevensey) on the edge of a marsh." (L. F. Salzman. Building in England? P. 84)

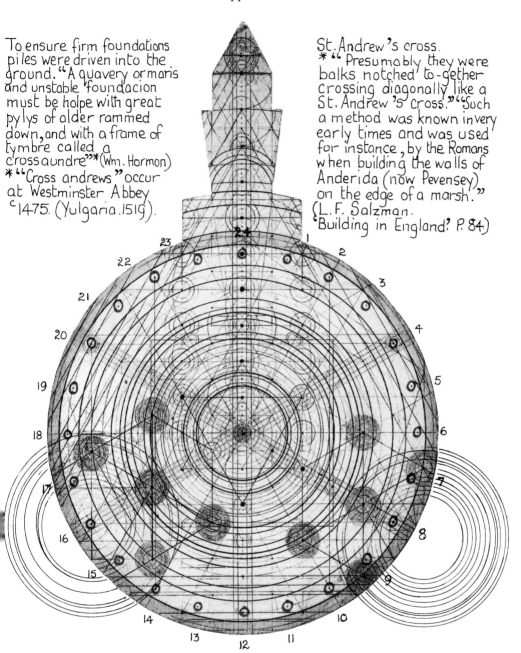

Figure 4: The Globe foundations and a twenty-four-hour clock. The group of circles extending from the main drawing suggests a possible position of extensions to the main building – e.g. external staircases.

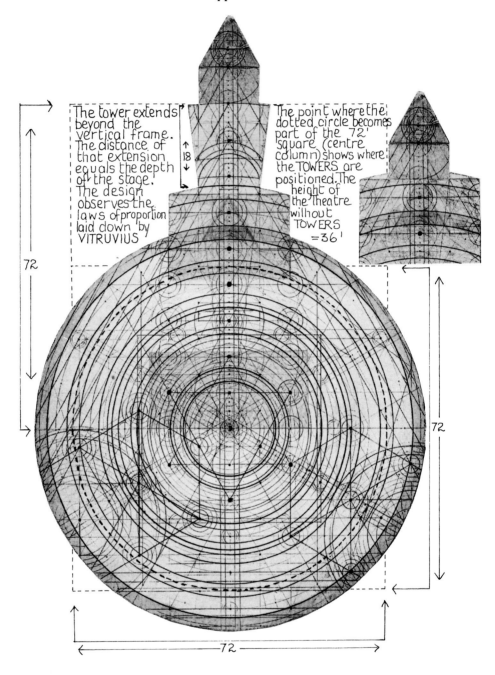

The tower extends beyond the vertical frame. The distance of that extension equals the depth of the stage. The design observes the laws of proportion laid down by VITRUVIUS

18

The point where the dotted circle becomes part of the 72' square (centre column) shows where the TOWERS are positioned. The height of the Theatre without TOWERS = 36'

72

72

72

Figure 5: The Globe towers. The broken line has been drawn on an existing circle for emphasis. The shading has been added.

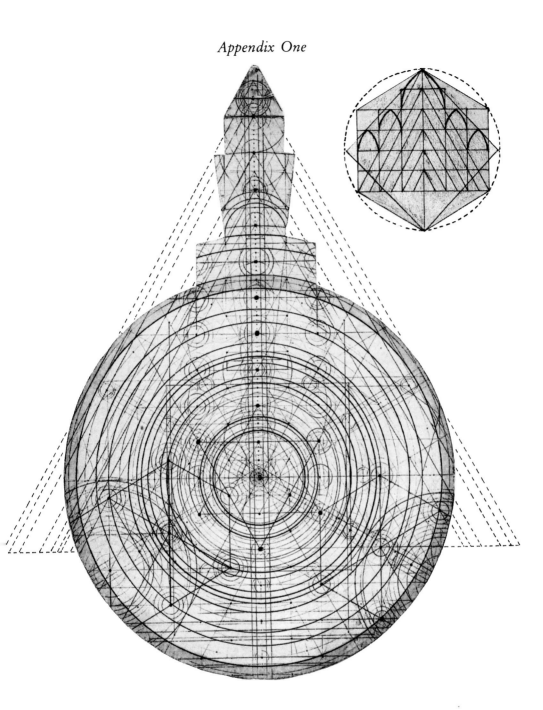

Figure 6: The geometry of the Globe theatre. The equilateral triangles (completed by broken lines) which rise from the circular ground plan to the elevation are a further illustration of the geometric design of the theatre. Compare with the figure top right. This is one of the proposals for the cross-section of Milan Cathedral by Stornaloco (1391) in which triangle, square, circle and hexagon were employed to illustrate the proportions of the design.

The Wooden Theatre Models

The collection contains drawings for seven theatres. Wooden models were made for six: the Theater, the Globe, the Fortune, the Rose, the Swan and the Hope. The seventh, the Bear Garden, has not been included because the drawings had qualities which I considered to be negative. These may well have arisen from the animal-baiting function of the building.

Since my brother had constructed a scale model of the Globe in detail which fully served its purpose, I considered it necessary to commission an impartial, professional model maker for any others. Accordingly I asked K. Peacock to build a model of one other theatre as a companion piece to the Globe. He looked at the original drawings, and, although they are not conventional architectural designs, he studied them sufficiently to recognise their purpose. He offered to make a sequence of models in wood. Because I wished to prevent any suggestion of collusion, we agreed that I should give him my interpretation of the originals in the form of prepared plans. I used metric measurements equivalent to my 72 unit measure. He then built geometric models to the exact size of the original drawings, fully aware of the magnitude of the enterprise and the need for absolute integrity. The first model constructed in this way was entitled 'Project No. 1'. On its completion he made the remaining models, the plans of which were likewise simply numbered 2, 3, 4, etc., to avoid the possible intrusion of any preconceived ideas.

This shared experience was one of the highlights of the venture.

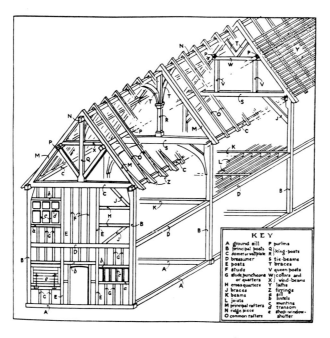

KEY

A ground sill
B principal posts
C corner wallplate
D breassumer
E posts
F studs
G studs, puncheons or quarters
H cross quarters
J braces
K beams
L joists
M principal rafters
N ridge piece
O common rafters

P purlins
Q king-posts
R
S tie-beams
T braces
V queen-posts
W collars and wind-beams
X
Y laths
Z firrings
g sill
b lintels
c munions
d transom
e shop-window-shutter

Figure 7: The structure of a timber framed house. The frame of the gable end should be compared with figures 8 and 9. This diagram by J. W. Bloe, OBE, FSA, is reproduced from *Building in England* by L.F. Salzman.

284

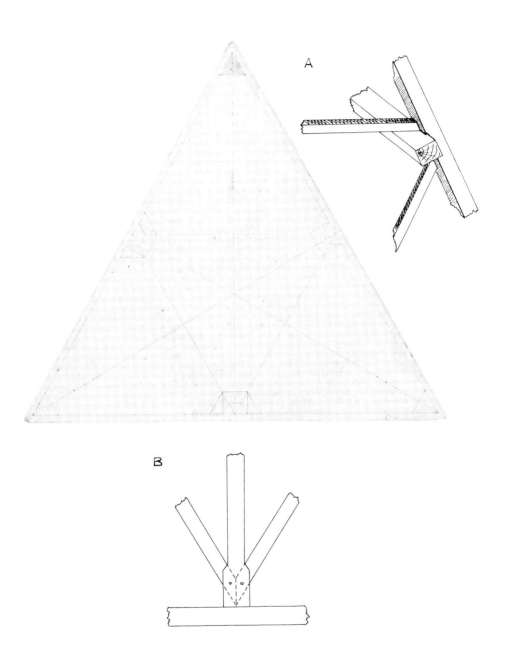

A

B

Figure 8: A gable end jointing. A and B lap joints, a feature of building practice
of the period, are seen in the main figure.

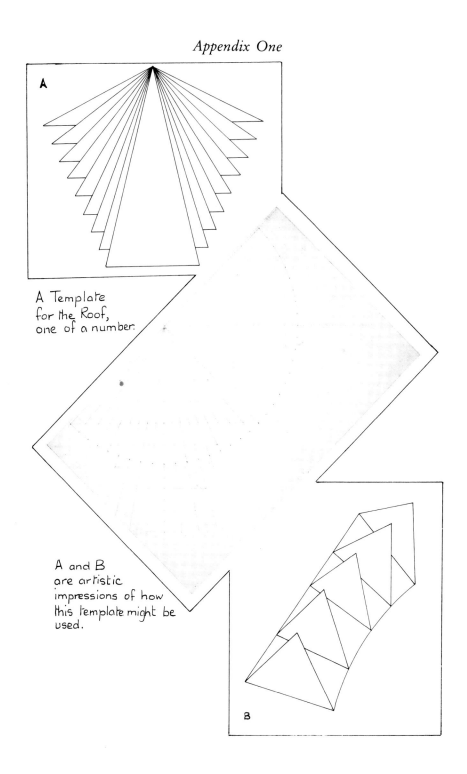

A Template
for the Roof,
one of a number.

A and B
are artistic
impressions of how
this template might be
used.

Figure 9: A and B are artistic impressions of how this template for the roof might be used.

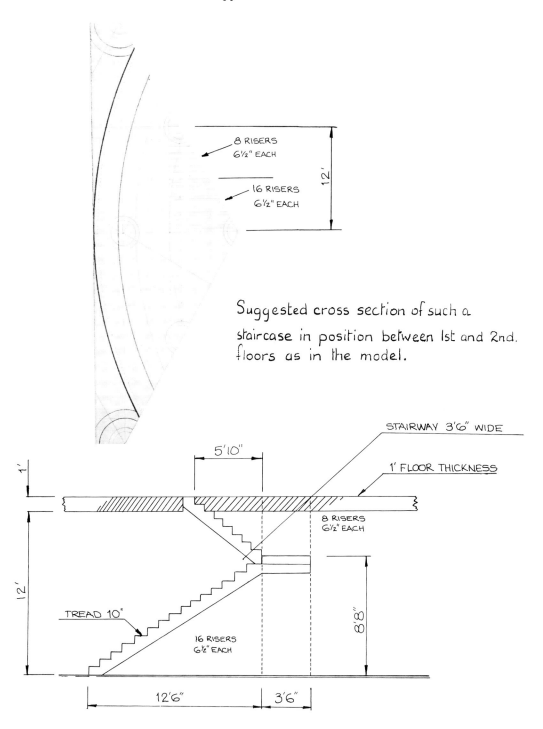

Figure 10: Part of a drawing for a staircase of 24 steps in the Globe.

Canons of Proportion

Special days come often from the blue – with no hint on their morning that today is to be such a one.

My diary now records that it was a Friday. Perhaps the date was significant. For me it was certainly so.

On that day I met, in the Library of the Theosophical Society, Joy Hancox, and was shown what she clearly considered to be a pearl of great price.

What was this puzzle she had laid before me? On the table was a – what? A bottle-shaped piece of card. Was it a plan?

Having drawn out in the past the enclosing spheres of the five regular polyhedra, my first thought was that I was looking at some similar scheme. But what was the significance of the projecting neck?

It needed Joy's explanation that here were two sets of relationships on one flat plane. Indeed, were one to bend this neck up, the object then revealed itself in three dimensions.

The lines and circles shown on the card had no dimensions, so what of the scale? From her years of study Joy pointed out that on attendant sheets was the dotted yardstick too.

And the structure for which this careful draughtsmanship was a blue-print? I had to be told.

The Globe. *The* Globe?! What, Shakespeare's Theatre?! WOW!

Where did the next hour go?

The fact that this bottle shape was only one of several 'plans' that had come into Joy's possession means that not only the Globe but other Elizabethan theatres could also be rebuilt. No conjecture. No need for expert consensus. Just an acknowledgment that these drawings are what they appear to be.

Moreover, with the name 'Globe' as our clue, it would seem that this famous building, like so many other well known structures of the past, was built to a canon of proportion that we have all but lost.

Architects today are so pressurised by the economics of a project. Every building must take stock of parking problems, available grants, change of use, policies A–Z (revised each year), and all those things Planners will not allow. Its size must be close to the maximum for that site to give the best return on the funds invested. And how shall we detail it? Make sure it meets building regulations and does not leak. Our premiums for indemnity are already far too high.

Were these the thoughts of architects of earlier times? We are informed by Vitruvius that there are, or were, other concerns. The size, shape and layout of a building should demonstrate a knowledge of certain rules of proportion and relationship.

And who first set out these rules? It is said that Vitruvius simply codified the earlier systems of the Greeks. So, Pythagoras and Plato were perhaps the source. Others will point to cabalistic lore or true masonry; to the Egyptian academics; to India, China or even back to pre-historic times.

Whence came this canon, then?

Whence came the rules for the processes and forms of nature?

In *De Architectura* Vitruvius sounds pessimistic about the state of contemporary Roman architecture because even then the rules were being disregarded.

What would he say of the way we build today?

In the reconstruction of the Globe Theatre we could have the opportunity to re-create precisely a famous building. We could also have a reminder that for a building to be a truly harmonious one, the design should reflect the way nature builds *her* structures; for be it atom, *globe* or solar system, the geometry is the same. The only difference is one of scale.

It is my hope that everyone who reads Joy Hancox's book experiences some of the excitement I felt on that October day.

ALAN HUGHES

Mathematical Aspects of the Drawings

Examination of the drawings brings to mind the great part played by geometry throughout the ages. Today geometry is much neglected by the population at large, and the neglect is seen by the almost total absence of geometry from the school syllabus. So it will not be easy for many people who examine the drawings to derive much meaning from them. This note aims to point out some of the salient geometrical features of the drawings and to give a summary of the long historical process by which geometry secured a leading role in architectural method, surveying and navigation.

A glance at the drawings shows at once the importance of the straight line and the circle. These two fundamental elements of Euclidean geometry take us back thousands of years to the time of the Egyptians, and, to a lesser extent, the Babylonians. Euclidean geometry, much revered by scholars throughout the ages, was a practical subject used in surveying, navigation, astronomy and architecture; but it was also of great religious significance (see, for example, *Sacred Geometry*, by Robert Lawlor, Thames and Hudson, London, 1982) and, of course, in this regard it was inseparably bound up with the mystical and sacred significance of number (see, for example, *Dimensions of Paradise*, by John Michell, Harper and Row, San Francisco, 1988).

Many of the drawings are connected with architectural design. Look at the use made of the points of intersection of circular arcs with other arcs or with straight lines, these points being of some particular significance in the design process. A surprising feature is the accuracy with which the tiny circles and the great circles are drawn, all, let us remember, by hand with the aid of the compass only. Equally surprising is the fact that the methods of printing and engraving used at the time were so accurate in reproducing the drawings. Many of the latter carry small holes at geometrically important points, and we must conclude that the draughtsmen of the times must have shown great dexterity in the use of the compass and the dividers.

Geometry literally means 'measurement of the earth', and this is a fair description of the subject as practised by the Egyptians from about 4000 BC. It was of great social and economic importance and was also essential in astronomy, which led to the introduction of the calendar, and was needed to predict religious holidays. Geometry was, of course, much used by the Egyptians in the design and construction of their temples and the pyramids. From Egypt the study of geometry spread to Greece. The Greek civilisation lasted from about 2800 BC to about AD 600 and included two periods of mathematical activity, the classical period (*c*. 600 to *c*. 300 BC) and the Alexandrian period (*c*. 300 BC to AD *c*. 600). A major school of the classical period was the Pythagorean (*c*. 585 BC to *c*. 400 BC). The Platonic school was established by Plato in Athens about 387 BC. The main centre for mathematics shifted to Alexandria about 300 BC and it lasted for 900 years until closed in 529 by the Christian Emperor, Justinian.

During the mediaeval period of about 700 years (400 to 1100) mathematics made no progress. There was some small-scale development in the period 1100–1450, but the rebirth of learning had to wait until the Renaissance period, 1400–1600. No outstanding development in mathematics occurred even over this period, but there was a marked rediscovery and absorption of Greek mathematics. The great achievements were in literature, painting and architecture, and the artists, in particular, were the first to apply seriously the Greek doctrine that mathematics is of the essence in the interpretation of nature. This was the prelude, as far as architecture was concerned, to the very considerable activity in design and construction which occurred in the sixteenth and seventeenth centuries.

The drawings are inseparably linked with John Byrom (1692–1763) but were made by others, and may have been produced long before his time. It may be relevant to note that Inigo Jones, the surveyor-general of royal buildings for James I, and the designer of a new palace at Whitehall, lived from 1573 to 1651; and Christopher Wren, who designed and built

51 parish churches in London after the Great Fire of 1666, lived from 1632 to 1723. So there was plenty of large-scale architectural design taking place in England during the century preceding the time of Byrom. Many of the drawings may belong to this century.

I conclude with a few remarks about three other items. Mention of the five Platonic solids occurs in a few places. This puts the emphasis upon Plato's dialogue 'Timaeus' where he develops a 'cosmology' linked to plane and solid geometry. He establishes a close relation between the four 'elements', earth, air, fire and water, and four of the solids. The fact that the solids appear in the drawings shows how strong was the Platonic tradition, even up to the time of the Renaissance.

Next is the occurrence, among the drawings, of a few examples of coordinate systems, that is, two systems of non-intersecting curves, with each curve of one system intersecting each curve of the other. These were clearly used in measurement and navigation, and in the determination of location. See, for example, the double horizontal dial shown in Chapter 8, figure 1. To understand this instrument from a mathematical point of view, it would be necessary to study the life and mathematical work of Oughtred.

Finally there is the intriguing regular nine-pointed star shown in Chapter 8, figure 19. How was this constructed? It is impossible to construct it by means of straight edge and compass alone. This impossibility arises from an amazing theorem found by the great mathematician, Carl Friedrich Gauss, at the age of only nineteen, in 1796. His theorem is too technical to record here but from it may be asserted the following result: for values of n up to, say, 12, a regular polygon of n sides may be constructed by straight edge and compass alone, if n = 3, 4, 5, 6, 8, 10 or 12, but not if n = 7, 9 or 11. So the nine-pointed star is non-constructible. This must mean that the star was drawn approximately, probably by drawing rays through the centre at mutual angles of 40°.

LAURENCE GODDARD

Parametric Diagrams

The drawings in question consist of a series of concentric circles at irregular intervals, with associated dots and lines. From the main body of these concentric circles emerges a linear component, whose divisions are related directly to the main body, but which extends beyond the circles themselves. These drawings are parametric diagrams, that is, a description of parameters in graphic form. They are a means of denoting the dimensions and proportions that can be used to construct a building, in the case of these specific diagrams, Elizabethan theatres in London, such as the Globe and Swan. In their form, these diagrams may be compared with Cesare Cesariano's diagram of Milan Cathedral (published in his 1521 edition of Vitruvius), which is an example of the use of plan and elevation based upon a series of concentric circles. Cesariano's engraving is more explicit than the parametric diagrams, for it shows the actual ground plan and elevation of the cathedral, superimposed upon the lines that define their dimensions.

The beauty of the parametric means of displaying information is one of elegant economy: the dimensions and proportions for an entire building are set forth in a single diagram, from which all dimensions, proportions and related geometrical forms may be determined readily. Parametric diagrams are the product of a traditional way of looking at the world which differs considerably from the modern approach. The modern way of thought is fragmental: it takes things apart in a reductionist way, and then considers the whole to be composed of an assemblage of those parts. Modern technical drawings, consisting of plan, elevation, etc., are an example of this. They are based upon a conception of cubic geometry that divides space into three dimensions at right angles to one another, the axes X, Y and Z. Every component of the machine or building is described then in terms of these three axes. But, although all modern technical drawing is based upon this principle, and it is a workable means of description, it should not be considered to be the 'correct' way of presenting such information. As the dominant means today, it is merely one of several possibilities. Parametric diagrams are another.

Ultimately, this modern means of diagrammatic description appears to have been derived from the techniques of industrial design, which require the manufacture of separate parts and then their assembly. Traditional building techniques need not use this means of portrayal of the information required to make a building. Parametric diagrams are pre-industrial in origin. They are the product of a more traditional, alternative possibility, a holistic vision in which the ruling proportional system of the building is not divided artificially into elevation and plan, but serves as the rule for all of the parts, wherever they may be located in the building. The parametric approach enabled the architect to incorporate the Vitruvian virtues of order, eurhythmy and symmetry into his buildings, for a correct application of proportional and harmonic parameters into the original diagram will necessarily produce these qualities and virtues in the final building. The use of parametric diagrams could be reintroduced with advantage in the design of new buildings. Their rediscovery at this time should be seen as an important contribution to a new understanding of the untapped potential that the Western Tradition of architecture still holds.

NIGEL CAMPBELL PENNICK

Appendix Two

Astrology

In the gradual emergence of a scientific method from the old mediaeval view of the world, one art or skill still retained its hold on the minds of most educated people: astrology. There is in the collection a drawing of an astrological chart (figure 1) on one side of which is the precise date and time of birth, 17 May, half past nine at night, 1650. It also bears the initials M.R. On the other side is the horoscope of the M.R. concerned. I first investigated the card when I came across the Schweighardt scrapbook, since there was a slight chance that M.R. might stand for Mr Rose, whose name appears in the front of the book. Sir Hans Sloane, who had owned it, had married the widow of Fulk Rose of Jamaica in 1695. However her name was Elizabeth. Aubrey in his *Brief Lives* mentions a jeweller called Rose living in Covent Garden *c.* 1633 but gives no initials for him, and there is no evident connection between this man and the drawings. I could not find a Rose with the right initials who was born in 1650. Another possible surname was Radclyffe, for the Radclyffes were a widespread dynasty with a Manchester branch known to Byrom, and I had already found Radclyffes living in, of all places, Rose Alley where the Rose theatre had once stood. A search through all the available family trees produced only one candidate, a Mary Radclyffe, but she turned out to be a married woman who died in 1651. Whether the horoscope had been constructed at the time of birth or later, M.R. would have been seventy-five years old at the time when Byrom formed his Cabala Club. Certainly the exquisite care expended on the chart shows the seriousness attached to astrology whenever the horoscope was drawn.

Jung is said to have constructed horoscopes of patients he was treating. More recently, the French psychologist and statistician Michel Gauquelin (1928–1991), who was highly critical of traditional astrology and its lack of scientific methodology, devoted much of his career to a rigorous examination of the subject to establish if there was indeed a correlation between the position of planets at birth, an individual's success in his profession and his personality. Using the births and careers of thousands of eminent people world-wide, Gauquelin did establish a highly significant relation between planets and the type of eminence. Fierce and prolonged criticism from astronomers, philosophers and physicists has not yet been able to discredit his findings, although their importance is open to question.

Discussions with a traditional astrologer enabled me to establish one or two facts about M.R.'s birth chart. It is in the customary form of a square with three triangles to each side, representing altogether the twelve signs of the Zodiac. It is an early type known as 'Decussata'. The first factor to look for in a birth chart is the sign rising on the horizon at the moment of birth, the Ascendant. Only seven planets were used in making the chart, which places it before the discovery of Uranus in 1781. This is what one would expect since the last known date on a card is 1732. Given the position of the Ascendant and other planets as indicated on the chart, it is possible to calculate, with the aid of an astronomical almanac, the approximate latitude at which the subject was born. Here that latitude would appear to lie between 6 and 16 degrees north of the equator. Both the British West and East Indies fall within these latitudes and can be considered as possible birthplaces for M.R., but there the trail must end. The card remains a puzzle I would like to solve.

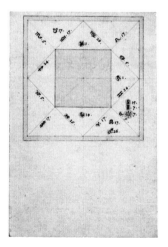

Figure 1: Horoscope for 'May 17, 1650'.

Notes

1   *Discovering the Collection*

1 Beatrice Stott, 'James Dawson and Thomas Syddall [sic]', Manchester, Lancashire and Cheshire Antiquarian Society Vol. XLVI, 1929, p. 14.
2 *Die Melancholie*, Nuremberg, 1514.

2   *The Challenge Outlined*

1 John Byrom, *The Private Journal and Literary Remains*, Vol. 1, Part 1, Manchester, Chetham Society, 1854, p. 83. Originally in shorthand, transcribed by Sarah Bolger.
2 Ibid., p. 90. I later came to the conclusion that this group met in London in rented accommodation to discuss the drawings. The choice of Byrom as the custodian of the collection may have been connected with the death of Sir Christopher Wren in 1723. 'Guessers' might be an error in transcribing the shorthand signs here by Sarah Bolger: because the shorthand is phonetic, instances occur where the sounds of certain words are misunderstood — vowels were indicated by slight variations in the position of a dot which in some cases was omitted entirely. This could easily lead to confusion even when the context of a word seems clear. For example on p. 107, Vol. 1, Part 1, Sarah Bolger transcribes a word as 'princes' whereas it should be 'princesses'. 'We saw the three young princes taking coach at St James's' makes good sense, except that the Royal Family at that time did not contain three young princes. What Byrom saw and reported on were the three young daughters of Princess Caroline. A hundred years later this fact was not known to Sarah Bolger, and so an error was made and perpetuated. The signs for both words are practically indistinguishable. Princes is: γ‿ princesses would be: γ⌐

Similarly in the present quotation 'guessers' hardly makes much sense. However the presence of Guises in Byrom's private London circle offers an alternative reading. The club could have been concerned with ideas or traditions which came from the Guises, or even Gisors.

3 Eliphas Levi, Paris, 1891 (quoted in Papus, *The Qabalah*, Wellingborough, The Aquarian Press, 1983, p. 84).

4 John Byrom, *The Universal Shorthand*, Manchester, Joseph Harrop, 1767, Preface p. ii.

5 Dionysius Andreas Freher, born in Nuremberg in 1649, a disciple of Jacob Boehme on whose work he wrote a detailed commentary. He moved to London in 1699 and died there in 1728.

6 Sir Lionel Brett, former Justice, Supreme Court, Nigeria, 1958-1968, died 1990.

7 Theophilus Schweighardt, *Speculum Sophicum Rhodo-Stauroticum*, Frankfurt, 1618.

8 Frances Yates, *The Rosicrucian Enlightenment* (paperback edition), London, Routledge and Kegan Paul, 1986, pp. 93-4.

9 Ibid., p. 94.

10 For a detailed analysis I refer the reader to Richard Foster, *Patterns of Thought*, London, Jonathan Cape, 1991.

11 The Bible, St Matthew, Chapter 5, verse 30.

12 Otto Lilien, *Jacob Christoph Le Blon*, Stuttgart, Hiersemann, 1985, p. 8.

13 J.Ph. Van der Kellen, *Michel Le Blon, Recueil d'ornements accompagné d'une notice biographique et d'un catalogue raisonné de son oeuvre*, The Hague, Martinus Nijhoff, 1900, p. 37.

14 Shakespeare, *Romeo and Juliet*, Act 3, Sc. 1, 103.

3   A Question of Origins

1 The Rate Books are in Chelsea Public Library, London. See Lilien, op. cit., pp. 60-1.

2 Otto Lilien, Ibid., p. 96.

3 John Byrom, *Remains*, Vol. 1, Part 1, p. 155.

4 John, Lord Percival, first Earl of Egmont, 1683-1748. British Library, Department of Manuscripts, Egmont Papers. Add. Ms 47029 Vol. CX (quoted in Lilien, op. cit., p. 39).

5 Huguenot Society of London Publications no. 10 *Returns of Aliens* Vol. 1, Aberdeen University Press, 1900, p. 399. 'Sensuyvent les noms de ceux qui se sont presentez avec bon tesmoignage pour estre receu en l'église depuis ung mois, fait ce 29 Janvier 1568.'

6 Ibid., Vol. 3, p. 444.
> James Debraie & Alse
> Picter Maker in England 21 yeres; free denizen; 1593.
> Frenche Churche; no servants.

At the bottom of the page is a note: As Greece had moreover their Painters, so in England we have also these; William and Francis Segar brethren, Thomas and John Bettes, Lockie, Lyne, Peake, Peter Cole, Arnold, Marcus Garrard, Jacques de Bruy, Cornelius, Peter Golchi, Hieronimo (de Bye) and Peter Vandervelde. Meres's *Wits Commonwealth*, 1598, quoted in Walpole's *Anecdotes of Painting*, Vol. 1, p. 159.

The evidence pointed towards Jacques de Bruy being a son of Theodore de Bry.

7 C.T. Courtney Lewis, *The Le Blond Book*, London, Sampson Low & Marston, 1920, p. 9.

8 Sir Christopher and Sir John Guise, *Memoirs of the Family of Guise of Elmore*,

London, Royal Historical Society, Camden 3rd series, Vol. 28, 1917.

9 Dorothy M. Owen (ed.), *The Minute Book of Spalding Gentlemen's Society, 1712-1755*, Vol. 73, Lincoln Record Society, 1981, Introduction, p. x.
10 John Byrom, *Remains*, Vol. 1, Part 2, pp. 599-600.
11 Ralph Straus, *The Unspeakable Mr Curll*, London, Chapman and Hall, 1927, p. 104.
12 Ibid.
13 John Byrom, *Remains*, Vol. 1, Part 2, p. 556.
14 Royal Society Minute Books, London, 6 November 1735.
15 John Byrom, *Remains*, Vol. 2, Part 1, p. 9.

> Mr Hauksbee gave me my account, viz:
> John Byrom M.A., admitted March 19th 1723/4.
> Paid to Mich[s] 1727 £9 4 0
> Contributions due Mich[s] 1735 £20 16 0
> which he said if I paid before Lady-day it would do.

16 H. de la Fontaine Verwey, 'Michel Le Blon, Engraver, Art Dealer, Diplomat', Amsterdam, Amstelodamum Jaarboek, 1969, p. 111.
17 In March 1616, two years after leaving school, he was apprenticed for 7 years to Thomas Man at Stationers' Hall, London. E. Weil, 'William Fitzer, The Publisher of Harvey's De Motu Cordis 1628', London, Bibliographical Society, 1944, p. 148.
18 H. de la Fontaine Verwey, 'Gerard Thibault and his Académie de L'Espée', Leiden, Netherlands, E.J. Brill, *Quaerendo* Vol. VIII, Autumn 1978, p. 288.
19 Biographie Universelle Française, Paris, 1829.
20 Martin Lowry, *The World of Aldus Manutius*, Oxford, Blackwell, 1979, p. 137.
21 This manuscript has now been re-catalogued as MS 2469[B].
22 H.B. Wilson, *A Genealogical Account of some families derived from Bedo Dee*, London, 1815.

4 The Globe and the Fortune

1 E.K. Chambers, *The Elizabethan Stage*, Vol. 2, Oxford University Press, 1923, p. 428, quoted in Frances Yates, *Theatre of the World* (paperback edition), London, Routledge and Kegan Paul, 1987, p. 130.
2 Vitruvius, *De Architectura*, Book 5, Chapter 6, translated by H.M. Morgan, Harvard, 1914, republished in New York in 1960 by Dover Publications, p. 146.
3 Frances Yates, *Theatre of the World*, pp. 132-3.
4 I.A. Shapiro, 'The Bankside Theatres, Early Engravings', Cambridge, Shakespeare Survey 1, 1948, pp. 25-37.
5 Dame Frances Yates died in 1981, having established herself as one of our leading historians this century.
6 Cecil Hewett, *English Historic Carpentry*, Chichester, Phillimore and Co., 1980, p. 15.
7 Ibid.
8 Ibid.
9 Peter Streete was elected Warden of the Worshipful Company of Carpenters in 1598, an indication of his high standing among his fellow craftsmen. Membership of the Companies was essential for proper employment and

jealously guarded. See Jupp and Pocock, *Historical Account of the Worshipful Company of Carpenters*, London, Pickering and Chatto, 1848.

The vigorous opposition offered by the City and the Companies to foreigners is shewn by abundant evidence. The term 'foreigner', however, is used in two senses − the one, its popular signification, designating persons not owing allegiance to the British Crown, the other, more technical and restricted, and applied to non-freemen of the City and the Companies. The former were constantly the objects of popular persecution, and sometimes fell victims in the unequal struggle. The latter were obliged to take up their freedom, or were fined for daring to exercise their calling. (p. 142)

In 1516 a feud broke out between City apprentices and foreigners on 1 May which was remembered as 'Evil May Day'. Later, in 1573, the Company records listed, among others, a fine imposed upon a 'foren carpenter for his sons for working without license, ijs' (p. 144). It was in the context of these practices and attitudes, I believe, that Theodore de Bry, while in England fulfilling his other commissions, furnished the designs from which the drawings for the theatres could be reproduced, probably with the help of Thomas Lant, draughtsman and 'servant of Philip Sidney'.

10 The writing on the sheet is not easily decipherable but appears to be:

♀▽♒△ this △ region under ☾ may probably be Purgatory △, called anima Messia by the Cabalists, and is the gate entrance to the Hevenly Orbs or Planetary Spiritual Sephirots, from wch you arrive to y^r Christeline Imperial heaven vide vide Sphere of Ptolomy etc. Boustlausta[?] 26: to the region of ♒, to y^r christalen Heaven from the Center of the ♀ the same distance DBr.

DBr − is this Dirk de Bry or simply de Bry ? Theodore de Bry is known to have called himself Dirk at times.

In the earth-centred planetary theory of Ptolemy the crystalline heaven was the ninth sphere between the fixed stars and the primum mobile.

11 See Appendix for additional information on the parametric drawings.
12 Fortune Contract, 1599, Henslowe Papers, *Dramatic Documents from the Elizabethan Playhouses* edited by W.W. Greg, London, 1931. Reprinted as Appendix F in Walter Hodges, *The Globe Restored*, Oxford University Press, 1968, pp. 163-6.
13 Experiments by Byrom Studios, Salford, with established photographic techniques to deal with the process of ageing were unsuccessful. This lent weight to my suspicion that the symbols had been inscribed by some form of invisible ink which responded to gentle heat.
14 John Byrom, *Remains*, Vol. 1, Part 2, p. 453.
15 Ibid., p. 587.

5 *Elizabethan Theatres − Patrons and Builders*

1 Pierre Colman, 'Un grand graveur-éditeur d'origine liégeoise, Théodore de Bry', La Wallonie, Le Pays et Les Hommes, Vol. 2, p. 189 *et seq*. Opposite is a family tree based on information in M. Colman's paper, provided for me by the University Library, Liège.
2 Andrew Gurr, *The Shakespearian Stage, 1574-1642*, Cambridge University Press, 1980, p. 30.
3 I am indebted in the following pages to the paper by Marie Axton: 'Robert

FAMILY TREE

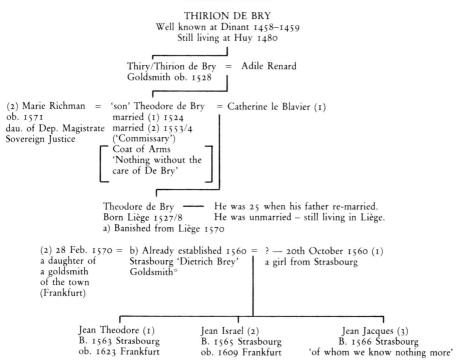

THIRION DE BRY
Well known at Dinant 1458–1459
Still living at Huy 1480

Thiry/Thirion de Bry   =   Adile Renard
Goldsmith ob. 1528

(2) Marie Richman   =   'son' Theodore de Bry   = Catherine le Blavier (1)
ob. 1571   married (1) 1524
dau. of Dep. Magistrate   married (2) 1553/4
Sovereign Justice   ('Commissary')
                          Coat of Arms
                          'Nothing without the
                          care of De Bry'

Theodore de Bry ——— He was 25 when his father re-married.
Born Liège 1527/8   He was unmarried – still living in Liège.
a) Banished from Liège 1570

(2) 28 Feb. 1570 =   b) Already established 1560 =   ? — 20th October 1560 (1)
a daughter of   Strasbourg 'Dietrich Brey'   a girl from Strasbourg
a goldsmith   Goldsmith*
of the town
(Frankfurt)

Jean Theodore (1)   Jean Israel (2)   Jean Jacques (3)
B. 1563 Strasbourg   B. 1565 Strasbourg   B. 1566 Strasbourg
ob. 1623 Frankfurt   ob. 1609 Frankfurt   'of whom we know nothing more'

* A census of 1562 lists in his home (Strasbourg) 3 servants (workmen) and a maid. Another (in 1569)
– document shows de Bry sheltering French refugees under his roof.

Dudley and the Inner Temple Revels', Cambridge, *Historical Journal*, 13 March 1970.
4 Alan Haynes, *The White Bear*, London, Peter Owen, 1987, p. 115.
5 According to his agent, Emmanuel van Meteren, who knew him well, Robert Dudley had been born in 1525 (Haynes, p. 20).
6 John Orrell, *The Human Stage*, Cambridge University Press, 1988, p. 20.
7 Peter French, *John Dee* (paperback edition), Routledge and Kegan Paul, 1984, p. 60.
8 John Orrell, *The Human Stage*, chapter 2.
9 It is worth noting that among the illustrations de Bry completed for the fourth volume of his *Grands Voyages* is one of Christopher Columbus discovering the New World. This is full of allegorical figures, one of which is a female in armour carrying a shield decorated with the Gorgon's head, in fact the shield of Pallas. The design is clearly visible and closely resembles that included in Legh's *Accedens of Armory*. The motif was evidently an important symbol for de Bry.
10 Lon R. Shelby, *Gothick Design Techniques*, Southern Illinois University Press, 1977, p. 46.
11 Marlowe, *Dr Faustus*, line 308.
12 Shakespeare, *As You Like It*, Act 2, Scene 7, lines 139-143.
13 Did Shakespeare name this character after Theodore's third son, Jacques, who,

it seems, was living in London when Lodge published his romance *Rosalynde* in 1590?

14 Adam McLean, 'Inner Geometry of Alchemical Symbols', *Hermetic Journal*, 1983, p. 11.

15 E.K. Chambers, *The Elizabethan Stage*, Vol. 2, Oxford University Press, 1923, p. 405.

16 *Henslowe's Diary* edited by R.A. Foakes and R.T. Rickert, Cambridge University Press, 1961, p. 304.

17 Fulke Greville, *The Life of The Renowned Sir Philip Sidney*, in *The Complete Works of Fulke Greville*, Vol. 4, The Fuller Worthies Library, 1870, p. 37.

18 Hope Contract, 1613, Henslowe Papers, reprinted as Appendix G in Walter Hodges, *The Globe Restored*, Oxford University Press, 1968, pp. 167-9.

19 Ibid.

20 Christopher Edwards, *London Theatre Guide*, London, Burlington Press, 1979, p. 22.

21 Jean Israel de Bry had died in 1611, leaving his brother, Jean Theodore, as director of the family publishing enterprise in Frankfurt. In 1613 Michel Le Blon was twenty-six, still unmarried and a free individual, although connected through his parents with the de Bry firm. He would be in a better position to undertake this commission than Jean Theodore whose commitments were now heavy. The presence of Michel's initials on other drawings favours this interpretation.

6 Sacred Geometry

1 Nigel Pennick, *The Ancient Science of Geomancy*, London, Thames and Hudson, 1979, chapter 8.

2 Z'ev ben Shimon Halevi, *kabbala, Tradition of hidden knowledge*, London, Thames and Hudson, 1979, p. 6.

3 Sir Nikolaus Pevsner, *Cambridgeshire*, London, Penguin, 1954, pp. 69 and 155.

4 B.W. Downs, *Cambridge Past and Present*, London, Methuen, 1926, p. 126.

5 David Lewer, 'Temple Church Guide', Andover, Pitkin Pictorials, 1971, p. 5.

6 C. Couäsnon O.P., *The Church of The Holy Sepulchre Jerusalem* (The Schweich Lectures of The British Academy, 1972), Oxford University Press, 1974, pp. 14-16.

7 C.G. Addison, *The History of The Temple Church*, London, Longman's, 1854, p. 103 *et seq.*

8 See chapter ten, pp. 266-8.

9 William Stukeley, *Diary*, Dec. 11, 1720, in *Family Memoirs*, Vol. 1, Surtees Society, 1872, p. 62.

10 Ibid., April 1 1726, p. 78.

11 B.E. Jones, *Freemasons' Guide and Compendium*, London, Harrap, 1956, p. 404.

12 The Holy of Holies measured 20 × 20 × 20 cubits. According to the Jerusalem Bible, the old Ezekiel measure for a cubit equals 21 ins or 533 mm. Converted into metric measure, the length of the Holy of Holies is 10,660 mm. The length of Byrom's cube equals 130 mm. This is a reduction of 10,660/130 or 82 times. Therefore the total volume of the Holy of Holies has been reduced by a factor of $82^{(3)}$.

13 Quoted in J.M. Landay, *The Dome of the Rock*, New York, 1972, p. 71.

14 Operative masons were certainly organised into a trade guild in England by the end of the fourteenth century. The Quatuor Coronati Lodge of freemasons published a research paper in 1928 by W.J. Williams which showed, according to the will of William Hancock, mason, that a fraternity of masons met or was founded at The Hospital of St Thomas of Acres, Cheapside, a branch of the Templars, in 1388. Not long after, the masons became one of the City of London's liveried companies. Williams quotes an account written in 1708 by J. Hatton:

> This Company was Incorporated about the year 1410, having been called the *Free Masons*, a Fraternity of great account who have been honoured by several Kings and very many of the Nobility and Gentry being of their Society. They are governed by a Master, 2 wardens, 25 assistants and there are 65 on the livery ...

7 The Search for Meaning

1 According to Frank Higgins (*Ancient Freemasonry*, New York, Pyramid Book Co., 1923, p. 285), there was an attempt in 1875 in Lausanne to draw up a plan to admit women into Co-Masonic Lodges. The famous theosophist Annie Besant is believed to have been supreme head at one time of the Co-Masonic Order. These groups, however, have no formal connection with Grand Lodge of England. Frank C. Higgins was a senior member of American Freemasonry. He reached the thirty-second degree and was past Master of the Ivanhoe Lodge no. 610, New York. His book, *Ancient Freemasonry*, began as a series of articles for the New York Herald and contains a wide range of illuminating insights into the history of early Freemasonry.
2 B.E. Jones, *Freemasons' Guide and Compendium*, p. 182.
3 Frank Higgins, *Ancient Freemasonry*, p. 462.
4 Ibid., p. 463.
5 Ibid., p. 462.
6 B.E. Jones, *Freemasons' Guide and Compendium*, p. 397.
7 The Pentalpha was chosen as the distinctive sign of the pupils of Pythagoras, who were known as the Order of the Pythagoreans. This brotherhood grew up around the mathematician in Southern Italy after he settled in Crotona in 529 BC. They were bound by oath not to reveal the secrets of their learning.

   The geometrical pattern of figure 10 is so positioned on the card that the invisible watermark fits exactly into the visible pattern. This shows deliberate and remarkable precision by the artist concerned. Undoubtedly the pentalpha was incorporated in this way yet again with some secret purpose in mind. This watermark was first noticed by Howard Colvin, St John's College, Oxford, in August 1988.
8 Milton, *Paradise Lost*, Book 7, lines 225-31.
9 B.E. Jones, *Freemasons' Guide and Compendium*, p. 299.
10 M. Baigent, R. Leigh, and H. Lincoln, *The Holy Blood and The Holy Grail*, London, Corgi, 1983, p. 494.
11 Writing in 1923 Frank Higgins noted 'a curious situation' which had 'recently arisen in English masonic circles through the protest of the London Church Times against the masonic order of Knights Templar worshipping in the famous old Temple Church in the ancient habit and insignia'. Did this group pursue the same interests as Newton centuries earlier? The secret tradition of learning which interested Newton and his study of the Temple of Solomon led

inevitably to the Cabala. The Templars, according to Higgins, came in contact with the Druses of Mount Lebanon, a religious sect who were 'heirs to the strange wisdom of the ancient East, the lore of the Chaldean seers and the secrets of their Egyptian and Phoenician neighbours' (p. 102). Furthermore, 'The typical Templar chapel of octagonal form has a solar significance which connects it with the special cabalistic wisdom of the ancient Chaldeans, which must have been communicated to them while in the East.' (p. 106).

12 The Royal Society Minute Books, London, 1727, p. 76.

13 Frances Yates, *The Occult Philosophy in the Elizabethan Age* (paperback edition), London, Routledge and Kegan Paul, 1985, p. 37.

14 Joscelyn Godwin, *Robert Fludd*, London, Thames and Hudson, 1979, p. 7.

15 St Michael and his knights continued to pursue me. In his recent book on the great pavement at Westminster Abbey, *Patterns of Thought*, Richard Foster included Holbein's painting of *The Ambassadors* (1533). Two men are portrayed standing on a patterned floor similar to that of the pavement. One is shown wearing the Order of St Michael (*op. cit.*, p. 57).

16 Joscelyn Godwin, *Robert Fludd*, p. 14.

17 John Stow, *Survey of London, 1603*, London, Dent, 1945 (Everyman edition), p. 215.

The following is a list of members of the Gisors family who held office in the City of London, extracted from Stow pp. 447-54. The register begins in 1190 and ends in 1602.

> 1240 John Gisors, Sheriff.
> 1245 John Gisors, Pepperer, Mayor. Reign Henry III
> 1246 John Gisors, Pepperer, Mayor. Henry III
> 1259 John Gisors, Pepperer, Mayor. Henry III
> 1311 Sir John Gisors, Pepperer, Mayor. Edward II
> 1312 Sir John Gisors, Pepperer, Mayor. Edward II
> 1314 Sir John Gisors, Pepperer, Mayor. Edward II
> 1319 John Gisors, Pepperer, late mayor of London and many other
>   citizens, fled the city for things laid to their charge.
> 1329 William Gisors, Sheriff, Reign Edward III

18 In 1350 a John Gisors 'gave to his son Thomas his great mansion-house called Gisors hall, in the parish of St Mildred, in Bread Street. This Thomas had issue, John and Thomas; John made a feoffement, and sold Gisors hall and other his lands in London, about the year 1386'. Stow, p. 222.

19 This man, Sir John Gisors, was buried in the church of the Grey Friars in Farringdon Ward. The church, originally founded in 1225, had become one of the most important churches in the city. It was the burial place for leading members of the nobility and royalty for several generations. Those buried there included Beatrix, daughter of Henry III, the wives of Edward I and II and the daughter of Edward III. John, Duke of Bourbon and Anjou, captured at Agincourt, was also laid to rest there. Edward II's wife, Isabel, was the daughter of Philip of France, the man responsible for the suppression of the Templars.

Much of this information would have been lost in the vandalism of the Reformation, if it had not been recorded by Stow. With his help we can begin to reconstruct the importance the Gisors once attained.

20 Edith Simon, *The Piebald Standard*, London, Cassell, 1954, p. 295.

21 M. Baigent, R. Leigh and H. Lincoln, *The Holy Blood and the Holy Grail*, p. 442.

8   Measures of Time and Space

1 A.J. Turner, 'William Oughtred, Richard Delamain and the Horizontal Instrument in Seventeenth Century England', Annali Dell' Istituto e Museo di Storia Della Scienza di Firenze, 1981.
2 David W. Waters, *The Art of Navigation in Elizabethan and Early Stuart Times*, London, Greenwich Maritime Museum, 1978, p. 22.
3 Eva G. Taylor, *Mathematical Practitioners of Tudor and Stuart England*, Cambridge University Press, 1973, p. 293.
4 W.E. May, *A History of Marine Navigation*, Henley-on-Thames, Foulis and Co., 1973, p. 56.
5 John Byrom, *Remains*, Vol. 1, Part 1, p. 266.
6 William Gilbert, translated by P. Fleury Mottelay, *De Magnete Magneticisque corporibus, et de Magno Magnete Tellure, Physiologia Nova*, Chicago, Encyclopaedia Britannica, 1952 (Great Books of The Western World Vol. 28).
7 John Byrom, *Remains*, Vol. 1, Part 2, p. 443.
8 John Byrom, *Remains*, Vol. 1, Part 1, p. 197.
9 V.F. Hopper, *Medieval Number Symbolism*, Columbia University Press, 1938, p. 41.
10 Christopher Duffy, *Fire and Stone*, London, David and Charles, 1975, p. 19.
11 Ibid.
12 Gerard Thibault, *L'Académie de L'Espée*, Leyden, Elzevier, 1628.
13 Ibid.
14 H. de la Fontaine Verwey, 'Gerard Thibault and his Académie de L'Espée', Leyden, E.J. Brill, *Quaerendo* Vol. 8, Autumn 1978, p. 314.
15 Andrew Gurr with John Orrell, *Rebuilding Shakespeare's Globe*, London, Weidenfeld and Nicholson, 1989, p. 22.
16 At the apex of this triangle the Hebrew letters proclaim the divine nature of that which is the beginning and end of all things. This drawing contains features which the reader will find explored in figures 21A and B, 22, 23 and 24 .
17 This symbolic representation of the three-fold nature of God by Robert Fludd is to be found in Volume 2 of *The Microcosm*.
18 The geometry in this drawing from the collection elaborates on the symmetry of Fludd's concept of God's three-fold nature. Fludd's name appears on the reverse (chapter seven).
19 The reader should note that the figure starts at the apex with a progression of triangles which form the sacred tetraktys of the Pythagoreans:

This was a triangular representation of the number 10, calculated as 1+2+3+4, the most revered numbers among the Pythagoreans. In figure 20 the tetraktys has been replaced by the Hebrew letters describing God.
20 Four drawings have been specifically included in this book, each of which is marked at some point with three dots in the form of a triangle. They occur in four different contexts: one, in the caption to a drawing, two, at the apex of a triangle; three (here) in the figure of the hexagon, and four, on the back of the

triangle with commemorative dates, illustrated in chapter ten. This variation in usage shows that the dots are not simply an obsolete form of punctuation, since three of the four examples occur in contexts without words. One purpose of the dots may have been to make the drawings immediately 'significant' to initiates who knew the sign. Alternatively the sign may have been included for reasons of secrecy or discretion.

21 This figure is an extraction from the geometry of figure 21B of the triangular structure of nitrate ion as it is expressed in modern scientific diagrams.

9 In Pursuit of Truth

1 Peter French, *John Dee*, p. 66 et seq.
2 Z'ev ben Shimon Halevi, *kabbalah*, p. 8.
3 Frances Yates, *The Occult Philosophy*, p. 22.
4 John Dee, *Monas Hieroglyphica*, translated by J.W. Hamilton-Jones, London, J.M. Watkins, 1947, p. 10.
5 James R. Newman, *The World of Mathematics*, Allen and Unwin, 1960, p. 79.
6 John Dee, 'Compendious Rehearsal', Manchester, Chetham Society, 'Autobiographical Tracts', edited by Crossley, 1851, p. 19.
7 Peter French, *John Dee*, p. 136.
8 Frances Yates, *The Art of Memory* (paperback edition), London, Routledge and Kegan Paul, 1984, p. 309.
9 This was the year that Thomas Lant died. He had worked closely with de Bry on the plates for Sir Philip Sidney's funeral procession (1587), and was also, I believe, involved in drawing up plans for some of the early theatres.
10 D.J. Bryden, 'George Brown, author of the Rotula', Basingstoke, *Annals of Science* 28, 1972.
11 M.S. Fisher, *Robert Boyle, Devout Naturalist*, Philadelphia, 1945, p. 162.
12 Quoted in M.S. Purver, *The Royal Society, Concept and Creation*, London, Routledge and Kegan Paul, 1967, pp. 194-6.
13 Stanley H. Redgrove, *Alchemy Ancient and Modern*, London, 1911. Republished by E.P. Publishing Ltd, Wakefield, 1973, p. 28.
14 Thomas Birch, *The Life of Robert Boyle*, London, 1744, p. 276.
15 Ibid., p. 277.
16 Roger Pilkington, *Robert Boyle, Father of Chemistry*, London, Murray, 1959, p. 90.
17 The alabaster monument can still be seen in the church of St Bartholomew the Great, London.
18 Ron Heisler, 'Michael Maier and England', *Hermetic Journal*, 1989, p. 120.
19 John Dee, *The Private Diary of Dr. John Dee*, edited by J.O. Halliwell, London, Camden Society, 1842, p. 63.
20 Public Record Office, List of Immigrants Ms 92, 1635.
21 John Wilkins, *The Discovery of a New World*, pp. 27-8, quoted in M.S. Purver, *The Royal Society, Concept and Creation*, pp. 106-7.
22 Frances Yates, *The Rosicrucian Enlightenment*, p. 187.
23 Peter French, *John Dee*, p. 11.
24 Ibid., p. 12.
25 Francis Bacon, *Novum Organum*, quoted in M.S. Purver *op. cit.*, p. 144.
26 Ibid.
27 Thomas Sprat, *History of the Royal Society*, London, 1667, pp. 62-3.
28 Horace, *Epistles Book 1*, Epistle 1, lines 13-14.

10 Influences for Change

1 Peter French, *John Dee*, p. 196.
2 Frances Yates, *The Occult Philosophy*, p. 91.
3 D.H. Wilson, *King James VI and I*, London, Jonathan Cape, 1966, pp. 298-9.
4 Christopher McIntosh, *The Rosy Cross Unveiled*, Wellingborough, The Aquarian Press, 1980, p. 55.
5 Joscelyn Godwin, *Robert Fludd*, p. 9.
6 Frances Yates, *Theatre of the World*, p. 89.
7 Frances Yates, *The Rosicrucian Enlightenment*, p. 84.
8 Christopher Hill, *Collected Essays*, Vol. 111, Brighton, Harvester Press, 1986, p. 278.
9 *Dictionary of National Biography*.
10 Ibid.
11 Frances Yates, *The Occult Philosophy*, p. 186.
12 The Jewish Encyclopaedia.
13 L. Couturat, *La Logique de Leibniz*, Paris, 1901, p. 131, note 3; quoted in Frances Yates, *The Art of Memory*, p. 387.
14 Frances Yates, *The Art of Memory*, pp. 384-5.
15 Frances Yates, *The Rosicrucian Enlightenment*, p. 81.

Bibliography

Articles and Essays

Axton, Marie, 'Robert Dudley and the Inner Temple Revels', Cambridge, *Historical Journal*, 13 March 1970.

Bryden, John, 'George Brown, author of the Rotula', Basingstoke, Taylor and Francis, *Annals of Science 28*, 1972.

Critchlow, Keith, Kairos, Worksheet no. 3, London, 21 Broomhouse Rd, SW6 3QU, 1970.

Crofton, Henry T., 'Broughton Topography and Manor Court', Manchester, *Chetham Miscellanies*, New Series, Vol. 2, 1909.

Heisler, Ron, 'Michael Maier and England', Oxford, P.O. Box 375, Headington, *The Hermetic Journal*, 1989.

Kohler, Richard C., 'Excavating Henslowe's Rose', Washington DC, Folger Shakespeare Library, *Shakespeare Quarterly* Vol. 40, Winter 1989, no. 4.

Lewer, David, Temple Church Guide, Andover, Pitkin Pictorial 1971.

Lloyd, H.A., 'George Graham Horologist and Astronomer', London, Journal of the Royal Society of Arts, 30 Nov. 1951.

McLean, Adam, 'Inner Geometry of Alchemical Symbols', *The Hermetic Journal*, 1983.

Shapiro, I.A., 'The Bankside Theatres, Early Engravings', Cambridge, *Shakespeare Survey* 1, 1948.

Turner, A.J., 'William Oughtred, Richard Delamain and the Horizontal Instrument in Seventeenth Century England', Annali Dell' Istituto e Museo di Storia Della Scienza di Firenze, 1981.

de la Fontaine de Verwey, H., 'Gerard Thibault and his Académie de L'Espée', Leiden, E.J. Brill, *Quaerendo* Vol. VIII, Autumn 1978.
'Michel Le Blon, Engraver, Art Dealer, Diplomat', Amsterdam, Amstelodamum Jahrboek, 1969

Weil, E., 'William Fitzer, The Publisher of Harvey's de Motu Cordis 1628', London, Bibliographical Society, 1944.

Williams, W.J., 'Archbishop Becket and the Masons' Company of London', Transactions of the Quatuor Coronati Lodge, Vol. 41, London, 1928.

Books: Primary Sources

Boissard, Jean Jacques, *Theatrum Vitae Humanae*, Metz, 1596.

Byrom, John, *The Private Journal and Literary Remains*, Manchester, Chetham Society, 1854.

The Universal Shorthand, Manchester, Joseph Harrop, 1767.

Dee, John, *The Hieroglyphic Monad*, translated by J.W. Hamilton-Jones, London, J.M. Watkins, 1947.

The Private Diary of Dr. John Dee, ed. J.O. Halliwell, London, Camden Society, 1842.

Gilbert, William, *On the Loadstone and Magnetic Bodies*, translated by P. Fleury Mottelay, Chicago, Encyclopaedia Britannica, 1952 (Great Books of the World Vol. 28).

Guise, Sir Christopher and Sir John, *Memoirs of the Family of Guise of Elmore*, ed. G. Davies, London, Royal Historical Society, Camden 3rd series, vol. 28, 1917.

Henslowe, Philip, *Diary*, ed. R.A. Foakes and R.T. Rickert, Cambridge University Press, 1961.

Khunrath, Heinrich, *Amphitheatre of Eternal Wisdom*, Hannover, Wolfart, 1699.

Legh, Gerard, *The Accedens of Armory*, London, 1568.

Lincoln Record Society, *The Minute Book of Spalding Gentlemen's Society, 1712-1755*, Vol. 73, 1981.

London Street Directories 1677.

Maier, Michael, *Atalanta Fugiens*, Oppenheim, 1618.

McLean, Adam ed., *The Magical Calendar*, Oxford, P.O. Box 375 Headington, Hermetic Sourceworks, 1969.

Plato, *Timaeus*, translated by B. Jowett, London, Sphere, 1970.

Ripa, Cesare, *Iconologia*, various editions: Rome 1593, 1603; Padua 1611, 1625; Amsterdam 1644; Venice 1645; Paris 1637, 1644, 1677; London 1709, 1779.

The Royal Society Minute Books, London, 1727 and 1735.

Schweighardt, Theophilus, *Speculum Sophicum Rhodo-Stauroticum*, Frankfurt, 1618.

State Papers Domestic, Vol. cccxi 1635-1636.

Stow, John, *Survey of London*, 1603, London, Dent, 1945.

Stukeley, William, *Diary, Family Memoirs*, Vol. 1, Surtees Society, 1872.

Thibault, Gerard, *L'Académie de L'Espée*, Leyden, Elzevier, 1628.

Vitruvius, *De Architectura*, translated by H.M. Morgan, New York, Dover, 1960.

Books: Secondary Sources

Addison, Charles G., *The History of the Knights Templar*, London, Longman, 1853.

The History of the Temple Church, London, Longman, 1854.

Anderson, James, *Royal Genealogies*, London, 1732.

Baigent, M., Leigh, R. and Lincoln, H., *The Holy Blood and the Holy Grail*, London, Jonathan Cape, 1982.

The Temple and The Lodge, London, Jonathan Cape, 1989.

The Bible

Bénézit, E., *Dictionnaire des Peintres, Sculpteurs, Dessinateurs et Graveurs*, Paris, Gründ, 1976.

Biographie Universelle Française, Paris, 1829.

Briquet, Charles M., *Les Filigraines: dictionnaire historique des marques de papier 1282-1600*, Geneva, A. Jullien, 1907.

Bryan's *Dictionary of Painters and Engravers*, London, G. Bell, 1903.

Churchill, W.A., *Watermarks in paper in Holland, England, France etc. in the 17th and 18th centuries*, Amsterdam, Menno Hertzberger, 1935.

Clulee, Nicholas H., *John Dee's Natural Philosophy, Between Science and Religion*, London, Routledge and Kegan Paul, 1988.

Couäsnon, O.P. Charles, *The Church of the Holy Sepulchre Jerusalem*, Oxford University Press, 1974.

Courtney-Lewis, C.T., *The Le Blond Book*, London, Sampson Low & Marston, 1920.

Craven, J.B., *The Life of Michael Maier*, 1910, republished London, Dawson, 1968.

Dictionary of National Biography, Oxford, 1917.

Dictionary of Scientific Biography, New York, 1974.

Downs, B.W., *Cambridge Past and Present*, London, Methuen, 1926.

Duffy, Christopher, *Fire and Stone*, London, David and Charles, 1975.

Edwards, Christopher, *The London Theatre Guide*, London, Burlington Press, 1979.

Encyclopaedia Britannica

Fisher, M.S., *Robert Boyle, Devout Naturalist*, Philadelphia, 1945.

Foster, Richard, *Patterns of Thought, The Hidden Meaning of the Great Pavement of Westminster Abbey*, London, Jonathan Cape, 1991.

French, Peter, *John Dee*, London, Routledge and Kegan Paul, 1948.

Godwin, Joscelyn, *Robert Fludd*, London, Thames and Hudson, 1979.

Green, M.A. Everett, *Elizabeth, Electress Palatine and Queen of Bohemia*, London, Methuen, 1909.

Gurr, Andrew, *The Shakespearian Stage 1574-1642*, Cambridge University Press, 1985.

Gurr, Andrew with Orrell, John, *Rebuilding Shakespeare's Globe*, London, Weidenfeld and Nicolson, 1989.

Halevi, Z'ev ben Shimon, *kabbalah, Tradition of hidden knowledge*, London, Thames and Hudson, 1979.

Haynes, Alan, *The White Bear*, London, Peter Owen, 1987.

Heawood, Edward, *Watermarks mainly of the 17th and 18th Centuries*, Holland, Paper Publications Society, Hilversum, 1950.

Hewett, Cecil, *English Historic Carpentry*, Chichester, Phillimore & Co., 1980.

Higgins, Frank, *Ancient Freemasonry*, New York, Pyramid Book Co., 1923.

Hill, Christopher, *Collected Essays*, Vol. III, Brighton, Harvester Press, 1986.

Hodges, Walter, *The Globe Restored*, Oxford University Press, 1968.

Hopper, V.F., *Medieval Number Symbolism*, Columbia University Press, 1938.

Hosking, G.L., *The Life and Times of Edward Alleyn*, London, Jonathan Cape, 1982.

James, E.O. (ed), *Jerusalem, A History*, London, Hamlyn, 1967.

Jenkins, Elizabeth, *Elizabeth and Leicester*, London, Gollancz, 1961.

Jones, B.E., *Freemasons' Guide and Compendium*, London, Harrap, 1956.

Landay, J.M., *The Dome of the Rock*, New York, 1976.

Lawlor, Robert, *Sacred Geometry*, London, Thames and Hudson, 1982.

Lilien, Otto, *Jacob Christoph Le Blon*, Stuttgart, Hiersemann, 1985.

Logan, Oliver, *Culture and Society in Venice 1470-1790*, London, Batsford, 1972.

Lowry, Martin, *The World of Aldus Manutius*, Oxford, Blackwell, 1979.

Manuel, Frank, *A Portrait of Isaac Newton*, Harvard University Press, 1968.

May, W.E., *A History of Marine Navigation*, Henley-on-Thames, Foulis and Co., 1973.

McIntosh, Christopher, *The Rosy Cross Unveiled*, Wellingborough, The Aquarian Press, 1980.

Newman, James R., *The World of Mathematics*, London, Allen & Unwin, 1960.

Norwich, John Julius, *Venice, The Greatness and the Fall*, London, Allen Lane, 1987.

Orrell, John, *The Human Stage, English Theatre Design 1567-1640*, Cambridge University Press, 1988.

Papus, *The Qabalah*, Wellingborough, The Aquarian Press, 1983.

Pennick, Nigel, *The Ancient Science of Geomancy*, London, Thames and Hudson, 1979.

The Mysteries of King's College Chapel, Wellingborough, The Aquarian Press, 1978.

Pevsner, Sir Nikolaus, *Cambridgeshire*, London, Penguin, 1954.

Pilkington, Roger, *Robert Boyle, Father of Chemistry*, London, Murray, 1959.

Porati, Alfredo et al., *The World of Science*, London, Macdonald and Jane's, 1978.

Purver, Marjery S., *The Royal Society, Concept and Creation*, London, Routledge and Kegan Paul, 1967.

Raistrick, Arthur, *Quakers in Science and Industry*, London, David and Charles, 1968.

Redgrove, H. Stanley, *Alchemy Ancient and Modern*, London, 1911, republished E.P. Publishing Ltd, Wakefield, 1973.

Shakespeare's England, Oxford University Press, 1916.

Shelby, Lon R., *Gothick Design Techniques*, Southern Illinois University Press, 1977.

Simon, Edith, *The Piebald Standard*, London, Cassell, 1954.

Smith, Charlotte, *John Dee*, London, 1909.

Sprat, Thomas, *History of the Royal Society*, London, 1667.

Stoudt, John Joseph, *Sunrise to Eternity*, Philadelphia, University of Pennsylvania Press, 1957.

Straus, Ralph, *The Unspeakable Mr Curll*, London, Chapman & Hall, 1927.

Taylor, E.V.G., *Mathematical Practitioners of Tudor and Stuart England*, Cambridge University Press, 1954.

Thimms, C.A., *A Complete Bibliography of Fencing and Duelling*, London, 1896.

Thomas, Sir Keith, *Religion and the Decline of Magic*, London, Weidenfeld and Nicolson, 1971.

Van der Kellen, J.Ph., *Michel Le Blon, Recueil d'ornements accompagné d'une notice biographique et d'un catalogue raisonné de son oeuvre*, The Hague, Martinus Nijhoff, 1900.

Waters, David W., *The Art of Navigation in Elizabethan and Early Stuart Times*, London, Greenwich Maritime Museum, 1978.

Webb, E.A., *The Records of St. Bartholomew's Smithfield*, Oxford University Press, 1921.

Webster, Charles, *From Paracelsus to Newton, Magic and the Making of Modern Science*, Cambridge University Press, 1982.

Wilson, Harry B., *A genealogical account of some families derived from Bedo Dee*, London, 1815.

Willis, R. and Clarke, J.W., *The Architectural History of The University of Cambridge*, Vol. 1, Cambridge University Press, 1886.

Yates, Frances, *The Art of Memory*, London, Routledge and Kegan Paul, 1984.
  The Occult Philosophy in the Elizabethan Age, London, Routledge and Kegan Paul, 1985.
  The Rosicrucian Enlightenment, London, Routledge and Kegan Paul, 1986.
  Theatre of the World, London, Routledge and Kegan Paul, 1987.

Miscellaneous Papers

Egmont Papers, British Library, Department of Manuscripts, Add. Ms. 47029, Vol. CX.
Huguenot Society of London Publications no. 10, Returns of Aliens, Aberdeen University Press, 1900.
Bartholomew Close – Scavenger Rolls, Guildhall Library.
St Bartholomew the Great – Church Records, Guildhall Library.
London Gazette 1721 and 1725, British Library.

Acknowledgments

The Byrom geometric drawings are in private possession and are reproduced by arrangement with the Trustees.

I would like to thank the staff of Jonathan Cape, in particular Tom Maschler for his vision, Hilary Turner, Pascal Cariss, John Caple, but above all Tony Colwell whose editorial skills have been much appreciated. I am also grateful to Julian Shuckburgh of Barrie & Jenkins for his interest and advice. Special thanks are due to the indefatigable energy, enthusiasm and great sense of humour of my agent, Anne Dewe.

I would like to express my gratitude to Leon Crickmore, Laurence Goddard, Alan Hughes and Nigel Pennick for their contributions to Appendix One and to Mr Neville Barker Cryer for his help with some of the masonic material in the text. My thanks also go to Kenneth Peacock and my brother, Malcolm Young, for the skill expended on their models of the Elizabethan theatres, and to Theo Crosby (of Pentagram Design Ltd) for his early expression of interest in and support for this project.

I owe a special debt to the staff of Kall-Kwik, Manchester, for their help in preparing so many illustrations of the geometric drawings, to Alison and Paul Swinnerton for their secretarial and graphic skills and to Byrom Studios, Salford, for their photographic help. Many others have helped to bring this project to completion: John Archer, Mark Ash, Michael Baigent, Professor Thomas Birrell, Howard Colvin, Michael Darlington, Anne Evans, Dr Gratton Guinness, Graham Handley, Dr Gordon Higgott, Dr Frank Hildy, Dr John Hinchcliffe, Miles Huntington-Whiteley, Stephen Johnston, Richard Leigh, Adam McLean, Dr Jennifer Montagu, Dr Alan Moreton, Lord Northampton, Elaine Ogden, Dr Michael Powell, Dr W.F. Ryan, Dr Simon Schaffer, Dr Harvey Sheldon, Lilian Storey, James and Eileen Sturzaker, Sir John Summerson, Ludovic Thijssen, Dr Roger Thomas, Ronald and Margaret Walker.

Finally, I must not forget my husband, Allan, for his patience, help and humour throughout.

I am indebted to several institutions for their help: The Quatuor Coronati

Acknowledgments

Research Lodge, London; John Rylands Library, Manchester; the Public Record Office; Salford City Library; staff of Salford Education Committee; Spalding Gentlemen's Society; the Spalding Local History Library, Lincs; the Theosophical Society Library, London; Warburg Institute; Whipple Institute, Cambridge; the University of Brussels and the University of Liège.

I would also like to thank the following for permission to reproduce illustrations: Ashmolean Museum, Oxford, p.222; Bible Society's Library at Cambridge University Library, p.168; British Library, pp.24, 42, 52, 55, 59, 60, 98–9, 105, 110, 160, 204, 206, 207, 211, 243, 252; the Governors of Chetham's Library, Manchester, pp. 2, 223; Keith Critchlow: Kairos Worksheet No. 3, p.152; English Heritage and the Museum of London, p.118; Richard Foster, p.274; Andrew Fulgoni Photography/MoL, p. 119; Guildhall Library, Corporation of London, pp. 87, 145; Adam McLean, pp. 183, 254; Manchester Central Library, pp. 107, 186; the Trustees, National Gallery, London, p.257; National Portrait Gallery, Picture Library, pp. 32, 257; Oxford University Press, p.284 (published 1952); Nigel Pennick, p.138; Priory Church of St Bartholomew-the-Great, London, p.51; Routledge and Kegan Paul, p.61; the President and Council of the Royal Society, p. 230; the Trustees of the Science Museum, London, p.233, 235; the Friends of Wells Cathedral, p. 208; Church of St Mary, Sompting, Sussex, p.71. The Rhenish helm illustration on p.71 is reproduced by kind permission from *English Historic Carpentry* by Cecil A. Hewett, published in 1980 by Phillimore & Co. Ltd, Shopwyke Hall, Chichester, West Sussex.

To these and all those others too numerous to mention I am deeply indebted.

Note on Contributors

Leon Crickmore was Dean of the Faculty of Arts and Head of the Department of Applied Philosophy at the North East London Polytechnic and is currently H.M. Staff Inspector of Music, Department of Education and Science.

Laurence Goddard was Professor of Mathematics at the University of Salford 1967–1982.

Alan Hughes is a member of the Royal Institute of British Architects and a Fellow of the Theosophical Society.

Nigel Pennick is the author of several books on sacred geometry.

Index

Note: *numbers in italic denote illustrations*

313

Index